IN GURKHA COMPANY

IN Gurkha COMPANY

The British Army Gurkhas, 1948 to the Present

Lieutenant Colonel J. P. Cross, O.B.E.

ARMS AND ARMOUR PRESS

LONDON   NEW YORK   SYDNEY

First published in Great Britain
in 1986 by Arms and Armour Press Limited,
2–6 Hampstead High Street, London NW3 1QQ.

Distributed in the USA by Sterling Publishing Co. Inc.,
2 Park Avenue, New York, NY 10016.

Distributed in Australia by
Capricorn Link (Australia) Pty. Ltd., P.O. Box 665,
Lane Cove, New South Wales 2066, Australia.

British Library Cataloguing in Publication Data:
Cross, J. P.
In Gurkha company
1. Great Britain. *Army* – History
2. Gurkha soldiers – History
355.3'1'0941 UA853.N35

ISBN 0-85368-865-6

The jacket illustration and the photographs in this
book are all reproduced by courtesy of Robin Adshead.

Designed by David Gibbons; edited by Debbie Fox;
typeset by Typesetters (Birmingham) Ltd., camerawork by
Anglia Repro Ltd., Rayleigh; printed and bound in
Great Britain by R. J. Acford Ltd., Chichester.

CONTENTS

PREFACE

The genesis of this history is to be found in a larger version produced for the Research Centre for Nepal and Asian Studies of Tribhuvan University in Kathmandu, Nepal, where I worked for some years after leaving the army. This shortened version also acknowledges the debt of gratitude to the following for allowing material that originally belonged to them to be used again by me: the editor of the journal of the Brigade of Gurkhas – *The Kukri*; the regimental associations of the 2nd, 6th, 7th and 10th Gurkha Rifles; and the individuals who answered my queries about 'what happened on the day'.

I served with the Gurkhas before they were made an integral part of the British Army on 1 January 1948 and for nearly 34 years afterwards. I experienced, at first hand, the traumas consequent on the end of the Burma War, the events before partition of the subcontinent and the bewilderingly difficult time after joining the British Army from the Indian Army, the Malayan Emergency and the Borneo campaign, as well as being a recruiter for the last five and a half years of my army service. That being the case, this history can neither be coldly objective nor utterly impartial. Subjective aspects colour my perception of the Gurkhas, seeing them and remembering them as I do. Not blind to faults and weaknesses, nor starry-eyed about undoubted sterling qualities and strengths, I like to think that what I have written truly reflects 'what it was like from the inside'.

A regiment is a closely knit group of people and the Gurkhas have a very strongly developed sense of family solidarity, with generation after generation serving in the army. Soldiering is seen as the one honourable profession open to the Gurkhas of Nepal, especially when under the British Crown. Many sons of British officers also follow their father's, and even their grandfather's, profession in the same regiment, cementing even harder the bond of comradeship that transcends the obvious differences that exist between Briton and Gurkha.

In my original dedication, I wrote: 'To the many thousands of Nepalese citizens whom I knew, loved, honoured, respected and worked with for the last 38 years of my army service, from 1944 to 1982, this work is dedicated in the hope that, with the recording of your deeds, devotion and dedication, your fellow citizens will have a deeper understanding and greater knowledge of the part you have played to make the name Nepal stir other men's hearts and to increase and strengthen the ties between Britain and Nepal.' This sentiment I also fully extend to my fellow citizens, many of whom have long realized just how much Britain owes to the Gurkhas and would like to know more about them, and to those countless thousands of others to whom 'Gurkha' is but a name that connotes outstanding bravery, sacrifices made for and friendship to Britain over many, many years.

To those people whose exploits I extol in the narrative, I salute what you have done; to the vastly greater amount of folk whose names have not appeared herein all I can say is that, without you, this work neither could, nor would, ever have been written. By no stretch of the imagination does not being mentioned imply any sense of ingratitude or non-recognition. By the same token, some units have been mentioned more than others: to be in the right place at the right time is not something that is granted to most mortals, nor to groups of mortals. It is a well-known fact of soldiering that, for most of the time, routine lays its steady and boring hand over all aspects of activity and, alas, this is not the stuff than attracts the attention of a wide public nor pages of a regimental history. Gurkhas are 'all-weather warriors'. It is wryly noted that 'fair-weather soldiers make gloomy regimental histories' – if nothing else this history of 'The British Army Gurkhas' is not gloomy. The Gurkhas 'say so much by leaving so much unsaid' – this book could have taken its motto from that sentiment.

Kathmandu, 1986

PROLOGUE
A BACKGROUND

Nepal, a land of contrasts and extremes, is landlocked, with the Chinese province of Tibet to the north and India on the other three sides. It is 520 miles long and nowhere exceeds 140 miles in breadth, averaging between 90 and 100 miles. It is the only Hindu monarchy in the world and has never been ruled by any other country. It still has very poor communications and, off the few motorable roads, the main beast of burden is human.

Beyond the flat southern rim of the part of Nepal that marches with India, the Terai, rise the foothills to the main Himalayan range, running up in ridge after ridge of steep-sloped mountains – steeper in the east than in the west – until the snows are reached. It is harsh, hard and beautiful country where man cannot win the battle for survival without incessant toil and crushing hardship – the odds pitted against him by nature, to say nothing of taxes and the repayment of debts. Virtually everything must be carried – men, women, and children, staggering along under cruelly heavy loads, are a commonplace.

This strip of territory, the Gurkha heartland, is inhabited up to a height of about 8,000 feet (rice does not grow above 7,500 feet), but grazing and the search for medical herbs in the warmer months go up to about 13,000 feet. The big rivers coming down from the snows and waiting to be harnessed to hydroelectric projects, cascade through deep gorges. Nature's moods can be sudden and cruel, and a generation's husbandry destroyed in hours.

Apart from land adjacent to the large rivers where wet paddy can easily be grown, hills are intensely cultivated and terraced, with some plots so small that only a dozen stems of paddy can be planted there. These very small plots are dug by mattock, while the larger plots are cultivated by a single-bladed wooden plough, pulled by a pair of oxen. Rice, wheat, buckwheat and maize are farmed on the lower slopes, millet and potatoes on the higher.

Villages of red and white, or terracotta-coloured houses, seem to hang precariously on the slopes or sit atop a ridge with pasture, firewood and water hundreds of feet below. Houses are designed for maximum utility only – 'homeliness' is beyond their reach. Leisure, as

9

such, is unheard of. Flat ground is so limited and unusual that, from the day a baby learns to walk, it becomes inured to the steep slopes and stony paths and, once grown up, that child will say that walking along level ground makes his legs ache!

Villages are connected by a network of footpaths. Movement is possible throughout the year, although in the monsoon rivers in spate, landslides, broken bridges, suspended ferries and leech-infested areas make detours necessary and time-consuming. In villages, shops are virtually nonexistent; rudimentary inns are found on the main trails, especially those the tourists frequent. Medical facilities are also very few and far between, except in the towns. Traditional shamanism is still widely practised.

The climate in the 'Hills', as they are known, varies according to altitude. Winter is not excessively cold and snow does not lie much below the 7,000-foot contour. Fires are an expensive luxury and one definition of hospitality could be 'to burn wood for someone when no cooking has to be done'. Spring and autumn are very pleasant, with warm, sunny days and cool nights, though during the monsoon it can quickly change from cold and clammy to hot and oppressive and back again. Hail is an annual occurrence and is greatly feared as it can severely damage crops.

Gurkhas are thick-set, stocky people, with an average height of about 5 feet 4 inches, with a wheaten to olive complexion, little body hair, almond eyes, high cheekbones, thick, black hair, very strong thigh and calf muscles, developed from carrying heavy loads up and down steep slopes from an early age. They are hard-working and have very strong family bonds, indeed not to accord one's family the highest priority is considered socially damning. They are normally cheerful, despite their hard lives, with a keen sense of humour and wonderful smiles. Their open characters invite an intimacy in their dealings with Europeans that is seldom achieved by other eastern peoples, certainly in the subcontinent. They are self-confident and independent, tending to be shy with strangers, but lively with friends. As education and tourism spread, the younger generation is becoming less reserved. Many are far from teetotal and smoking is prevalent. They can be extraordinarily brave, as their army record shows. Normally frugal and abjuring waste, they can be generous to a fault with their hospitality.

A Gurkha's strengths are physical and mental stamina, a desire to improve himself, an ability to be a productive member of an extended family yet retain his individuality, experience of pain and deprivation, an ability to improvise, resourcefulness, uncomplaining dependability and being inately the stuff good soldiers are made of. These character- istics, fostered by a society that knows how to be pragmatic yet is bound by strong communal constraints, have developed over the centuries. So it is that a poor youth, with nothing more than basic grit and guts, experienced only in survival and hard work, is willing to leave his all behind, to change his lifestyle, to suffer again and to improve himself through a lot more pain and hard work. Realizing this can account for his weaknesses: a tendency to be unenterprising, unimaginative, slow in the uptake and not using his initiative for fear of being held responsible to the extent that he might jeopardize whatever security he has, and so have to reduce his circumstances even more.

For these people, as well as for the great majority of all communities in Nepal, life is one long struggle, with hunger and suffering never very far away. Almost all of them are materially poor and far too many in vassalizing debt. The very nature of the countryside, the poverty, the ignorance, the superstititions, and an all-pervading realization that, however hard they try, release from hunger, tiredness, aching limbs and drudgery can only, at best, be temporary, if at all. The dust, the dirt, the mud; the lack of roads, of transport facilities, of sanitation; the debilitating effects of undernourishment, of a poor and monotonous diet, of inadequate clothing; the debts, the need for cash and other pressures all occupy a father's energies to such an extent that the odds are heavily stacked against a new-born babe having a decent start in life. Unrelenting effort is required to maintain what advantages there are, but a bad harvest caused by hail or drought or floods, acts of God that destroy land, property and homes, injuries and illnesses, or the rapacious mendacities of a semi-literate, petty-minded functionary all mock these efforts so that enhancement for self and family is still farther away. As the saying has it, 'If I want to live, I just can't cope; if I want to die, I have to wait my time.'

Happily unaware of this the pot-bellied, snotty-nosed and grubby-faced child continues to play with stones, sticks and mud, crying when it hurts itself, running to mother for comfort and knowing when it is naughty – just like kids anywhere. And like any other child, it remains blissfully ignorant of the stark and harsh realities it will have to face – all too soon.

Young Gurkhas become inured to hardship, they accept it and expect harsh conditions as part of the natural order of things. Their apparent callousness to man and beast stems from this. Even if their children do get enough to fill their tummies, a poor diet will result in stunted growth and undeveloped mentality. An apparently healthy-looking youth will lack stamina for 'those last few yards' and will burn out prematurely. It is not at all uncommon for people to eat meat only about six times a year and for sure food supplies to be available for only three months in every twelve. Those lads who tend cattle, often in upland pastures, away from their villages, can grow very strong, as there is plenty of milk to drink. The survival of the fittest is no empty saying.

To reach the age of four in a well-nourished condition is a victory hard to attain. Not to succumb to the disadvantages of life but to overcome them is a constant challenge to all growing people, whether they are conscious of it or not. As they grow up in their Gurkha heartland, they will become aware of what being a 'Gurkha' involves: it is the touchstone, the magic wand, the talisman for changing their lives. They are fired by it, only gradually realizing the slender chances against fulfillment of such an ambition.

So they grow up, absorbing all those invisible qualities that toil, poverty and battling against the odds instil. In the evenings they will listen to their elders talking about that most honorable of professions, soldiering, 'service', 'promotion', 'pension' and other matters with stories of derring-do, battles fought, strange places with stranger-sounding names, bravery awards and what the 'Commanding Saheb' said . . . and their imaginations will be fired as never before. They will also come across lads older than themselves who have tried for such a life but, thwarted by fate from any fortune, have returned to their villages, disconsolate. They may hear about others who disappeared to India where the shame of failure to enlist does not matter and, whatever the conditions, hunger might be assuaged and a pittance might be earned. To attain the second victory in life – a decent job with a pension at the end – is even harder and more elusive than the first.

Many a young Gurkha does not want to spend the rest of his life subsistence farming and is frustrated by his lot at home. Prevented from obtaining employment elsewhere in his country and imbued with the tradition of leaving Nepal for self-advancement, a Gurkha will see foreign army service as the only method open to him to improve himself, to get out of debt and pave the way for his children's enhancement. However, this means leaving the familiar and journeying into the unknown, to face the problems of changing one's habits, being willing to face different types of pressures so that, despite the trauma, his lot will eventually be better. Not that a hungry lad analyses it all so clinically – he just 'knows' that it surely cannot be worse than it already is. He therefore sets his sights on the British Army, and then on the Indian Army, before trying his luck as a soldier or policeman in Nepal, or a watchman in India.

Unlike many other races, Gurkhas have an inherent and subtle chemistry that allows their natural characteristics of sturdy independence, patience, inurement to hard conditions, loyalty to a family – nuclear or extended – to be blended successfully with all that is required to be a good soldier, which can be described as an indeterminate mix of self-discipline, self-confidence, loyalty, guts, determination, motivation, a good appearance, correct temperament, a strong though malleable character, and a cheerful personality. Thus it is that service in the British Army, with good pay and conditions, opportunities for travel, sport and adventure, medical and educational facilities for single men and families, a chance to make one's name as a 'bahadur' – a brave man – and serving under dedicated and impartial officers, is as strong a magnet in the 1980s as it ever was before.

All this, enshrouded in the knowledge that the Gurkhas produce brave men who prevail under unlikely circumstances in greater abundance than most, has produced an aura of mystique and legend that, to an extent, feeds on itself to such a degree that, when a Gurkha does misbehave (and he will be the first to agree that this can and does happen) many of his British admirers feel let down. However, their military excellence is undisputed and has become a byword, making the Gurkha larger than life in attribute, exploits and panache, all carried with a confident modesty, refreshing in a world of increasing brashness. Indeed, the national weapon – the curved knife called 'kukri' – similarly suffers from this aura, turning it from 'just another knife with a different shape' to something that must draw blood before being returned to its scabbard and that can be used as a boomerang when thrown at an enemy to decapitate him. Both points are untrue!

The bond between Briton and Gurkha started at soldier level and is still strongest there, but it has spread far and wide, ever since and especially after the Gurkhas became part of the British Army. Paradoxically, the name and fame of the Gurkhas are more widespread outside Nepal than in it. Just as only a member of a masonic lodge is critically interested in what being a mason entails and implies, so too, in Nepal, except for a very few 'fringe' thinkers, precious little notice is taken of the fact that a few Nepalese citizens serve in a foreign army – it does not concern the majority of society as the 'martial classes' are a minority. In simple terms, Nepalese are divided into Mongolian and Aryan, with Gurkhas drawn from the former.

The relationship between Britain and Nepal is unique. On 18 November 1980, at Buckingham Palace during a state visit to Britain, His Majesty King Birendra of Nepal said:

'. . . the people of Nepal began to admire fairness, justice, discipline and tenacity in the British character just as the British, I am sure, must have admired some inherently good disposition in the character of their Gorkha brethren. The Anglo-Nepalese encounter [of 1814–16] thus turned out to be a voyage of discovery of each other's ideals and values. This has another advantage too. It proved that Nepal rejects, totally and unequivocally, any idea of subjugation, thus stubbornly refusing to

become a province of any other country. It was based on these
cherished principles of non-interference, sovereign equality and un-
questioned independence that Nepal became a close friend of Great
Britain.'

This history puts flesh on the bones of His Majesty's contention.

1
THE SHAKY START

The Gurkhas of Nepal have been comrades in arms of the British since 1815, when the Bengal Presidency Army of the Honourable East India Company defeated them during the Anglo-Nepal war of 1814–16. Mutual empathy between each side was such that service was offered to the Gurkhas under British officers as Company troops, and was accepted.*

Forty-two years later, in 1857, Indian units of the Bengal Presidency Army mutinied, resulting in Company rule being superseded by British government rule, with delegated authority vested in a viceroy representing the Queen Empress Victoria and with a separate administration based in New Delhi, the capital of British India. Gurkha units had shown such loyalty and Nepal had supported Britain so well during the mutiny that Gurkhas were incorporated into the Indian Army, which was raised from the remnants of Company troops. It is worth noting that Nepal has never been under the domination of a foreign power and has always been grittily independent.

By 1902 there were ten regiments of Gurkhas, with an eleventh regiment raised in both world wars. Known as the 'Gurkha Brigade', regiments were numbered from one to ten and, in peacetime, each comprised two active battalions and a training organization.

During 1947, very delicate and protracted negotiations took place between senior representatives of the governments of the United Kingdom, Nepal and India about the future of the Gurkha Brigade after India became independent. In the event, six of the ten Gurkha regiments were detailed to stay in the Indian Army, while the other four, the 2nd, 6th, 7th and 10th Gurkha Rifles, became an integral part of the British Army on 1 January 1948. The 2nd had been raised in 1815, the year of Waterloo, the 6th in 1817, the 7th in 1902 and the 10th in 1890, although the origins of the last two can, in fact, be traced as far back as 1776.

The background and events leading up to this most unusual happening were set against the cataclysmic upheaval of the British leaving

*See chapters 9 and 10 of *Gorkha – The Story Of The Gurkhas Of Nepal* by Frances Tuker, Constable, London, 1957.

15

India and the subcontinent being partitioned into a smaller India and a new Pakistan. Until then the Gurkha Brigade had always had British officers, never Indian. Ever since the end of the Second World War in 1945 it had been obvious that tremendous changes were in the air and, once they had come into effect, nothing would ever be the same again as far as Indian matters were concerned. Independence had been set for 15 August 1947, but it was only one week before this date that any announcement was made about the future of the Gurkhas, who were to be unequally divided between the armies of Britain and India, with the British Army units to serve in Malaya, Singapore and Hong Kong. Apart from listing which regiments had been chosen for the British Army, with the vaguest of details about their new conditions and terms of service, the announcement said that every single Gurkha officer and soldier of all ten regiments would be given the choice of which of the two armies he wished to serve in, or to serve in neither and return home. 'Whatever they do will be of their own free will' was written in a letter sent out by the Adjutant General of the Indian Army, dated 14 August 1947. This was declared British government policy and became known as the 'opt'.

By then conditions in the subcontinent were volatile at best, untenable at worst. Gurkha units were spread over central and northern India and all were faced with trying to maintain even a semblance of law and order in a world gone mad. Normal army organization creaked drastically – signals frequently arrived late and garbled. One message, sent from GHQ in New Delhi to a Gurkha unit on the North-West Frontier and graded 'Operational Immediate', took six weeks to arrive – the same time as it did for any mail that was not lost to arrive from England. Logistical shortages of clothing, transport, equipment, fuel and rations were commonplace and could be got used to; lack of any directions about the future was more insidious.

As soon as possible after the announcement that a choice of regiments had, at last, been made, plans were drawn up for those British officers of Gurkha units staying in the Indian Army to join the British Army Gurkhas. As long as British officers remained in battalions the men were patient and trusting in their acceptance of the situation, despite the appalling disarray and turbulence that were sweeping the land. However, many officers who had served with the soldiers during the war and who, therefore, were tried and trusted, were being sent home as their demobilization dates drew near, while pre-war regulars were posted to other British Army units. At the very end of 1947 some battalions had only two officers and by then they were mentally exhausted and emotionally drained. Small wonder if, in some cases, they hit the bottle harder than was good for them.

Between the initial announcement and the opt being made, conditions deteriorated even more, from serious but localized breakdowns in law and order on a large scale to widespread abominations and chaos as a seething mass of millions of refugees, whose only crime was to be a Muslim in a Hindu country or a Hindu in a Muslim one, struggled painfully to reach a sanctuary. Killings, rapings, mutilations, mayhem and unchecked blood lust of a scale seldom seen before or since abounded, mindless, sickening and utterly irrational in its ferocity. Bullock carts with refugees in nose-to-tail convoy stretched for over a hundred miles; the stench in the worst hit areas was in the air for months. Normal life came to a halt. All that mind-boggling shambles and savagery, added to an obvious desire to get right away from such horrendous goings-on, created stresses and strains among the Gurkha soldiers that had seldom, if ever, been met with in so-called peacetime. Old norms vanished and, in their place, life became a day-to-day burden of patchwork plans and groping guesswork. For days on end Gurkha soldiers found themselves having to escort tens of thousands of pitiable refugees, hundreds of whom lay down at night by the side of the road and died of sheer helplessness having nothing left to live for.

Seldom before had the troops' discipline and loyalties been more severely tested. There were cases of indiscipline among a few Gurkha units, caused more by pro-Indian troublemakers taking advantage of British officers' inability to reassure the men about their future than by anti-British sentiments. There were, regrettably, some isolated nastinesses but, in the main and for most of the time the Gurkhas did not waver. It speaks volumes for what the British had done in the old Indian Army that, during those months, every unit, Gurkha and Indian, stayed true to its salt. Faith in Britain's ability to manage a crisis, though, had been shaken and morale suffered accordingly.

All through the latter part of 1947 Indian and Indian-domiciled Nepalese propaganda and threats against the proposed British Gurkhas worked at two levels – unabashed, unsubtle and unending outside a unit but insidious, sly and full of half-truths within. Small wonder that, when the opt was concluded, it showed a direct ratio between the few men volunteering for the British and the nearness of that unit to Delhi. Apart from everything else, it has to be remembered that, before this time, no Gurkha had ever been asked to serve permanently outside the Indian subcontinent. Being Hindus, they were in spiritual, if not moral, danger of becoming contaminated from living and having their being 'over the black water', which necessitated particular cleansing ceremonies of ritual purification before such a man could cross over the border into Nepal and be reaccepted as a caste Hindu.

In the event only those of the four regiments chosen for the British Army were asked if they wished to stay in their units and so join the British Army or go to a regiment staying with the Indian Army. That took place at the end of the year. By then there were very few British officers left whom the men knew and could turn to for advice and the officers had been strictly forbidden to talk to the men about anything to do with the opt. This lack of interest, as it seemed to the Gurkhas, was yet another instance of the British having lost control of the situation and no longer caring what happened on a personal soldier level; in other words, all-essential trust was being eroded.

By the time of the opt the original promise of those not wanting to stay in either army being allowed their discharge was either forgotten or withdrawn, and a man who did want to go home knew it would be possible from India and not from overseas. Some of those who opted for the British Army did so from an aversion to serving under Indians, others because their friends said they were going to, and some who saw a chance for promotion where none had existed before. In addition, an attempt was made by a handful of communist sympathizers to infiltrate the ranks and form cells within units. I discovered this in 1949 and cleansing action was taken. This took the form of immediate discharge for the ringleader and the presence of cells in units being exposed. The incipient danger then fizzled out. In units destined to remain in the Indian Army there were those who went on home leave in 1948 and, instead of rejoining their battalions, joined the British Army as recruits – many of these formed the nucleus of the Gurkha Engineers.

The result of the opt was not nearly as good as tentative results had indicated from battalion straw polls taken in August 1947 but, despite acute disappointment felt by some officers who had thought that their men would go wherever the regiment went, it has to be said that the final tally could have been worse. The average strength in each of the eight battalions was around the 300 mark, a third of their full complement. Two units, 2/6 GR and 2/7 GR, came across to the British Army with about a hundred men each while, over in Burma, where three battalions, 1/6 GR, 1/7 GR and 1/10 GR had not had the experience of the holocaust in India, results were much better. Apart from a paucity of riflemen, there were, naturally, very many promotion gaps in each unit waiting to be filled as a result of those Gurkha officers, warrant officers and NCOs who had opted for the Indian Army, to say nothing of the loss of specialists and 'tradesmen' – clerks, drivers, fitters, signallers, medics, mortarmen and many others. In 2/6 GR, where all the clerks had opted for India, an arrangement had been made to borrow them back in order to complete essential documentation, without which the units could not have moved. When the time came for 2/6 GR to leave

India, every single one of those clerks had changed his mind and begged to be taken, some even shedding tears in their remorse in having opted the way they had, having been unduly influenced by the anti-British propaganda. The great majority of clerks were Indian-domiciled and did not come from Nepal, so were significantly influenced by the anti-British propaganda. But it was not to be as the die had irrevocably been caste.

The 'home' of each regiment, the Regimental Centre, also suffered acutely. Not slanted to be operational, these units had had to provide operational help before partition, quelling riots and trying generally to keep the peace. Their opt had also left many gaps in the senior ranks, and the packing up and leaving period that took place in early 1948 was made far harder than otherwise by the petty-minded officialdom of low-level functionaries. Much that could go wrong did. Part of the deal reached bilaterally between the British and Indian authorities was that, as long as units destined for the British Army were on Indian soil, stores, rations and services would be provided on repayment. Alas, even when arrangements were simple, the lower echelons of Indian bureaucracy often prevented their realization.

For the 2nd Gurkhas – the 2nd King Edward VII's Own Gurkha Rifles (The Sirmoor Rifles) to give them their full title – leaving their Centre in Dehra Dun was traumatic as it had been their home for 130 years. For the 6th, who had been in Abbottabad, now in Pakistan, a double move was needed. In the 7th and 10th Centres, clashes broke out between those who had opted for India and those staying with the regiment and, to cap it all, when the 10th Centre was trying to leave, after only three days' notice, postal services broke down, there was no signal traffic, food was in short supply and, once the journey had started, floods washed away roads and a bridge. When, finally, the unit had got into the train to take it to the port of embarkation, there was a derailment. From start to finish it was an agony of frustration.

Only when they got to their new destination did many of the British officers feel that they were waking from a bad dream that had gone on too long. Their state of mind had been conditioned by the war, in effect, never really having stopped. Mini-wars had been fought in Greece, Palestine, Dutch East Indies, French Indo-China and Burma, and yet in reality the war had ended some 30 months before. It had been a time that showed once more how discipline and loyalty were the bedrock and hallmark of a good unit, despite the horror that was felt by the officers having somehow let their men down. To take but one example, 1/1 GR: they were in tribal territory – where government had no writ in areas away from off the main road – on the North-West Frontier, which became, on that fateful day of 15 August, Pakistan. The Union Jack gave way to another flag, a brand-new one. In October the battalion moved to Pakistan proper, in December to India where all the British officers had to leave their men on a war footing in the disputed territory of Jammu, south of Kashmir, without being able to hand over to any Indian officers as none had arrived by that time. 'You have been with us since 1815,' a senior Gurkha officer said to me, 'what are a few days more so that you can hand us over properly?'

The British officers then left their men and India for good (a paradoxical expression!) and went across to Burma to join their new battalion, 1/7 GR, just as the opt was taking place, on 27 December 1947. There, on 4 January 1948, the Union Jack was hauled down yet again and, five days later, the three Gurkha battalions in the Rangoon area left for their new homes in Malaya. Three days after that the boat arrived off Penang and all breathed a long sigh of (premature) relief as the friendliness of the people and the green, calm stillness of the place became apparent – so completely unlike anything anybody had experienced for the past 30 months. It was dawn after a long, long night. Then, as an officer of 1/10 GR so aptly put it, '. . . and where we settled, our tents rose like mushrooms in the new, green land we had come to. We had suffered disruption, depletion, disorganization and depression, but one thing Malaya offered was the hope of peace and tranquillity in which we could sort ourselves out and "get back to pre-war standards", as the Old and Bold used to say . . .'

The undermanned, travel-weary and still bewildered battalions, feeling very much like pioneers reaching a new frontier after tremendous difficulties, had all arrived at their new locations by April 1948. 1/2 GR went to a tented camp at Ulu Pandan, on Singapore Island; 2/2 GR went to Ipoh in Perak; 1/6 GR went to Sungei Patani, not all that far from the Thai border; 2/6 GR, originally destined to go straight to Hong Kong, were so thin on the ground that they were sent to Kuala Lumpur, the capital of Malaya, instead – and went on to Hong Kong that December after they had absorbed some recruits; 1/7 GR went to Seremban; 2/7 GR also went to Kuala Lumpur; 1/10 GR went to Johore Bahru, near the causeway linking Singapore to Malaya, after a short spell in Kuala Lumpur; and 2/10 GR, who had been in Pakistan before their move, went to Hong Kong.

To add to all the other difficulties already thrust upon them, three battalions were faced with additional problems: 2/2 GR had been prisoners of war in Malaya, had suffered under Japanese brutalities and had not properly recovered, while the two 7 GR battalions were made into gunner regiments. Indeed, Royal Artillery officers were posted in and 25-pounder guns were issued. 2/7 GR found the only common language with their gunner instructors was Italian, which the Gurkhas had learnt during the war. This transformation was the first step in trying to form an all-Gurkha division, an idea that was later revoked. 7 GR, breathing a collective sigh of relief, reverted to being infantry within a few months.

A new army in a new country – a fresh start to be made. There was an overwhelming desire for a period of stability, to take stock of it all, re-attest the men, re-equip them, re-document them and, when the inevitable fatigues allowed, to re-start training. There were countless siting boards, survey boards, promotion conferences and planning conferences. The strain on the British officers was hectic but there was a determined air about all that was done. Before, all had been disintegration, now it was purposeful rebuilding. Settling in became the order of the day. Apart from such things as the army forms and procedures being different from the old Indian Army ones, military law was not the same and the 'army language' changed to English from Roman Urdu (the lingua franca of the days of the Raj) when such people as the doctor and visiting staff officers needed to talk with the men although, of course, battalion officers always spoke Gurkhali, and to Malay (which the men picked up in next to no time) when the local shops were visited. There were new ranks: gone, for instance, were Jemadar and Naik. Now it was Lieutenant (King's Gurkha Oficer), or Gurkha Lieutenant for short, and Corporal.

No battalion, however, could really get to grips with reforming itself until it had been made up to strength again. For this, many recruits were needed from Nepal to be trained by one of the four training wings that had been formed from the regimental centres. The one British Gurkha organization that had to stay in India was the recruiting set-up, as it was not then allowed on Nepalese soil. (That did not come for another eleven years.) This was divided into a western and an eastern depot and in each place the Indians took the lines over. In Jalapahar, above Darjeeling, conditions were described as 'Bedlam', while for the western depot at Kunraghat, very roughly half way between Kathmandu and Benares, tents had to be pitched on a disused rifle range. Difficulties seemed never-ending and the depot staffs were very hard-pressed as only nine of the original 54 clerks on the staff of the western depot remained. Six days after the depot became part of the British Army there were over 10,800 Indian Army pensioners who had nowhere else to draw their pensions. The tented camp was swamped, with all meagre facilities ludicrously extended, before arrangements were made for these people by the Indian Army. It was a minor miracle that the small staffs coped as well as they did, having the burden of recruiting also. So hectic was the recruiting side that some of the first recruits reached their training centres in Malaya dressed in nothing but a towel and a blanket.

Before absorbing these men into battalions, training them was a task of the very highest priority. Nothing was expected to distract from this. The official words of welcome by the Governor of Singapore were still ringing in people's ears after he had said, '. . . I trust that you will receive in peace, in this part of the world, the rewards of your hard work and courage during the war. I wish every one of you a happy and interesting life as members of the British Army serving directly under our King. I am confident that your bearing in peace will be no less distinguished than your bearing in war.'

The very last thing anyone wanted or expected was a war. Yet, by June of that year, 1948, that is just what did break out, never to be called by anything so rude or direct as war, though, only to be known as an Emergency.

2
MALAYAN EMERGENCY:
THE CRITICAL YEARS, 1948–1951

It is strange, looking back on it all with the gift of historical hindsight, to think that such an uninspiring start to a twelve-year campaign would see the only time that the communists were beaten in Asia in an armed struggle of their choosing. Certainly the bruising that the French, and later the Americans, suffered in Indo-China, to say nothing of the defeat of the Dutch in the East Indies, did see tactical military victories against Asian guerrilla armies many times during the fighting. The Dutch, French and Americans lost, in the end, because the political bases from which they operated were not as strong as were those of their adversaries. Even if Gurkhas had been deployed in the Indo-China struggle after, say, 1954, they could only have caused a delay in the inevitable.

The communist opposition in Malaya was based militarily on what happened during the Japanese war when the legendary Spencer Chapman and others like him trained, then deployed, Chinese communist guerrillas against the Japanese in a common cause. After the Japanese surrender the strange bedfellows, Chinese communists and British imperialists, got out from opposite sides and started chasing each other once again, but this time not for reasons of courtship.

The overwhelming initial Japanese victory against the Western powers during the Second World War had shown the frailty of the colonial masters. Communists in Asia were just as ready to take advantage of an opportunity to increase their hold over the masses as they were in Europe. Indeed, it is now open knowledge that the Soviet Union was active in formulating policies to deny the Western colonial powers their former territories. In 1948, 'colonies' and 'empire' were not dirty words. At that time, though, the Western powers did not understand about communist expansion. Thirty-six years later, in Nepal, I heard a senior Soviet 'intellectual' boast to his Nepalese audience that the Soviet Union was not only responsible for the Western powers losing their colonies in Asia and Africa, but was also at the bottom of getting the British to hand over power in India in 1947!

It was certainly the case that the Soviets were meddling in the area. At one level policy was being formulated and orders given by them in Calcutta in early 1948 under the guise of an Asian Youth Congress, although 'hard proof' of this is still disputed, to rid Malaya, French Indo-China and the Dutch East Indies of their colonial masters. On a lower level, I clearly remember a case in Cochin-China, in late 1945, when my Gurkha unit went there to disarm the Japanese and two Japanese battalions had to be retained to keep the Viet Minh at arm's length. The Japanese brought in a Russian they had captured when he was advising the Viet Minh. The man was indeed a Russian, was dressed in khaki uniform and had hammer-and-sickle badges on the lapels of his shirt collar.

It is not easy to tell when the communists had finally worked out their revolutionary strategy and tactics; certainly Mao Zedong, during the 'Long March' of 1934–5, was working from proven principles of communist revolutionary warfare. As regards the campaigns that developed in post-war colonial territories, communist revolutionary warfare was divided into three distinct phases that merged from one to another as violence escalated. First there was the Passive Phase, which consisted of the penetration of such organizations as trades union movements, local government, student unions, touring repertory groups and the like. In Malaya this phase can be said to have started in 1928, by which time communist agents from China had established a South Seas Communist Party in Singapore although the Malayan Communist Party itself (MCP) did not start up until 1930. Throughout the 1930s its main form of action was disruption of the two major industries of rubber and tin. As its aim had more of a personal sacrifice motive than one of personal gain it did not achieve much success but, helped by the conditions of the war against the Japanese, the communists managed to forge links with the local villagers as well as with many townsfolk. Natural antipathy between the Malay – easy-going, lacking any great interest in commerce but having some latent ability for organized work and in a position of political power – and the Chinese – extremely industrious, money-orientated but with no political power – had been exacerbated to a great extent by post-war conditions of near breakdown of the civil administration. These factors prompted the communists to launch into the second of their revolutionary phases, the Active Phase.

As its name implies, the Active Phase is where the revolutionaries would take positive action to increase their influence. This consisted of coercion, intimidation, acts of banditry, sabotage to weaken the economy (slashing rubber trees, for instance) and generally making life uncomfortable for those who did not admit to such pressures. At the same time it would become impossible for the government forces to give the protection necessary for the ordinary citizen to go about his business undisturbed as the communists had the initiative. Recruits would be attracted, numbers swell and elementary training given to militant activists. The type of person attracted by a spirit of adventure joined, so did many criminals 'on the run' from the police. The other two classes of person consisted of those who had had wives, mothers or sisters threatened if they did not join the cause and, lastly, the genuine zealot who, though few and far between, was the most dangerous of them all. Such a situation provided the 'sea of people' for the communist fish to swim in. Detection was very hard, as was discovered in the Vietnam conflict – an 'innocent' labourer, rubber-tapper or tin-miner by day could, in fact, be the hard-core fighter of the night, who had managed to spy out juicy targets during his normal work in daylight hours.

Gradually, like the widening ripples of a stone thrown into a pond, the influence of the communists would spread to swathes of territory, which would then be taken over and become 'liberated zones' in which the government had no influence except when it sent in large numbers of troops. As these zones were increased in size and number, so the third phase of revolutionary warfare would emerge, the Counter-Offensive Phase (so called, presumably, because by then the communists were in a position to counter the government's security forces successfully). The communists would topple the government by defeating it militarily and take over responsibility for running the country. This was the phase of Mao's struggle in China when the Malayan Emergency started with the communists on the verge of beating the nationalists, politically and militarily. This third phase never happened in Malaya. In fact the second phase, conducted from 1948 to 1960, revealed that not only had the communists overestimated themselves, their political base was never as strong as that of the government, so they failed and reverted to phase one. Although they were an expensively hard nut to crack, they were still cracked.

On my way through Delhi, in December 1947, to join my new Gurkha unit, I was told by the commander of the British Gurkhas, India, Brigadier R. C. O. Hedley, CBE,DSO, that he had been approached by a senior Indian official with the incredible suggestion that the British Army Gurkhas should all stay in India for another year so that their accommodation could be made ready for them. This offer, that could hardly have been initiated by the official himself, was looked upon with extreme distaste and was completely ignored, to the eventual cost to the communists.

At that time there were two British battalions in Singapore and one in Penang, an island off the north-west corner of Malaya, and a gunner regiment in Tampin, about 160 miles north of Singapore. There were two battalions of the Royal Malay Regiment (RMR) that were still recovering from the war years, so not orientated sufficiently towards an operational role to be immediately effective, while the Malayan Police had neither jungle squads nor special police for guard duties. In other words, depleted – without any Gurkhas to call on – the communists would have had the run of the country virtually to themselves.

Luckily for the peace of mind of the Gurkha battalions, nothing of the communist plans was known about and, certainly in those very early days, no thoughts of war or even of being deployed on operations were in anyone's mind. Everybody's aim was for a period of stability and achieving a standard that their 'new' army would be proud of. The inexperience of many of the rank and file was an extra, unwanted factor when operations started in June, less than two months after the arrival of the last unit from India.

The deployment of the Gurkha battalions had covered areas of the country that had previously been a military vacuum. To the top military brass, unrealistically over-confident and complacent, looking at their wall maps with coloured pins denoting battalions, it must have seemed of no operational consequence whether the units were under strength or not. On the ground the Gurkhas set about establishing themselves as best they could under the circumstances, blissfully unconcerned with any of the problems facing the top military planners or the apathy and lack of any coordinated policy on the part of the colonial government – there was no Special Branch, counter-subversion being the concern of the Criminal Investigation Department – and blithely unaware of any hostile elements, which were just about to disrupt their lives for a decade.

THE GREEN HELL

The Malayan peninsula stretches for about 400 miles from north to south, lying strategically between Thailand and Singapore, dividing the Indian Ocean and the South China Sea, and never more than 180 miles wide. So near the Equator is it that the climate is wet and hot (around 30°C) all the year round – there are no seasons and it rains a lot. Four-fifths of it were then covered in jungle, either tropical rain forest or, where the virgin forest had been cut down, thick, and in places, impenetrable, secondary growth. Down the middle of the country, especially in the northern part, is a range of mountains, rising to 8,000 feet, with, on either side, a profusion of broken country, often steep-ridged hills, which descend to flat and swampy plains sweeping to the coast. The terrain to the south is generally much flatter and swampier. Rubber estates and tin mines had been established off the main road that runs from north to south. In 1948 the ownership and management of these enterprises were almost entirely European; palm oil, pineapples and timber had not started to diversify the economy to any significant extent.

Movement through the jungle was normally restricted to about a thousand yards an hour, while in swamp it could be as slow as a hundred. Game tracks and, where aborigines lived, paths could be used but were an invitation to be ambushed. Following water courses allowed no quicker movement and the undergrowth on either side was probably thicker than elsewhere, while the steep banks of many streams were obstacles. Under the canopy of trees visibility was also heavily restricted, often being no more than a few yards in any one direction, although places where there were more panoramic vistas did exist. At man height much of the light is shut out by the trees, which can grow to over 150 feet tall. Seedling trees, creepers and undergrowth in tangled profusion made all progress very slow, especially as men had to keep their eyes skinned so that they could shoot instantly yet look where they were treading so as not to trip up. Commanders also needed to keep a constant eye on map and compass. Leeches, hairy caterpillars, ticks, wasps, hornets, along with the occasional scorpion and snake, all added to the hazards if not the misery, which induced an enervating and all-pervading weariness. This was exacerbated by the weight of the man's pack and, very often, being wet through with sweat or rain added to the strain in the seemingly endless patrolling and ambushing – a major tactic to dominate the jungle, so often with no visible result.

This was the terrain that the troops had to operate in for weeks on end against an enemy who became more experienced, cannier and, after the first three years of the Emergency, far harder to exterminate.

This enemy, known to the Gurkhas as 'dushman' or 'daku' – from the word 'dacoit', were the remnants of the wartime Malayan Peoples Anti-Japanese Army, with the 'J' changed to 'B' for British. They were the armed wing of the MCP and soon changed their name once again to the Malayan Races Liberation Army (MRLA). This 'army' followed the British pattern of regiments, battalions, companies and platoons, some of which operated independently. It consisted of ten regiments, numbered accordingly, deployed country-wide, based in deep jungle camps cleverly sited and well hidden, with the approaches carefully guarded. Strengths varied considerably and, at the start of the Emergency, numbered about 5,000 active 'soldiers', far fewer than the armed forces, which, with the police, were collectively known as the 'Security Forces'. The 'soldiers' were regarded as 'bandits' until it was discovered that that term had adverse nationalist Chinese connotations, when they were officially designated 'Communist Terrorists' or CT for short.

There was also a civilian side to the MRLA, called the Min Yuen (Masses Movement), who were outwardly ordinary citizens. Their task was to provide the CT with food and information. Their method of obtaining food was to take it from other citizens, without payment and often by the use of threats of severe punishment for non-compliance. As regards information, such people as rubber-tappers, shopkeepers and Public Works Department labourers were used as 'screens' to report security force movements. Without the Min Yuen the MRLA would have been very severely restricted.

Being a communist organization there was a strong political chain of command that worked in tandem with and had authority over the military commanders. From the Secretary-General – Chin Peng, MBE, who had marched in the London Victory Parade in 1946 – at the top, the command stretched through regional and district to branch committees, whose members were fanatical.

The Malayan Emergency was a guerrilla-orientated campaign. Malaya had no fixed lines, stable fronts or firm boundaries in the accepted military sense, as the enemy were all internal, less a few who came over the Thai and Singapore borders. The Malayan campaign was conducted in support of an established government, so the all-important political stability was never seriously threatened, unlike in Vietnam and the American involvement. After 1949 the MRLA rarely took any form of offensive action against the army and so had to be sought out by relentless cunning, and time-consuming and patience-testing efforts at all levels. However, success did not essentially depend upon high command – although correct policy was of paramount importance – but rather on the man on the spot, in the jungle or rubber estates, whose initiative, resourcefulness, self-reliance, sustained courage, stamina and instantaneously correct reaction to a situation could be, and often was, decisive. Thus it was ultimately the junior leaders and riflemen, seldom above company level, more often at platoon strength, who slogged it out and bore the brunt of it all. This was a testing call to the best-trained troops even under normal circumstances.

1948: NO POLICY AT THE TOP

When the Emergency was declared by the High Commissioner of Malaya on 17 and 18 June the die seemed very heavily loaded against the Gurkhas being able to answer the call to action against the English King's enemies as was generally expected of them. Despite a dearth of experienced NCOs and trained riflemen, some battalions were ordered to send soldiers to form Force Ferret,* which operated in some parts of

*Force Ferret: special groups operated in the jungle against the CT. One group would be split into four teams, e.g., from Ist Seaforth, 2/6 GR, I/7 GR, Royal Malay Regiment, with

the country for three months, thereby reducing rifle companies to below fifty men. Before the recruits had even learnt how to fire their rifles they were sent to guard key points in the towns, where their orders were 'to refrain from loading rifles but to use the kukri or bayonet instead' and, sometimes, on tactical operations in the rubber plantations or the jungle. That they did all that was expected of them and, on occasions, gave their lives so doing, probably saved Malaya from falling to the communists during that most insecure period. It was a most critical time as, had the communists realized how weak the Security Forces were, they could have gained an irreversible momentum. Emphasizing this aspect of effort on the part of the Gurkhas in no way belittles the amount of hard work and sacrifices of the Malayan police and the Royal Malay Regiment – who were so very nearly engulfed by the communist impetus – nor the work of the troops from Britain, Australia, New Zealand, Rhodesia, Nigeria, Kenya, Fiji and Sarawak, all of whose time came after the initial momentum of the communists had been broken by the Gurkhas. It was more 'touch and go' than anyone appreciated. Instead of there being 'mind against mind' as each side tried to read the enemy's intentions, the British officers' minds were as much, if not more, attuned to starting up the British Army's Gurkhas virtually from scratch than seeing themselves as the one, fundamental link between carrying out government policy as it evolved and communist aggression as it became manifest, to prevent Malaya from being overrun. Indeed, in 1948, most of the senior British officers, with the Burma campaign fresh in their minds, had no idea that they had a different sort of war, a revolutionary war, on their hands, so they drastically underestimated the CT's ability to stick it out. 'It'll be over by Christmas' were words that had to be eaten more than once.

This was the background to the start of a decade's deadly game of hide-and-seek. Communist policy on operations against the Security Forces was on two levels: they would concentrate on 'soft' targets, such as small groups of policemen guarding European-owned plantations and tin mines or on road ambushes against 'soft-skinned' vehicles. The establishment of a Chinese Home Guard in the early 1950s, as opposed to an all-Malay police force, was regarded with much greater virulence and attracted many attacks. As regards the army, the communists would turn aggressive only when they were certain of success in capturing arms and ammunition, and only retaliate if surprised, when they would fight hard to make a clean break. The military

Chinese liaison officers, Dyak trackers and a detachment of Royal Signals and it would be commanded overall by a European rubber-planter who knew the district well and had a fund of invaluable local knowledge and jungle lore. The force was, however, expensive in manpower and was, in any case, no long-term solution.

were the hunters, the CT the hunted. The main aspect for the Security Forces was the monotonous, uncomfortable, unpleasant, physically exhausting slog of it all, rather than the danger and fear associated with a conventional war.

Because there was no Supremo there was no coordination between the military, police and various other organs of government. This meant that troops were called on at short notice, often on spurious grounds, often too late and were, far too often, unsuccessful, hampered as they were by the inexperience of their junior ranks. Initially operations consisted of sweeps designed to flush the CT into stops, normally time-consuming and ineffective, or small sub-units, mostly of platoon strength, were 'lent' to a district to see what could be done to help the police or the hapless planters, who were lonely on their estates and still bitter about the military defeat only six years before. They and their workers were prime targets and many ghastly acts were perpetrated against them in an effort to disrupt the economy. They were easy targets so troops were needed to escort them until Special Police had been enrolled for this task. However, all such employment was so haphazard and lacking in organization, besides being wasteful of military resources, that they were soon abandoned in favour of patrols of small strength, based on plans laid at company level.

The CT kept mostly to the jungle, coming out from time to time to commit atrocities. Food was then no problem; the main sources of supply were the Min Yuen-dominated 'squatters' and estate labourers. The 600,000-odd squatters were illegal Chinese immigrants who had settled in remote areas without land title. Over the years the government had done nothing about them, if only because it could not cope with the immensity of the problem. Despite the CT effort forcibly to dissuade the European tin-miners and planters from staying at their work, there was no wholesale evacuation from mining areas or plantations, which the CT had optimistically forecast. So, from the very start, the communists failed to achieve the disruption of the economy that was essential to their success. They also operated in units too large at that time for the accepted methods of guerrilla warfare. Contrary to guerrilla tactics, by pressing on indiscriminately with their policy of terrorism, arson and murder, they failed to 'swim in the waters' of the local people.

The overall communist planning and strategy were approved and orders promulgated by June 1948, yet the opening of the communist offensive seemed to take the authorities by surprise, although warning had been given that something nasty was in the wind. The senior general in Kuala Lumpur did not endear himself to the planting community when in response to the question of what he did when he received news of bandits from the planters, he said he took the last nought off and acted accordingly. 'I can tell you,' he said to one press conference, 'this is by far the easiest problem I have ever tackled . . .'

Battalions found themselves guarding vital points in towns, escorting the nightly mail trains, searching villages and patrolling rubber estates. 2/6 GR had the dubious distinction of having the first fatality of the Emergency when a Gurkha soldier was killed and 2/7 GR, shortly afterwards, suffered the first fatal casualty of a British officer. Rocket-firing aircraft and resupply by air were first used in July for 2/6 GR who were sent on a punitive expedition to the borders of Pahang and Kelantan states. They had to follow up the bandits who had entered a valley that was, rather unusually, controlled so strictly by Chinese who had been living there for a couple of centuries that, during the war, even the Japanese had had to get permission to enter the area. When aircraft supported 1/7 GR for the first time, recognition of the target proved so difficult to the pilot that it was the troops who were strafed. Helicopters were very few and far between to start with and were not a factor in planning operations for some years.

All the stories that follow can only be tiny glimpses of how the British Army Gurkhas responded to the various and varying situations. Interspersed among them are short explanations of any changes of policy that altered the pattern of action on the ground, as well as any other points pertinent to operations.

Probably the neatest operation of those days involved surprise and secrecy in the deployment of troops interposing between the guerrillas in the jungle and their civilian helpers by themselves living in the jungle and sending patrols forward. That does not sound anything out of the ordinary, but the strange thing about operations in those very early days was that none of us thought in terms of jungle warfare or even of spending nights away from base. This was partly because the myth of the Malayan jungle's impenetrability still lay heavily on people's minds and had yet to be dispelled, and partly because no one was geared up for jungle operations then. In the case I am describing, a company of 1/10 GR, under Major J. A. Castle, spent about three weeks in the area of Poh Lee Sen, a 'squatter' village fifteen miles northeast of Kulai in Johore state. Under cover of darkness, the Gurkhas entered the jungle four miles south of Poh Lee Sen and made a base. Despite appalling weather conditions, they spent the next two weeks combing the area, finding an armourer's workshop complete with tools and small arms, ammunition, radio sets, grenades and massive quantities of communist literature. This led to the arrest of 67 Chinese squatters. Enemy attempts to ambush one of the Gurkha patrols failed. In all, it showed how prepared the bandits were and how much they had penetrated the local population. Major Castle was made MBE.

A far less clinical operation was when I was sent for and told to take a platoon (of 1/7 GR) and go to a small village, Sepang, in Selangor state and show ourselves to as many people as possible, as well as look for a group of bandits that was being organized for operations: I was told I'd be away for a week and to do what I could.

Sepang was a typically rural Malayan village with a couple of streets, a district office, a police station and a few shops, all owned by Chinese. The Malay community was to be found in even smaller villages, 'kampongs', in the neighbourhood. I learnt that the bandits lived in a large squatter area that lay between the European-owned rubber estates and the jungle. The chief bandits were known as the 'Killer', the 'Extortioner', 'Quartermaster' and the 'Drill Master' – the latter exercising his charges in weapon training and drill, even summoning his recruits by bugle.

I spent the week taking a section or two of Gurkhas to the various estates, visiting the planters and being briefed on the situation as they saw it – uniformly abysmal! We 'showed the flag' and familiarized ourselves with the countryside, which was dull, flat and, being near the coast, apt to be swampy. We made foot patrols off the estate roads and on the fringes of the squatter area. The more we showed ourselves, as indeed were our orders, the more we jeopardized any chances of concrete results.

On our last morning, patrolling at dawn behind one of the estates on the fringe of the squatter area, we were surprised to hear, in the distance, faint but clear, a bugle being blown. Moving slowly towards it – the going was slow – we heard volleys of firing, still far away, which we put down to range practice. With no Security Forces within many miles it had to be bandits, but we found nothing.

I was given an extension of two weeks and flew over the area which was much larger than I had expected. It was a patchwork of tangled scrub, tapioca plots, vegetable gardens, scattered dwellings and deep-green swamp areas. The jungle, with its foreboding, unbroken canopy, stood proud, extending to the north while, to the south, lay the tidier patches of rubber and coconut estates. My twenty-odd men could be there for years and never get a smell of the bandits unless we were incredibly lucky.

I then led a patrol back to the area where we had heard the firing, not knowing really what to look for, nor what to recognize if we found it! We did find some strips of raw meat laid out in an otherwise empty booth that might have been a bandit collecting point. Just up the track were two huts, which we investigated. Nobody was inside. One of the Gurkhas standing by a tree took up a firing position aiming along the track and hit his leg on something hidden in the undergrowth. This turned out to be a sack containing a large tin brimming with packets of documents, weapon-training pamphlets, histories of communism complete with pictures of Karl Marx and lists of monies. Although everything was written in Chinese, the pictures, diagrams and columns of figures were, to me, positive proof that we had stumbled into the home ground of the bandits.

I then split my force into two; with no radio I told the senior man of the other group that I would make a noise like a cuckoo from time to time to maintain contact. Some time later the ground rose to a small hill and at the top we found an empty sentry post with a kettle simmering on the hob. An alarm device had been rigged up outside, while inside the hut we found some army blankets and a wooden bugle. I 'cuckooed' to the others to join me. We were still checking the area when we heard a bird call from the jungle that lay, dark and foreboding, a hundred feet below us. A short while later there was an answering call. Ten minutes after that, further away and fainter, came two more calls, one answering the other and, even more faintly, another two calls ten minutes later still. I knew they were men, not birds, as the call each was using was of a bird that only ever called at dawn and dusk. It was not for some years that I, in my turn, realized that, as there are no cuckoos in Malaya, my signals must have alerted the bandits! On our way back to Sepang I mentally equated my wooden bugle as only one better than a wooden spoon.

There was no more excitement until two days later when I was contacted by an excited and blood-thirsty planter who told me that one of his labourers, a Sumatran, had been captured by the bandits, blindfolded and abducted to the far end of the squatter area where there was an arms cache. He had been held for a week, escaped and now offered to lead us back. Despite doubts, I decided to go with the planter and have a look. Although we were all tired, the local planting fraternity was still anti-army as a result of the British defeat at the hands of the Japanese six years before and I felt it right to lean their way. I took fifteen Gurkhas and the planter had five special constables, all Malays, and his tame Sumatran. It was 8 p.m. when we set out and the night was pitch black.

The Sumatran was in front and insisted that I walk directly behind him. Four hours later he seized my hand and held on to it so hard that I could hardly get out of his grip. Convinced that I was being led into a trap I wrenched my hand away. Very soon afterwards we had reached the place the Sumatran said the weapons were stored, behind two huts. Crossing over a small, wooden bridge we heard the sounds of a man running away – probably the sentry – and, against all orders, from directly behind me and missing me by inches, the planter opened fire.

Loud groaning was heard from inside the huts and there we found a wounded man. The weapons were nowhere to be seen.

Before we started back I checked my fifteen men, asked the planter if he had checked his and, on being told he had, we moved off. I had been warned that there were about 60 bandits in the vicinity so, with our presence now betrayed by the shooting, I wanted to get back to Sepang as fast as possible. After a short while I heard a scuffle to the side of the track. We froze, then took up prone firing positions facing the noise. There was a whispered 'Captain! Captain!' and, mindful of Japanese ruses in Burma, I gave my torch to the Gurkha on my right and whispered to him to shine it at the noise, at arm's length. The beam revealed two men, clasped together, one in front of the other. The man behind wore light-coloured uniform and the man in front wore Security Force green. It seemed, as the light flickered over them, that the man behind was using the man in front as a shield. I hissed to the Gurkha to put the light out and before I could decide what action to take a shot rang out, followed by a rasping sigh and the hurried movement of someone running away.

The wounded man proved to be one of the planter's special constables, so he could not have checked his men as he said he had. We gave him what first aid we could and carried him to the nearest house where he could stay until help was sent. I never did discover who the other man was nor what the pair of them were doing.

By the time we got back to Sepang I was nearly asleep on my feet. I went to the police station to give in my report and found that news of the incident had already reached the police. I learnt that the special constable had died during the night and, besides the wounded Chinese in the hut, the planter's burst of automatic fire had killed a woman, none other than the Quartermaster's wife. For my part I was told that I would have to stand trial for murder. I felt this to be an inappropriate reward for all we had tried to do but, having only had four hours' sleep in just under four days, did not argue. While I could just, but only just, see the police point of view, to my Gurkhas it was utterly incomprehensible. This not particularly exciting incident was typical, given the absence of overall firm policy.

I then left on home leave and the murder charge was quietly dropped. However, a row blew up as a result of troops from one state, Negri Sembilan, being sent to another, Selangor, without permission or operational clearance. It was symptomatic of the lack of any coordination at any level and the planters 'calling the shots'. Junior British officers would have much responsibility put onto them that would normally have been shouldered by NCOs and this would continue to be the case for as long as the Gurkhas were not up to their traditional peak of formidability and efficiency.

Towards the end of 1948 the planting community bitterly complained to the Govenor of Malaya, Sir Edward Gent, that not enough was being done for them and they demanded that an all-out war be declared against the communists.

1949: THE MAKINGS OF A POLICY

By early 1949 the CT had become more daring in their methods. On reflection it could be because they underestimated the Security Forces' potential, which had in no way been fully realized – so many teething troubles had there been and still were for the Gurkhas in their 'new' army.

Security Forces' weaknesses at ground level were obvious and were exacerbated by a combination of the following factors: no joint planning between the police, who had their ear to the ground but lacked the ability to take enough advantage from it, and the military who were in the reverse situation; a wrong appreciation of the long-term gravity of the communist insurrection that resulted in only short-term measures being taken; a paucity of trained soldiers; and many commanders thinking in terms of a 'hot' war with 'front lines' and other conventional aspects, as opposed to thinking in a guerrilla or communist revolutionary warfare context so, in turn, underestimating the communist terrorist potential.

Thus it was, in January 1949, 1/6 GR suffered a major setback when a platoon of 'A' Company was ambushed at Sintok, north of Alor Star, two miles from the Thai border; Major R. E. Barnes, Captain (KGO) Tulparsad Pun and nine Gurkha soldiers were killed. The incident happened because too few precautions had been taken during the jungle warfare training that all soldiers were being put through before being committed on 'serious' operations. The first contact of the platoon patrol was when the leading scout saw the enemy coming down a path towards him. The Gurkha managed to kill one of the enemy with his first burst of Sten gunfire, which seemed to be the signal for the terrorist ambush to open fire on the whole platoon who had been advancing up an enclosed path. Barnes and all but one of the leading section were killed immediately and the Gurkha officer was killed within minutes.

The middle and rear sections quickly returned fire and the battle went on for half an hour, when Lance Corporal Gaine Gurung was killed; whereupon the survivors withdrew, taking their wounded with them. It was then found that eight other Gurkhas had also been killed and three wounded. One of the wounded riflemen was in the leading section and

In the first six months of operations, the British Army Gurkhas were awarded 1 MC and 5 MM.

was hit three times but when the terrorists closed in to collect the dead men's weapons he feigned death. It worked, and when it became dark he managed to walk the four miles back to camp. Lance Corporal Gaine Gurung, who had seized an LMG from a wounded rifleman, played a major part in keeping the enemy at bay until he too was killed. He was awarded a posthumous Mention-in-Despatches.

This whole incident was a serious warning that the enemy were highly skilled jungle fighters (the ambush position could not have been bettered) and that they had a first-class Intelligence system. Before this incident, there was no separate military doctrine to counter the concept of revolutionary warfare as opposed to conventional warfare in the jungle, as had been developed during the Burma and Pacific campaigns. Counter-revolutionary warfare slowly developed, in its own right only after this sad display of military incompetence.

Two government measures taken during the first part of 1949 were of the greatest significance. Mr. C. C. Tan, the brilliant Chinese who became Head of Psychological Warfare in 1956, wrote:

'It took the British time to realize the futility of blaming the defenceless squatters for non-cooperation and fence-sitting . . . [and] to wake up to the fact that such a policy had the effect of playing into the hands of the communists. [Some squatters] were initially attracted by the MCP's programme of "land for the landless" and political enfranchisement for their own "people's government". Since without protection the public could not be expected to resist the communist terrorists, the idea was soon conceived that individual members of the rural population could be brought to places where protection could be given. On 1 March 1949 the government introduced national registration . . . every adult had to register and was issued with an identity card. The communists and their supporters dared not present themselves for registration. On 28 May 1949, a regulation was promulgated providing the authorities with the power to settle the squatters.*

Registration separated the sheep from the goats and provided useful information on the distribution of the squatters, which could be used as a basis for resettlement planning. Even though lack of experience and inadequate staff hampered initial planning, this was a truly crucial decision against which the MCP was forced to mount an extensive pro-paganda campaign encouraging the squatters to resist resettlement. It was the start of a two-pronged campaign plan – military action to wipe out the terrorists and administrative action to protect the population – the basis, in fact, of victory.'

*Concentrations of resettled Chinese squatters were known as New Villages and the Home Guard that was raised to protect them was formed from the ex-squatters themselves.

By this time the CT had found out that the Gurkhas were having difficulties at junior command level and that planning and determination could provide a reward in gaining arms and ammunition in road ambushes. These became more and more frequent and were only successfully countered when armoured lorries, scout cars and strict convoy discipline had been introduced.

Large-scale operations appreciably increased. 1/6 GR were the first unit to be airlifted to an operational base and 1/10 GR the first unit to make significant use of aerial resupply. Air strikes were used more and more frequently against suspected terrorist hideouts.

The High Commissioner, Sir Edward Gent, lacked the ability to direct events as they should have been; he was recalled to London for dismissal but he never reached England as he was killed when his aeroplane crashed on the way back. His successor, Sir Henry Gurney, also found it almost impossible to inject any sense of urgency or reality into his subordinates in the Kuala Lumpur secretariat and this soon became obvious to the thousand-odd 'front line' planters who bitterly commented upon it. All this had an adverse effect on the conduct of operations.

Sir Henry did, however, have an imagination for far-sighted plans. Soon after he became High Commissioner a retired officer, General Sir Harold Briggs, who had much Burma war experience, was recalled to be the Director of Operations. Despite resentment being shown by the then radical departure from normal government procedure, he was given authority over all Security Forces and also power over civil departments in so far as the Emergency was concerned. Not obvious to others at that juncture, both these men saw that the key to the problem facing the Security Forces was to prevent the CT from getting vital support from the Min Yuen and, at the same time, to protect the squatters who faced torture and death if they refused to cooperate. Several military commanders at battalion level had already taken what steps they could in this direction but they had never had any backing from the top. Now they had.

Briggs reached the conclusion that the country should be cleared of terrorists systematically from south to north, simultaneously isolating them from the people and so forcing them into the open. The plan that was evolved and that carried his name more than any other paved the way for final victory. The decision was taken to lift the squatters from their dwellings on the jungle fringes and resettle them in New Villages – an enormous task. Once inside the villages the Chinese still had to be protected, which tied down police inside and troops outside. The CT reacted violently to the Briggs Plan by trying to break the morale of the villagers through attacks, murders and intimidation as well as through propaganda directed against the Security Forces. Shrill claims of brutality, theft and rape were made, to say nothing of plain downright heavy-handedness and lack of concern. In reality, all the soldiers, British and Gurkha, had behaved scrupulously fairly and many Chinese were, in fact, very impressed by the troops' patient impartiality and humane behaviour towards the squatters during the removal operations.

The second part of the Briggs Plan, which was to deprive the CT completely of their food supplies, made them change their operational methods. They had to go into the deep jungle and grow their own crops and this, in turn, critically affected the pattern of operations for the Security Forces. Naturally none of all this happened quickly; more than two years were needed to complete such an ambitious scheme. Nevertheless another phase of the Emergency had begun.

The Gurkhas have a saying that well exemplifies the type of burdensome, sweat-stained, frustrating, tiring, normally low-key, often unsuccessful, sometimes very dangerous and occasionally dramatically won mini-battles that comprised jungle operations, known as 'ulu bashing' to the British troops, that were a constant of 1949: 'To work in the dark and to sing beside a river.'*

Over in Hong Kong 2/6 GR and 2/10 GR manned police posts on the border as the battle raged in China between nationalists and communists. However, the requirement for more troops in Malaya saw both battalions directed there, a Gurkha presence in Hong Kong being provided by men who had recently been formed into the Gurkha Engineer Regiment. The embryo Gurkha Signal Regiment remained in Malaya for all their training.

In 1949, by Royal Command, The Gurkha Regiment was renamed The Brigade of Gurkhas; 10 GR received a royal title and became the 10th Princess Mary's Own Gurkha Rifles in recognition of outstanding service in the Second World War.

1950: GETTING TO GRIPS

Johore State had always seen more communist activity than elsewhere. It was the military area of 1/2 GR who had been trying, all through 1949, to get to grips with the terrorists, especially 7 Company, MRLA, probably the most ruthless and militant group, which operated in north Johore in the Labis area. On 5 January 1950 the terrorists ambushed a train near Labis and, although extensive follow-up operations were mounted, no contact with them was made. Information of the CT's hide-out reached Special Branch.

---

*'Ulu bashing' from the Malay word 'ulu' meaning 'the headwaters of a river'. Honours and awards in 1949 included 4 DSO, 10 MC, 8 DCM and 30 MM.

A message was passed to Major P. Richardson, commanding 'B' Company and, in the small hours of the 22 January, a 2-platoon-strong force moved out. As it happened the telephone was used to pass the details and the line was bad. Richardson, tall, shy and adored by his men, had received a garbled version of the message and did not go to the place intended. Had he gone there the Gurkhas would not have found any enemy. As it was, it turned out to be the largest contact in the whole Emergency! The area the Gurkhas went to was a mixture of rubber, swamp and paddy and, as dawn broke, their visibility was severely restricted by a thick, ground mist.

There was still a shortage of senior ranks and platoon commanders so both platoons were commanded by corporals; Richardson had the company sergeant major with him in his group. Soon after it was light they started to advance, Richardson in the middle with a platoon on either flank. After advancing only a hundred yards Rifleman Bombahadur Gharti saw a terrorist run towards a squatter's hut fifty yards further on. The Gurkha opened fire and was answered by the appearance of several terrorists who came at him out of the mist, firing. Bombahadur, firing from the hip, charged into them and killed at least four of them.

Close behind, slightly in front of the right-hand platoon, Richardson saw a CT coming towards him, armed with a rifle. Both fired at each other and both missed. Immediately afterwards, Richardson was engaged by two more Chinese, both of whom he killed. At the same time he heard a blood-curdling shriek from behind and turned to see a CT slashing at a body lying partly-hidden in the long grass. Instantly realizing that it must be one of his Gurkha bodyguards who had been overpowered, Richardson took aim and shot the man who was hacking at the Gurkha with a 'parang' chopper. The Gurkha had been badly cut, suffering extensive injuries to his neck and skull. Evacuated as soon as possible, he died in hospital that evening.

While this was happening the rest of the terrorists tried to move off in the other direction. The mist had lifted by this time and the CSM, Warrant Officer Bhimbahadur Pun, having taken over the other platoon, carried out a deft flanking movement, forcing the rest of the terrorists into an area of swamp and paddy between the two platoons. The slaughter was swift and bloody.

After the battle had died down the killing ground was searched. Twelve bodies and some weapons were recovered. The ground being swampy a number of bodies and weapons could have remained hidden. Several months later it was established that 35 terrorists had either been killed outright or been mortally wounded, including the commander of 7 Company,

Major P. Richardson was awarded the DSO and WO II Bhimbahadur Pun the DCM, the first ever to 2 GR, because Gurkhas did not become eligible for the decoration until 1948.*

Another example of fighting at company level was provided by 1/6 GR, who were in the Jerantut district of Pahang and much wiser now than had been the case the previous year. Information was received about a large force of terrorists having moved through a nearby rubber estate and 'C' Company, commanded by Major E. Gopsill, MC, was detailed to investigate. The company commander went and made a reconnaissance while the company was getting ready for a follow-up, drawing rations, weapons and ammunition. He found fresh tracks of an estimated 150 to 200 men.

'C' Company moved off, temporarily losing the tracks when the CT had left the rubber estate and gone through a squatter area, finding them again once they were in the jungle. They followed the tracks until night-fall when it was reckoned that the Gurkhas were about four hours behind the terrorist group.

All next day the tracks were followed but it was only late in the after-noon that contact was made – by an enemy sentry, sitting astride a log, firing a burst of Sten gun at the leading scout. Gopsill appreciated that a frontal attack was his best option; it was a wise decision as the camp, consisting of about thirty huts, was on the reverse side of the hill in front of the Gurkhas, running down to a large swamp. It had been well sited as, on the right of the company, was a steep ridge, covered with thick, thorny creepers and the left side was also protected by very dense jungle.

The Gurkha scout returned the fire, killing the sentry. 8 Platoon then charged to their front, with 7 Platoon on the right and 9 Platoon on the left. Firing broke out everywhere. 8 Platoon, along with company head-quarters, reached the enemy camp and engaged a platoon's worth of terrorists. Six were killed and the rest escaped, covered by their own supporting fire from further down the slope.

Luckily, fire directed at 7 Platoon mostly went overhead, the CT misjudging the steepness of the slope. 7 Platoon were finding the going difficult as the thorny growth severely impeded movement. Some 25 minutes later a bugle call sounded from the direction of the enemy; this was the signal for a protracted burst of shooting at 7 Platoon, prior to a charge at them. The terrorists came down the slope, screaming and shouting.

They were about 30 yards from the Gurkhas before they were forced back up the hill, dragging their wounded with them. Another bugle call

*Certain British Army awards, pre-1948, were only made to Gurkhas when they were part of a British Division, e.g., 36 British Infantry Division, in Burma.

was blown and the enemy charged at 8 Platoon who were still in the camp. This was repelled, with several of the enemy being wounded, as their shrieks indicated. 8 Platoon then counter-attacked but got bogged down in the swamp at the bottom of the hill. They stayed there and the action continued on either side, as a third bugle call was sounded and the enemy charged on 9 Platoon. The sounds of the Gurkha charge 'Ayo Gorkhali' (Charge) were heard.

The commander of 9 Platoon, Captain (KGO) Dalbahadur Limbu, IOM – the platoon was detached from 10 GR to make up numbers – had lost contact with the rest of his men in the half-light and, with three men, was attacked by thirty or so CT on a small path at the edge of the swamp. Calling to an imaginary lot of Gurkhas to charge, Dalbahadur and his three men charged the enemy, putting them to flight, killing two and wounding six of them.

The pursuit was taken up and the camp was searched, yielding arms, ammunition and loot from previous raids. Blood was everywhere. A careful check resulted in only four bodies being found, but bloodstains showed that 25 men had been wounded. The Gurkhas had had no casualties and had only expended 700 rounds of ammunition.

The citation for the award of the DCM, the first ever won by 1/10 GR, by Lance Corporal Sherbahadur Rai, is given as it shows how the junior NCOs were recovering from the traumas of the previous two years:

'On 1 March 1950, Lance Corporal Sherbahadur Rai was returning from local leave in Johore Bahru, accompanied by some other leave details, on the civil train from Johore to Mentakab.

Between Bahau and Kemayan the train was derailed and ambushed at about 10.30 hours by a large party of bandits, positioned on both sides of a cutting. The carriage in which these Gurkhas were travelling came to a halt in the middle of the cutting. Hence the full force and volume of enemy fire was directed on this carriage as a result of which four Gurkhas were wounded, one seriously. The fire was so heavy that the men were pinned down. The enemy called upon the men to surrender and under cover of withering fire, one bandit, armed with a Sten gun, approached the carriage. Lance Corporal Sherbahadur immediately shot and wounded him and the latter withdrew. A second bandit tried to follow suit and was shot in the mouth by Lance Corporal Sherbahadur Rai.

Lance Corporal Sherbahadur Rai seized the chance to jump out of the train and charged the enemy. His action inspired the four wounded men to follow him. One was so badly wounded in the chest that Lance Corporal Sherbahadur was compelled to place him under suitable cover from fire. With the remaining three, however, he charged round the flank of the cutting, straight at the enemy who immediately withdrew. Lance Corporal Sherbahadur Rai and the three wounded men followed the bandits for one and a half miles, firing as they went. Eventually, on account of the wounded men, Lance Corporal Sherbahadur Rai was compelled to call off the pursuit. On the way back, he picked up the dead body of the bandit he had shot and, returning to the railway line, handed the body over to the police. He also dressed and bandaged the wounded Gurkhas. The highly courageous, bold action and inspiring leadership on the part of this young Lance Corporal undoubtedly prevented a serious incident from becoming a major disaster. As an example of offensive spirit in the face of great odds it is second to none . . .'

In 1950, after two years of the Emergency, matters hung in the balance, although there was some optimism, as shown when Major General Sir Charles Boucher, KBE, CB, DSO, the Major General Brigade of Gurkhas (as the senior officer was known) and the officer who took the brunt of the initial communist outburst, said, among other things in his farewell message to the Brigade on the eve of his retirement, that the Gurkhas 'have played the leading part in saving Malaya . . .'

The communist terrorists were being eliminated at a rate that out-numbered the military casualties but the police were losing more than the terrorists were, while over one hundred civilians were being murdered every month. Although the troops held the initiative to a great extent, there were many instances of there not being enough troops to contain the communists sufficiently to prevent their attacks on civilian targets.

The realization by authority that planning at all levels was needed led to the formation of War Executive Committees at state level (SWEC) and at district level (DWEC) at which the administration, police and military were appropriately represented. This was essential if efforts were not to be frittered away by lack of coordination. Special Branch Intelligence gathering, psychological warfare, food-denial operations, New Village defence and a host of other problems could not be the concern of only one element of government.

Company bases started to be a feature of battalion life. These were defended outposts, of anything up to fifty miles away from battalion headquarters, where a company, sometimes with an armoured car troop and a gunner detachment, was given its own area of territorial responsibility. Based in some buildings of a rubber estate, with maybe the soldiers under canvas or in portable shelters, they allowed a much greater and more intimate knowledge of the terrain and of the pattern of terrorist movement to be acquired, besides allowing time for members of the local DWEC to get to know and trust each other. Also it made the planting fraternity much more settled to have their own 'tame' soldiers nearby. Operations at company level became known as 'framework' operations, as they took place within the framework of DWEC's plans.

As the conduct of operations became better organized, so emerged tactical formations where none had been before. The name 'Brigade of Gurkhas' has no tactical significance: it is a title, the generic term for the Gurkha presence in the British Army and is analogous with the Brigade of Guards. Every Gurkha is a member of and every Gurkha unit is part of the Brigade of Gurkhas, no matter what tactical formation or static organization is served under. The senior tactical formation set up for operational command was 17 Gurkha Division and it became operational in 1950. Named after its famous Indian wartime forebear, it had its brigades similarly numbered: 48, 63 and 99, with an independent 26. It was normal to have two Gurkha and one British battalion in each brigade. Artillery and armoured support were entirely British; engineer and signal support were almost entirely Gurkha, while provost support consisted of equal Gurkha and British representation.

The commanders of these tactical brigades, not having known the jungle as did the men who had been operating in it, favoured large-scale operations, designed to disrupt, then separate, the communist guerrillas from their support in the New Villages. Named 'Jackpot', 'Avenger', 'Stymie' and other similar enigmatic titles so dear to the military planners' hearts, these operations lasted over a period of weeks, if not months, and, apart from tying troops down in large numbers, were often more successful in disrupting communist movement than in eliminating the CT by kills, captures and surrenders. Sweat, toil, discomfort and effort expended during these sweeps, ambushes, roadblocks and searches were not to be measured or reflected in tangible results. During 1950 rewards for information on kills and captures were introduced. Several CT took advantage of this scheme by ratting on their comrades; troops were never entitled to any monetary awards.

During the year there was trouble in Singapore. Riots erupted when a 13 year-old Dutch girl called Maria Hertogh, who had been separated from her parents in Java by the Japanese invasion, and had lived ever since with a Malay woman, was married to a Malay school-teacher. Her parents in Holland then found out about their daughter and claimed her, appealing in the Singapore Supreme Court. The marriage was declared illegal. This decision caused riots, with violent and ugly scenes disrupting normal life to such an extent that 2/6 GR and 2/10 GR were withdrawn overnight from jungle operations and sent to help in Singapore. It is only of academic interest to know that the hierarchy on the island had as much to learn about keeping the peace in a city as had their counterparts on the mainland about keeping it in the countryside, and had as high a proportion of 'dead wood' among their senior ranks, probably as a result of having been prisoners of war under the Japanese and never really having recovered.

1951: THE COMMUNISTS' NEW STRATEGY

Some time in 1951 a new, world strategy was put into action by the communists. As far as Asia seems to have been concerned, priority was now given to attracting and making use of nationalist sentiments to build up a communist-neutralist bloc against the Western powers.

This coincided with a changed situation in Malaya where, by mid-year, Security Force action had made such an impression on communist plans that not only were their tactics changed as a result but also efforts were made to draw off the Gurkha soldiers from the scene of the fighting and to discredit them as well.

As regards the changed tactics, there were wild reports circulated from Sarawak saying that Gurkha troops were wanted there, from Malaya; and once leave men were in the Transit Camp in Barrackpore, Calcutta, jute-mill coolies were paid 8 annas each from party funds to demonstrate outside the camp, demanding the returning leave men 'to throw away their weapons [they did not, in fact, carry any. The Gurkha guard commander showed considerable presence of mind by telling the leader, who called at him from the perimeter fence at the other side of the camp, that the Gurkhas would not fire if the demonstrators could not be heard. Accordingly, the main effort went off a couple of miles away] and not to rejoin their units.' Both these facts were experienced by me.

As far as the discrediting went, a perfectly normal leave party comprising 1,237 men, women, and children from all the units of the Brigade of Gurkhas travelling by boat from Singapore to Calcutta, called in at Rangoon. After a lapse of four days, a party from the Nepalese consulate visited the passengers on board. I was in charge of the troops and, after showing the Nepalese party round the decks, I was invited to return to the consulate. Once there I was told about a letter sent to the consulate saying that the boatload of Gurkhas was a battalion that had mutinied and was being sent home, in disgrace, to Nepal on disbandment and was not to be visited while in dock. I asked where this battalion was supposed to have been based and was told Kota Bahru, a small town near the northeast border of Malaya with

Honours and awards in 1950 included 1 DSO, 10 MC and 12 MM. At the first investiture to be held in Kuala Lumpur, 37 out of the 51 recipients were from the Brigade of Gurkhas.

Thailand where, except for a brief operation involving 'A' Company, 1/7 GR, that had only recently been concluded, no Gurkha unit had been since 1941, and then only briefly. (Most interestingly, in Kathmandu, in 1985, I could re-check this with the personalities of that time.) This pattern of diverse efforts to keep Gurkha troops away from trouble spots was again to be observed some years later, in 1962.

Details of the new policy only slowly seeped down to the CT in the jungle during which time there were many sharp little skirmishes between the Security Forces and the guerrillas, with much bravery being show on both sides. One such skirmish occurred in August 1951. 2/7 GR was stationed near Seremban, at Paroi, where there was a New Village next to the military camp. On the 17th, two platoons of 'A' Company were on patrol within two miles of the camp, in undulating scrub-covered terrain that gave longer fields of fire than could be found in jungle. The force was commanded by Lieutenant (KGO) Dhanbahadur Gurung, MC, IDSM, a man of unusual forcefulness, tactical talent, and courage, who was respected and feared by his men.

The Gurkhas were moving cautiously, on either side of a track – always a danger to walk along – with LMGs ready to give instantaneous covering fire, when they were ambushed by over 80 terrorists who were lying in wait in well-camouflaged positions sited on high ground, with an unprecedented five machine-guns, all pointing in the direction of the Gurkhas' advance.

The CT opened fire, killing two Gurkhas in the first burst. The Gurkhas charged and one man was wounded. Dhanbahadur was forced to withdraw to cover. During the next three hours both sides strove for an edge that would give them victory; Dhanbahadur led three more charges, with a man being wounded each time. The Gurkhas' ammunition began to run low – the CT seemed to be very well supplied – and Dhanbahadur, refusing to take cover himself, walked up and down in front of his men, barking out encouragement loudly enough for the enemy to hear. They tried to kill him, but in vain; they did not realize that 'the Gurung' was indestructible.

The messages sent by the radio operator, who showed considerable initiative when putting up his aerial, took time to be responded to as there was initially no reserve in camp. The company commander, Major E. Gopsill, DSO, MC, recently transferred from 6 GR, gathered a group of reinforcements and ran towards the firing. As he approached the fighting he saw, in the encroaching darkness, that the Gurkha position was about to be overrun by the CT – in fact Dhanbahadur had already given the order to counter-attack with kukris as they were too short of ammunition to be effective. Luckily, these reinforcements arrived in the nick of time to save the situation.

The bar to his MC that Dhanbahadur Gurung won might be thought inadequate recognition of such bravery. Two MMS were also awarded, one of them to a young rifleman, Harkabahadur Rai – during one of the CT charges a Chinese had tried to snatch the Gurkha's weapon from him and had his arm completely severed by a kukri stroke. Such hand-to-hand fighting rarely occurred during the Emergency. It was later learnt that the enemy lost eight killed with a further ten wounded.

Such spectacular contacts were infrequent high spots in the long and normally unremarkable run of trying to keep the terrorists away from their 'lifeblood' – supplies and information – provided by the Min Yuen. Squatters were still being resettled, Chinese Home Guards had been established (not without considerable misgivings) and national registration cards were being issued to all Malayan citizens. This was bitterly opposed by left-wing elements and the CT all over the country were constantly stopping buses and contacting estate labourers in order to get people's cards and burn them. The message was that, without cards, the 'running dogs' could neither call up the individual for military service (which had never been an intention) nor get hold of a person when they wanted to impose taxes. All this resulted in there being labour troubles on rubber estates, including strikes. Troops had to be used to escort tappers to work, put out mobile screens between them and the estate boundaries near the jungle and escort them back afterwards. All such activity took place between dawn and noon.

The rubber industry, then, was composed of certain large concerns or 'companies', with their head offices in Britain, normally consisting of many more than one 'estate' or 'plantation' in various parts of the country. The expatriate staff were known as 'planters', the labourers as 'tappers'. The larger the estate, the more senior the manager and the more 'divisions' and the more assistants to run them. Some divisions were co-located, others were separated by up to, maybe, ten or more miles. Being the only primary source of income (other than tin), it was essential for overall business confidence that levels of production be maintained as high as could practicably be expected; it was equally essential that financial returns be boosted as much as possible.

A rubber estate has a disquieting sameness – long lines of trees, stretching for miles, onto which are attached little porcelain bowls to catch the rubber sap, latex, as it drips down when the bark of the tree has been pared, 'tapped' in the jargon, by a sharp blade. The latex half-fills the bowls and a rubber tapper will have an area of trees, first to tap, then from which he will pour the latex into buckets. A network of laterite roads spreads over the estate, connecting tappers' 'task' areas, latex-collecting sheds and the estate factory that processes the liquid rubber into 'sheets'.

On well-managed estates the ground is planted with a cover crop, which holds the soil, prevents leaching and, being only a few inches high, gives an uninterrupted view. Mosquitoes thrive in the rain water that collects in empty latex cups, and make life misery.

Escorting the labourers was unpopular among the troops; it was boring work with little to show for it and the soldiers felt that they could be better used in a more positive role. If they were not visible to the tappers, work was suspended until 'protection' was in evidence – the estate managers were not keen on this. If troops ambushed the jungle fringes, in properly pre-selected ambush positions, they were more likely to have a successful contact, which the labourers with communist sympathies did not like. It was a messy situation.

My company was based in Rompin, a small village in the state of Negri Sembilan. My orders were to co-operate with the planters and, where possible, to act according to their wishes, which was not always possible. I had been contacted by one assistant planter with information that CT might try and approach the tappers near the jungle edge in one particular part of the estate, and asked if I would lay an ambush there. He would bring his manager to the area and point out that, although the place seemed deserted and so might be thought dangerous, in fact some Gurkhas with their British officer were, even then, observing them. The manager could then convince his labourers that they were being guarded although the soldiers were not visible, which meant that some of the remoter parts of the estate could be properly tapped.

I agreed to the scheme. On the appointed day, I took a dozen men, left camp soon after midnight, made a long approach march and, soon after dawn, reached the specified area. Camouflaged and having left no traces, we took up all-round fire positions. We were on a slope, at the bottom of which was a stream and a short rise on the other side where a red laterite road terminated.

I had been told that my particular area would not be tapped that day but plans had gone awry; I heard the banging of tins at a latex collection point then saw tappers flit from tree to tree. I was horrified to see that we were going to be discovered as one young Chinese tapper, a girl, was descending from the line of trees where the ambush lay in wait. At one spot she bent down, lifted her skirts and pulled down her knickers to relieve nature. Rifleman Bhimbahadur Limbu's self-control was tried to beyond its normal limit when, hidden in a thicker than usual clump of undergrowth, he saw this girl approach him, turn round before she saw him, move a pace backwards and squat. Bhimbahadur had just enough time to move his head to avoid the jet. The girl got up and moved away, unaware of any captive spectators. She was the only tapper on our side of the stream and she did not tap every tree. That probably spared us from discovery.

We all wanted to fidget as the mosquitoes were dreadful. After being in ambush for three hours two Europeans and a small armed escort approached us from the other side, from the estate road – the manager, who was armed with a shotgun, had a large Alsatian and his assistant with him. Stopping some sixty yards from us the assistant asked his boss if he could see anything in front of him. 'No', was the reply, so the assistant, with a touch of justifiable pride and a sweep of his arm, announced that 'John Cross and his Gurkhas are in ambush on the far bank.'

The reaction of the manager, who had spent three years in solitary confinement as a Japanese prisoner of war for reasons of conscientious objection, was understandably 'nervy' and was far from what had been expected. Angrily saying that he had not given any permission for the military to come onto his estate, he brought out his weapon and aimed it in our direction, vehemently declaring he would shoot anyone he saw, and then told his dog to go and smell us out. I quivered as I witnessed this, wondering how on earth we could remain undetected. The dog came over to our side, sniffed around but kept twenty or so yards below us. Five minutes later we were alone once more. Soon afterwards we withdrew.

That evening I went round to the manager's bungalow, some ten miles away from the morning's incident. 'I was told you were on the other division of my estate this morning. I went up there. Just as well you weren't there as my dog would have found you and I would have shot you first and asked questions later.' He grinned maliciously, meaning every word he said. His face dropped the proverbial mile when I repeated his conversation, word for word, back to him and described all that he and his group had done! He visibly blanched. Although maybe the CT were none the wiser that day, at least one European planter was!

General Sir Harold Briggs retired at the end of 1951, sadly dying soon afterwards. On 7 October of that year, a communist platoon was in an ambush position on the winding road leading to the hill station-cum-holiday resort of Fraser's Hill. Its target was any military convoy that might pass by, hoping to replenish its stock of weapons. The ambush was on the point of being lifted when, to its utter amazement, a large, black car, flying the Union Jack, followed by an escort vehicle, drove along the road below it. Realizing that the occupant of the car, a Daimler, could be no other than the High Commissioner, Sir Henry Gurney, they decided to open fire. The car stopped when fired on and, for a reason never discovered, Sir Henry got out on the side of the firing and stood there, as if asking to be shot, which he was, being killed instantly.

That day had been set aside for as many Gurkhas as possible to observe the holiest day of their most holy feast but it was cancelled, partly out of respect to Sir Henry and partly so that as many troops as possible could be used in the pursuit of the CT who had shot him. This sad event proved to be the turning-point of the Emergency; no longer could Whitehall delay in providing a Supremo to combine the duties of both High Commissioner and Director of Operations. The Commonwealth Secretary was sent out by the prime minister, Mr Winston Churchill, to make an on-the-spot assessment of the situation. At the end of the year it was announced that General Sir Gerald Templer had been chosen for this awesome and onerous task. He later became Colonel of the 7th Gurkha Rifles.

On his arrival Templer was displeased with what he found: morale was low, complacency in high places rampant, and that the Briggs Plan, although in theory a winner, was being delayed its full implementation to its detriment. With a determination and a vigour that the sleepy administration had never experienced before, nor which it believed could be sustained, Templer managed drastically to change the situation so much for the better that, within 32 months, there was no more need for a 'benevolent and paternal dictator'. Those who served under him, certainly at company commander level, were in complete awe of and had absolute trust in him.

Templer brought the message that the British government would declare its intention to grant Malaya democratic independence, but he had to convince everybody at all levels that it was in his own interest to work for, by helping the government and not the communists. In pursuance of this policy he coined the famous phrase, 'winning the hearts and minds of the people'.

Major General R. L. Clutterbuck who was, as a Lieutenant Colonel, the General Staff Officer Grade I on the Director of Operations' staff, 1956–8, wrote in the *United States Military Review* of 1965:

'The real crisis in Malaya occurred between 1948 and 1951, when the guerrillas operated in bands of 100 or even 300, numbers which enabled them to overwhelm any small village police post – maybe a sergeant and ten men – and to murder all government officials and known supporters in the village. It was vital that these police posts should hold out or, if overrun, be replaced; it was important that they had sufficient confidence not to succumb to the communist offers of a 'live and let live' deal. The call for platoons to bolster up every village police post had to be resisted. The solution was to position the infantry in company-sized camps from which they could respond for help . . . patrol the jungle fringes . . . react to raids . . . [make it hard for] large bands of guerrillas . . . to withdraw quickly enough to avoid casualties. These big bands suffered a constant drain [and] gradually split up into small groups, twenty or thirty strong [against whom] the village post could hold out with confidence.'

By the end of the year the Brigade of Gurkhas were told that they 'were firmly established [in the British Army] with an enviable reputation.'

Honours and awards in 1951 included 2 DSO, 4 MC, 5 DCM and 22 MM.

3
MALAYAN EMERGENCY: RESURGENCE OF HOPE, 1952–1956

1952: A NEW BROOM

Almost as soon as he arrived, Templer's influence began to be felt. He was a dynamic man and, from a mere company commander's level, he seemed exactly the breath of fresh air that was wanted – in any sense, a rare commodity in tropical Malaya. He managed to stir those in the secretariat and at lower levels of the government to such a tune that it was difficult to tell, during his first few months, whether the ordinary civilian functionaries or the CT hated and feared him the more.

The political assurance of Malaya's independence from Britain knocked out the main plank from the MCP's platform. Militarily, Templer ensured that cooperation at all levels was strengthened by allowing prominent citizens into the deliberations of the War Executive Committees (WECs). At soldier level he introduced the procedure of analyzing the techniques and tactics used during operations, especially when the CT and the Security Forces clashed. This he did by the introduction of a form called ZZ and this had to be filled in by the commander of every patrol when contact was made. There were many questions to answer and sketch maps to make. Questions such as where the sun was shining, who saw whom first, how long had the soldiers been away from their overnight base, when had they last had a break at the crucial juncture, and many others. All these forms were scrutinized by Templer's staff and weaknesses current to all missed contacts were the subject of special attention. Slowly, slowly, the ratio of kills-to-contacts improved.

This ratio was a measure of the standard of the soldiers. I myself was a company commander from late 1951 to mid-1956 and was always grieved when we muffed a contact. What had to be got used to was the monotony of the jungle, the patrolling, the ambushing, the dampness, the living in dirty clothes and, at the same time, the constant striving for professionalism and the necessity to be ready at all times for the unexpected. The statistics still haunt me: for every million hours of security-force endeavour in the Federation of Malaya the enemy was in the sight of a soldier's weapon for twenty seconds; the other is that, during the 438 days I was in the jungle, I spent a total of 5/9d – about 29p! One was either hot and sticky, or chilled to the marrow when it rained, always weighed down by equipment and a weapon, always having to move as though on glass, one had to be so cautious yet, in the moment of action, be as lissom as a goalkeeper trying to save a penalty kick, and as quick off the mark as a hundred-metres sprinter. Out of the jungle, in camp, just to walk about unencumbered was a joy.

We all felt sorry for the 1948 recruits, who were just returning from their first home leave when I took over the company. They had been recruited when everything was such a rush that quality had had to be sacrificed for quantity. Many of the missed contacts were directly con- tributable to them or to those NCOs who had been 'overpromoted' to fill gaps caused by the opt.

By 1 April, by which time the Brigade of Gurkhas had passed their fifth anniversary of joining the British Army, they had accounted for over a quarter of the Emergency 'bag' of CT eliminated, although the Brigade's strength did not represent a quarter of the Security Forces. The Emergency also passed the 5-year mark, with 814 of the elimina- tions, which reached the 1,000-mark on 3 December, resulting from Gurkha contacts.

Food denial operations continued to be a constant feature of deploy- ment with situations that called for a high standard of individual initiative arising, but there were many incidents where bravery was shown that were not connected with that aspect of operations but occurred while on routine patrol, as was witnessed on 20 August, in the jungle of Johore, to the east of Kota Tinggi.

It was the operational area of 'A' Company, 1/2 GR, and Corporal Hoshiyarsing Gurung was commanding a twelve-man patrol that was following up the tracks of a terrorist wounded the previous day. The track led up the side of a hill to the top. Someone noticed a branch, obviously recently broken by a man – a sure sign of human movement in the vicinity. The patrol commander immediately ordered the patrol to open out and move in extended formation.

A new footprint was detected but, before anything further could be done, a whistle blast shrilled and heavy fire, with at least three LMGs and many other automatic weapons, was opened by about thirty CT who were in a well-prepared position further up the hill. The initial burst of fire wounded a Gurkha Bren gunner and a rifleman; the rest of the patrol took up positions and returned the fire. Another rifleman was wounded and the patrol commander's arm was smashed by a bullet, but he continued to direct the patrol's fire.

Hoshiyarsing realized that, as the patrol was outnumbered, it was useless lying pinned down – bold action was needed. A lance corporal was ordered to make a charge against the enemy, covered by fire from the wounded man's Bren gun and the rest of the Gurkhas who could still use their weapons. The five unwounded men charged up the hill but were caught in crossfire and were forced to withdraw, only the lance corporal not being hit.

As the position was hopeless the patrol withdrew, taking their weapons with them. Hoshiyarsing managed to drag a wounded soldier about 60 yards and hid him in the undergrowth. The lance corporal and the remaining Bren gunner, Rifleman Bhaktabahadur Pun, helped to bring back the other wounded – Bhaktabahadur managing to carry his own Bren gun and the weapons of the two men he supported, all at the same time.

As this was happening the terrorists went down to the other three wounded and the two dead, and removed their arms and equipment. Somewhat surprisingly they did not kill the wounded men, nor did they follow up the rest of the patrol.

The regimental history states that the conduct of the wounded Gurkhas evacuated with the corporal was outstanding and their uncomplaining courage was 'overpowering' to those engaged in the evacuation. The worst hit, Rifleman Kharkabahadur Pun, was the best behaved, despite half a dozen separate wounds. He had to have a leg amputated.*

Companies would normally operate from temporary camps away from battalion for eighteen months, then return to the battalion's peacetime location for retraining. This would be a frantically busy two months, by the end of which time everybody would be glad to escape back to his company base. Sometimes an operational headquarters would be set up by a battalion away from its main location. One was 1/10 GR who had been sent to a notoriously bad area in Pahang, called Bentong. When it was time to leave, a farewell address was presented by the public and read:

To the Commanding Officer, Lieutenant Colonel J. S. Bolton, DSO, Officers and Men of the 1st Battalion, 10th Princess Mary's Own Gurkha Rifles.
Sir,

Your battalion arrived in Pahang over a year ago when spirits were low; we need not remind you of those days of terror, of murders and ambushes which took their dread toll of all nationalities. Through the skill and energies of your men the District has been improved beyond

*He was awarded the MM, while Corporal Hoshiyarsing Gurung received a bar to his MM, the only bar to the MM ever recorded as having been awarded to 2 GR up to that time.

recognition. The name of the Battalion has struck fear into the hearts of the Bandits, many of whom have fallen to your guns. It would be foolish of us to say that the District has been entirely cleaned up, for much remains to be done, but during your stay you have achieved one important thing, you have won the complete confidence of the people.

Never before, we believe, has so mixed a community taken a Battalion to its hearts so readily. The Battalion has been integrated with the Civil population quite spontaneously at all levels. There has never been the slightest friction. Nothing but continual display of mutual trust.

We are grateful to you. We shall never forget you. We know that our sincere and lasting gratitude will be some consolation.

Signed by the leaders of the four races of the town, Chinese, Malay, Indian and Ceylonese.

28 February 1952*

Later on in the year, on 1 September, 17 Gurkha Infantry Division became tactically operational. Gurkha sappers and signallers were fully deployed operationally, both in the field and at headquarters. This was the first time that Gurkhas, always renowned for being ace infantrymen, were used in other roles permanently.

Being away from officers who spoke Gurkhali, the English name for the debased Nepali spoken by the martial classes of Nepal when in the army, caused problems. In the old Indian Army Urdu was the lingua franca and all officers were expected to speak Urdu or the language of the ethnic group concerned. Not so after 1 January 1948. British officers with the corps units made valiant attempts to learn Gurkhali, but those who came into contact with Gurkhas only occasionally obviously spoke English. This problem was recognized and tackled, but it was only after the Falklands crisis that it was seriously remedied. In Malaya the pace of operations in battalions was controlled by Gurkhali-speaking British officers and the men in the communication centres did speak English, so people managed. However, there were occasions when a knowledge of English at soldier level would have paid dividends. I particularly recall a battle of wits during one operation when we had to have aerial

---

*1/10 GR also made history with the award of the DSO to a Gurkha for the first time ever: the recipient was Major (Gurkha-Commissioned Officer) Purne Rai, Sardar Bahadur, DSO, OBE, MC, OBI, who was also the first Gurkha to be made OBE; this is the full title of Gurkha Officers (38 between 1948 and 1984) of equivalent status to British officers, who receive their commission direct from QGO, as opposed to those who receive their training in the United Kingdom (19 in 37 years).
Honours and awards in 1952 included 1 DSO, 7 MC, 5 DCM and 23 MM.

resupply. I was away from the set but the following conversation was monitored by Tac HQ after contact had been established by the RAF Valetta pilot and my radio operator. Dropping Zone recognition was always difficult. In those days only smoke marked DZs; panels, and marker balloons came later.

'Valetta for Ground. Put up smoke!' called the pilot.

'Ground for Valetta. Wilco Out,' answered the Gurkha.

Nothing happened for a while and that conversation was repeated twice more. Finally the angry voice of the pilot came crackling through, 'Valetta for Ground. Smoke . . . Smoke . . . Smoke . . . Smoke . . . Over.' It was getting late.

'Ground for Valetta,' said the Gurkha. 'Wilco. Wait out.'

I got back to the set just as the aircraft flew away, still with our rations on board, to find a puzzled Gurkha signaller lighting the cigarette the pilot had insisted he smoke, then calling '. . . Smoking. Over.'

1953: FOOD DENIAL OPERATIONS

By 1953 the increased use of aircraft – helicopters for troop carrying, fixed-wing craft for supply dropping and reconnaissance work – was greatly helping troops in their mission of dominating the jungle and their search for terrorists who, denied supplies from the Min Yuen, were forced to withdraw into deep jungle and spend much time and effort in growing their own food. For this they would cut down small patches of jungle, thus exposing them to God's sun and the Security Forces' air, and plant crops. One day, on a routine flight, the pilot of an Auster aircraft, Captain Metcalf, thought he saw the tell-tale signs of one such cultivation. Knowing that he would alert the enemy were he to investigate, always provided they were there in the first place, he made a rough 'fix of the position on his map as he flew on without deviating from his course. Back in base he worked out how best to get an accurate fix without frightening any terrorists away. He decided to make a series of flights, at dawn, over the next five days, flying on a route that would not appear too obvious. On the sixth day he flew nearer to the spur where he thought the target was, delighted to find that his original fix had been accurate – a most difficult feat when obliquely observing anything from a flank in thick jungle – and that there was indeed a clearing the size of a tennis-court, planted with rows of vegetables. Under the trees he saw what he thought was a small 'basha' – a crude hut built of cut fronds and small trees. All this he took in from a height of 1,500 feet, again from a flank.

As the camp lay just inside the operational area of The Gordon Highlanders, planning for the ensuing operation fell to them. They planned to assault the camp with two platoons, with one platoon in ambush position to the east. To cover the approaches from the north 'C' Company, 2/7 GR, under command of Captain J. Thornton, was detailed to set up ambushes. For this Thornton took 43 men.

One of the problems of leaving a company base camp was that the alert could be given to the MRLA by the Min Yuen. Deception measures were vital and took, for instance, the forms of moving out at night, using a roundabout approach, one platoon lying down and one platoon standing up in the same vehicle, and not stopping the vehicle for debussing – to name but four. When Thornton and his men moved out it was in the dark and raining (Chinese seem to hate getting wet) and their entry into the jungle was unobtrusive. By 1600 hours that same day they made their base about a mile or so from where they thought the camp was. Patrols on different compass bearings were immediately sent out to reconnoitre the area, to ensure there was no enemy movement in the immediate vicinity and to get an idea of future ambush positions.

One of these 'fan' patrols, as they were called, was led by Lance Corporal Rabilal Rai. After only about 300 yards he and his two riflemen heard voices. Moving cautiously closer they saw two terrorists washing in a stream; they seemed so confident that the camp had to be nearer than the mile away they had thought it was, unless it were a different camp. More voices could be heard and Rabilal decided that the camp had to be 'recced', which was in accordance with standing operational procedures. He also felt that he was more likely to succeed in keeping quiet and leave fewer tracks if he undertook the 'recce' alone. On crawling forward he found the camp, occupied by some dozen communists, all dressed in their khaki uniform. He returned to the other two men, told them to go back and brief Captain Thornton while he himself made a circuit of the camp area to discover where the sentry posts were. He also suggested that the company commander meet him at some specified rendezvous for an immediate assault.

It was 1730 hours when Thornton received the message. The cultivation had been spotted, thereby confirming it was the camp they thought it was. However, all the plans, including the clearance given for sub-unit boundaries, had been meticulously laid down before the operation started and it was a foolhardy commander who ignored such details. Besides which, it was getting late for such an attack; better to wait until the morning, although this did increase the likelihood of the terrorists picking up the patrol's footprints. On balance, delay was preferable and, waiting for Rabilal to return, Thornton contacted the Gordon's CO, who gave him permission to assault the camp, keeping his own troops where they were, in an ambush role.

Thornton decided to lead the assault himself with a small group, the majority of his men laying ambushes on the other side of the camp, the idea being that, on the sound of fire being opened, the enemy would probably try to escape away from the noise. Next morning, at first light, they moved off, dividing into two groups not far from the camp, the cordon group being given time to get into position before the assault was launched. The assault party crawled to a position at the top of the hill until they were within five yards of an enemy sentry. At that stage of the Emergency there were no silencers fitted to weapons, except in exceptional cases. Experiments had been tried, certainly with the Sten gun, but the movement of the working parts was considerable, so the idea was dropped. Some silenced weapons were kept centrally and used for very special occasions. Thornton did not have any, so had to move, then shoot, only when the noise of firing did not matter. It had taken his group an hour, by which time the cordon should also have been in its ambush position. Thornton suspected that the camp was a hundred yards to his left, but had to wait until the sentry moved away before they could assault the camp with the maximum chance of success. The sentry was not so obliging and kept on looking around suspiciously. As he seemed likely to stay there until relieved, it was decided to kill him prior to the final assault. Rabilal's fatal shot alerted the enemy in the camp; after a hundred-yard dash it was found that the camp was surrounded by a barricade of felled trees. A Bren gun was fired but nobody was hit. It was completely silent and Thornton felt that the enemy had managed to escape unharmed. Then there was the sound of firing from the cordon at the bottom of the spur as some of the terrorists ran into the Gurkhas' positions. Eight dead were found, with the Gurkhas suffering no casualties.

Thornton's main impression about the operation was the 'complete and clinical silence of it all. No-one shouted and there was no excitement: just quiet, determined competence by the Gurkha soldiers', as the regimental history records. Thornton's final words on the operation were, 'One thing I was quite sure about – I would never like to have Gurkhas on the other side.'*

By the middle of 1953, many terrorists were not prepared to fight; some still were. In June, some twenty CT carried out a road ambush on a rubber estate in Johore. It was in 1/10 GR's area of operational responsibility and a platoon, under command of Lieutenant (QGO) Dhojbir Limbu, was deployed in an effort to come to grips with the terrorists. The platoon was inserted in a neighbouring rubber estate to try and pick up tracks, as it was thought there was a better chance of a successful

---

* Captain Thornton was awarded the MC, Captain Metcalf the DFC and Lance Corporal Rabilal Rai the DCM.

follow-up that way. Tracks were indeed found and Dhojbir was ordered to keep on the trail. The CT moved cunningly and tactically, splitting up into groups three or four times each day and then joining up again at a predetermined rendezvous. The terrain was swampy jungle, never a pleasant combination, and was made harder to navigate in and follow up tracks because of heavy rain. The platoon's rations were running low, so Dhojbir ordered his men to eat only once a day and to keep tracking the enemy from dawn till dusk.

On 8 July, with the men very hungry, the tracks were lost for the twenty-third time since the operation started. Dhojbir realized that, if they did not make contact with the enemy that day, they would have to abort their mission – men can go only so far on no food. He split his men into groups and sent them off to search for the terrorists, instead of looking for their tracks.

It was the patrol that Dhojbir was leading that suddenly came across the main enemy camp, which was sited on an island in the swamp and was barricaded by felled trees to prevent its being rushed. The terrorist sentries and the Gurkhas saw each other at one and the same time and, although he was greatly outnumbered, Dhojbir ordered a charge. Three machine-guns were brought to bear on the small group of Gurkhas, as well as grenades being thrown at them. With the Gurkha officer in front, the attackers penetrated the barricade and entered the camp, killing two terrorists before the rest of them fled into the swamp. Much food and ammunition, as well as some weapons, were found there. One of the dead was later identified as a political commissar who had a large price on his head.

It later transpired that none of the terrorists knew that they were being tracked by the Gurkhas during the 25-mile long slog. It was a very good example of Gurkha tenacity and tracking skills, to say nothing of a very high standard of jungle-craft generally. Lieutenant (QGO) Dhojbir Limbu was awarded the MC.

It was during Operation 'Sword', in the jungle near Kulim in Kedah State when tremendous guts were shown by a rifleman of 2/10 GR – a patrol of only four Gurkhas bumped into a strongly fortified terrorist camp, more reminiscent of a Japanese bunker position during the war in Burma. In mountainous country and occupied by about 30 CT, the small patrol had virtually no chance. The commander was killed and two men wounded, but the remaining rifleman, Narparsad Limbu, put up such a brave and determined fight that the terrorists eventually fled, but not before Narparsad had used up all his ammunition and collected more from the dead man and his wounded colleagues.

Honours and awards in 1953 included 1 DSO, 7 MC 2 DCM and 10 MM.

After the enemy had fled Narparsad tended one of the wounded, leaving him hidden with a rifle, food and water; he also hid his commander's corpse and, as soon as it was dark, set off for his own base camp, carrying a Bren gun and magazine in addition to his own rifle. He reached his platoon at dawn, having had to climb a steep hill in the dark. He then led another patrol back to the scene of the battle and, after searching around, found the other wounded Gurkha who had rolled down a slope. The men took both the two wounded soldiers and the dead patrol commander back to base that same day.*

By now the Emergency had been a feature of everyone's everyday life for five years, only a year less than the Second World War. The original weaknesses of the Brigade had been overcome to a very large degree by training, by experience and by the natural process that is a constant always, especially under hard and dangerous conditions, promotion to the worthy, and elimination of the slowest by the increased awareness: 'if it's not going to be me, it's got to be him'.

However, underlying weaknesses still remained and, in the case of 2/2 GR, symptoms of its having been captured by the Japanese still pertained, especially in the more senior ranks who had lost out over the years. A policy of 'roulement' was introduced, with battalions being sent to Hong Kong for a complete change, although many wondered if it were for the better. 2/2 GR were the first to go and they benefitted enormously.

1954: PROFESSIONALISM PAYS OFF

By 1954 riflemen throughout the Brigade were responsible for raising the kill-to-contact ratio that, while aeons away from the fumbling British officer-led patrols of 1948, were, in fact, only what had always been expected of the Gurkha soldier. A fine case in point occurred on 12 January when Rifleman Birbahadur Rai, 1/10 GR, showed courage, presence of mind and spot-on marksmanship. 1 Platoon, 'A' Company were returning in trucks from zeroing their weapons on a makeshift range when information of CT having been sighted was given to the platoon commander, Sergeant Hardan Rai, DCM, MM, by a police officer. The platoon drove as near to the southern, marshy end of the estate in question and searched from well before noon until dusk was beginning to fall. The platoon was suddenly fired on with automatic weapons and rifles from the edge of the swamp, 200 yards away. Immediate Action drill was put into effect, with the Gurkhas turning and making a charge. The terrorist fired once more and disappeared into the swamp.

*For his courage and devotion to duty Rifleman Narparsad Limbu was awarded an immediate DCM.

The Gurkhas came up to the stream and crossed it; Birbahadur found himself the only man on solid ground, the rest of the soldiers were floundering. Birbahadur carried on alone and under fire from other CT. He was fired on from about 30 yards by one man, armed with a Sten gun, whom he killed. With fire still being directed at him he advanced until he came across two of the enemy armed with pistols, both of whom he shot. A fourth terrorist appeared from behind a tree, fired two shots, missing both times. Birbahadur turned and killed him. Thirty yards further on he came upon a fifth terrorist, who was firing a carbine at him; he too was shot.

Birbahadur Rai had, by himself, accounted for five terrorists. He was under fire for most of the time and never knew the strength of the enemy. He never hesitated. Behind him the rest of the men were hampered by more difficult ground and, although they accounted for at least four of the terrorists being wounded, they acted only in a supporting role to the lone rifleman.*

At the top end of the battalion spectrum, the CO of 1/6 GR would also go into the jungle. The battalion was engaged on a series of missions, codenamed Operation 'Hunter', that relied heavily on obtaining and using Special Branch information.

1/6 GR had its headquarters at Kuala Kangsar in Perak. The CO was Lieutenant Colonel W. C. Walker, DSO, OBE, who later commanded a Gurkha Brigade, the Gurkha Division, became Major General Brigade of Gurkhas and then the Director of Borneo Operations. One of his first moves in the area had been to establish close liaison with the police, because it was from them that much of the information, upon which to base his operations, would come.

On one occasion Mr Cyril Keel, the Special Branch officer who dealt mostly with 1/6 GR, received a tip-off that a courier on a bicycle was due to pass through Kuala Kangsar at a certain time. A random, snap police roadblock and search was organized and the suspect was duly brought in. Routine searches ended fruitlessly, but Keel persevered. At last, after every item of the man's clothing had been shredded and every component of the bicycle had been dismantled, the vital rolled slips of paper were found. They were in the man's shoes, stuck along the inside edge and covered by a glued-down inner sole. Special Branch needed no more. Interrogation quickly brought forth the information that there was a courier post in a certain house in a village near Ipoh, to the north. The hiding-place was found under the hearth of a live fire, where further

*Rifleman Birbahadur Rai was put in for an immediate MM but this was upgraded, at a higher level, to the award of the DCM.

messages were detected in a storage jar of rice. In the face of such incriminating evidence the individual in charge of the post agreed to remain active and to let Special Branch see all the messages before they were passed on. Keel was able to feed his own letters into the network to contact CT using this method.

Several military operations were planned and mounted as a result of the information this system produced. The terrorists were so astute that it was most difficult to get hard and fast facts around which to plan with any degree of certainty. However, one day a message did arrive that gave details of a jungle meeting of terrorist leaders, the venue and the period of four days during which it would be held. A reconnaissance patrol was sent out and, working meticulously and with the utmost caution, did such a fine job that the information they brought back was good enough for a sand model to be made for further briefings.

Mindful of disappointments in the past, Walker was determined to have enough troops to surround the area of the meeting so that the six leaders could not escape even if the initial contact were not completely successful. Seven platoons were involved. The entry into the jungle was made as unobtrusively as possible by elaborate feints, a night move and the crossing of a large river with muffled paddles. A two-day march brought the force into the area of the meeting on the first evening.

The meeting-place was a deserted hut in a clearing in thick jungle. In the open space was a clump of scrub in which the killer group, two Gurkhas, was completely hidden, with a vine, lying carelessly on the ground attached to both the killer group and the commander of the assault platoon. The other six platoons formed a cordon, so well concealed that the terrorists entering the area could have no idea of its presence.

The Gurkhas settled down to a four-day wait, but the killer group heard people approaching after only four hours. They could not turn round and see who was coming up behind them and could not tell if their camouflage was good enough to keep them completely concealed. It was a most nerve-racking time. An armed Chinese padded past, followed by another, a third and eventually all six expected men entered the hut. They took off their packs and, with weapons at the ready, scanned the surroundings then, very deliberately, the leader moved towards the killer group. As he approached, the killer group opened fire and Walker, hidden with the assault group, shouted 'Charge!' The platoon came into the clearing to find the bodies of two of the terrorists and the rest of them scuttling into the jungle where they were all cut down by the cordon. Among the dead were a political commissar and a senior committee member.

Recognition of dead CTs was reduced to a fine art. Dead bodies were recovered whenever possible and cameras and fingerprint outfits were carried for use before a CT was buried. Special Branch recognized one CT killed by 1/10 GR who had been in London for the Victory Parade in 1946, had gone on afterwards to a convention in Prague and had attended the youth rally in Calcutta in early 1948 when the communists had planned their campaign of violence in south-east Asia.

Although the jungle was frequently bombed and shelled, there were vast areas where the ecology remained undisturbed. Big game was to be found: tiger, elephant, bison, bear and even rhinoceros. The bison, 'seladang' in Malay, was probably the most aggressive animal and the others would normally try and avoid contact with man. Elephants, however, were in a special category.

A soldier of 2/10 GR was one of two who were trampled on by an enraged elephant when on operations in the jungle. As one man escaped the other was seized yet again and impaled on one of the tusks, suffering severe injuries. The regimental medical officer walked in when news reached the battalion and gave a blood transfusion. There was a three-hour wait for a helicopter and when it did arrive it could not land because of tree stumps on the landing site. It would return the next morning when the stumps had been cut off. The man was too ill to wait so was carried out, using makeshift firebrands, with the doctor holding up the transfusion apparatus, through 3,000 yards of jungle, arriving at the head of the road at 2115 hours where the ambulance was waiting. The tusk had passed through the right lower ribs, perforated the right lung and caused a deep wound. The soldier was critically ill in hospital for two weeks but, six months later, had made a complete recovery.

It was care, such as instanced here, that was so essential for the maintenance of high morale – itself so necessary in a campaign such as the Malayan Emergency.

At other times, men were not hurt, but frightened. On one occasion I took some men from 'A' Company, 1/7 GR, out for a night ambush on a rubber estate. I put the Gurkhas into three groups, with myself at the furthest end of the line. Nothing had happened by the time set to lift the ambush, so I started back to meet up with the other groups. Even in the waning moonlight I could see that one man was extremely shaken.

I asked him what the matter was but he was unable to speak. His friend told me that he had been lying motionless, watching the road to his front, listening to the noises that never cease – twigs dropping, branches snapping, insects, animals. Suddenly he felt warm air in his ear and thought it was his section leader who had come quietly over to see if he were awake. He put his hand up and there, Glory Be! was an elephant's trunk. He glanced up and saw the animal standing over him, investigating him tentatively.

The Gurkha whispered to his section commander, agonizingly, 'Send it away, send it away!' The NCO, acutely conscious of what an angry elephant could do, responded by collecting as many twigs as easily came into his reach without moving his body and threw them, almost conciliatorily, at the elephant. Agonizingly slow seconds passed. The elephant lifted one of his front legs and stepped over the recumbent Gurkha, now emulating rigor mortis – so petrified was he. Then the other front leg and finally, after an eternity of a few more seconds, both back legs. The elephant then moved off across the road where it was joined by its mate and offspring. That was at 9 o'clock; by midnight, when I met him, the man was being helped along, still almost in a state of trance, unable either to believe his luck or, in his heart of hearts, that it hadn't all been a frightful nightmare.

In 1954 General Templer left Malaya, having prepared the ground for final victory. With his departure Sir Donald MacGillivray became High Commissioner and Lieutenant General Sir Geoffrey Bourne the new Director of Operations.

General Bourne continued to apply the strongest pressure on the CT. His tactics were to concentrate on the weakest areas first, ridding them of all the insurgents and then to lift all the tiresome restrictions so people could lead normal lives once more. Such an area was then declared 'white', the first being Malacca, and this would, of course, be heralded as a major propaganda victory for the government and celebrated as such with considerable public participation.

Concentration of forces in areas relatively near a road was instrumental in denying freedom of movement to the CT; deep jungle, however, was a different problem. There is an aboriginal population in Malaya, living in remote jungle fastnesses, shunning civilization and being used as sources of information, food and shelter by the CT. These people, generically and incorrectly known as 'Sakai', lived in rural slums known as 'ladangs'. They were timorous folk who had a marked antipathy towards the Malays and considerable empathy with the Chinese, who treated them well and spoke their languages. Government realized that these aborigines would have to be wooed from the communists and did this by establishing police posts, grandly known as 'forts', in certain strategically sited places in the deep jungle. The troopers of 22 Special Air Service Regiment were also engaged on operations in support of this policy. These forts had medical posts and encouraged barter for jungle produce. At that time the aborigines did now know what money was all about and could only count up to three. Gradually shyness gave way to confidence and information about terrorist activity in the very deep jungle began to be gleaned and analysed.

UNDER THE CANOPY

The basic problem in the jungle concerned how to fight in it, live in it and move through it so as always to be ready to better the other man. It may be glorious to die for your country but it is far more glorious and very much more satisfying to make the other man die for his. That was my philosophy and I took pains to learn from my Gurkhas, whether it was refinements in navigating in featureless country, improvisation or aspects of jungle lore. The latter was particularly impressed on me when we were chasing some bandits – MRLA's 3 Platoon, commanded by an exceptionally brave man called Tan Fouk Leong (an open invitation to be renamed Ten Foot Long!). They were in a bad way and had been on a diet that must have consisted almost entirely of leaves, as we found green faeces. We were moving along in the jungle when suddenly the platoon commander of the leading platoon, Gurkha Lieutenant Tulbahadur Rai, DCM, made the sign for the men to stop. He stared at the ground and then called me up to him. 'See that?' he asked. I looked at the ground, seeing nothing but a tangled mass of dead and dying leaves. Pretending to be bright I said that I did, but Tulbahadur must have noticed I was looking at the wrong place. He pointed out a patch of ground that did not look any different from the rest of the jungle floor and said, 'Of course, you think this is the mark of a tiger.' I hadn't, but I let it pass. Tulbahadur then showed me how like a tiger's pug mark it was and why, in fact, it wasn't a tiger's, but that of a man, the rear man of the bandits, making a mark like a tiger's pad and then haphazardly laying leaves over it. And how had Tulbahadur known this? Because the man had made the spoor from in front of where the tiger would have trodden and, from that angle, he had made the 'tiger' walk backwards. Nobody else, not even the lead scout, had cottoned on to this. We continued tracking 3 Platoon.

Tulbahadur had an uncanny knack of instant analysis, so to speak. On another occasion we were sent to an area to follow up a contact made by another company. The area seemed 'cold' by the time we were deployed in it although there were plenty of signs that the bandits had spent time there. Walking along I saw some ash by the side of a track but ignored it, as the terrorists were supposed to have left the area at least two days before. Tulbahadur, walking just behind me, bent down, felt the ash and, almost in one movement, dived into some undergrowth and dragged a wounded bandit out. He must have been there some time as maggots were eating his wounds. 'But how on earth did you manage to bend down so low as to see him hidden under that mass of bush?' I asked.

'The ash was still warm to the touch,' he answered, 'and the length of time the 'daku' were reported to have left the area and the warmth of the ash didn't correspond. As there were no tracks leading away, the odds were heavily on there being someone hidden nearby.'

Clearance and operational boundaries were always a matter of great concern, especially when troops were operating close to the edge of their boundary. I was under command of another battalion on one occasion, during one of those operations when food control and 'swamping' an area seemed a good idea.

I'd taken a patrol of four men, moving on a compass bearing of 10° away from the patrols on either side of me. We came across a large enemy camp, empty, but well laid out with strong defences and primitive facilities for repairing weapons. Eighty to a hundred men could have been accommodated there easily.

A little further on at the top of a small rise near a swamp, we all heard a noise from the north, the far side of the swamp. Opinion was divided, I thought it was man-made; the Gurkhas thought it was a bird. A few minutes later we heard it again, much nearer this time – and definitely man-made. I looked at my map. The company boundary was some half mile to the north along a small river, so the noise had to be CTs'.

There was little chance, so I thought, that the enemy would cross the swamp, so I decided to take my men over it and see what we could find on the far side. It was about 30 yards wide, little more than a water-logged creek full of a type of cactus that consisted of giant fronds that had barbs on the edges, were twice as tall as a man and which made a great noise when brushed against anything. We went down the bank and very, very carefully started towards the far side.

About half-way across there was a noise like a tin being pierced, then the unmistakable clink of a water-bottle stopper hitting the side as it dangled. We heard muffled Chinese tones and, before we had a chance of moving on, the gang on the far side slid into the swamp and came towards us. We froze and lifted our weapons up to our shoulders, taking aim, and waited.

It was mid-afternoon but, in the swamp, it was gloomily dark. One, two, three men came into sight, a dozen yards away, dressed like soldiers but with a red emblem in their hats – no recognition sign any of us knew about – seven, eight now. I whispered to the man on my right, 'Be ready to fire,' and tensed myself.

As if on a sudden impulse the men we were watching turned and saw five men facing them, all in the aim position. In a flash they were aiming at us but the man on my right urged me not to shoot, hissing out the name of the battalion to our north.

For a dreadful, loaded second, thirteen men stood poised. I was in an agony of doubt. In a flash I saw that there might be a mistake and the men facing me in the gloom might just somehow be Gurkhas with a bandit hat sign, rather than Chinese in security force-uniform, with captured equipment, as had been known in the past. If I shouted, 'Don't shoot!' in Chinese and they were Gurkhas, they were much more likely to shoot and not to miss than if they were Chinese and I shouted 'Don't shoot!' in Gurkhali. I chose the former, took my hat off so they could see my face, lowered my weapon and moved forward, shouting 'Don't shoot, don't shoot!' in Gurkhali.

They were Gurkhas; they were from the battalion to the north (our sister battalion) and the signs they wore on their hats were intended to mislead, as indeed, some years back, the communists had misled them by using a crossed kukri motif sewn onto stolen jungle hats.

The tense atmosphere relaxed and mutual recrimination set in until we realized that neither of us had strayed – the operational commander had given us different boundaries, despite my having asked him to verify this two days before. (Two weeks earlier a British battalion had killed six of each other in a similar situation.) The noise we had heard was the patrol finding sealed tins of rice which they had slashed with their kukris so that the rice would become uneatable, and it so happened that the Chinese-type voice was the patrol commander's, whose vile Gurkhali accent had earned him the nickname, in his battalion, of 'Chinaman'.

Back from patrol in our jungle base I opened the radio set, having found out that there had been three other instances of patrols clashing, and said, 'Fetch Sunray.' After I had got the senior officer on set I started my transmission: '. . . by the grace of God you have just been saved the onus of many Gurkhas' unnecessary deaths . . .'

That evening, after stand-down, I called the soldier who had been on my right in the swamp and asked him why he had urged me not to open fire.

'Because I recognized my brother,' came the devastating reply.

1955–1956: READY FOR POLITICAL TRANSFER

The British Government had promised to let Malaya govern herself once the terrorist threat had been seen to have abated to such an extent that communist victory was no longer possible and military defeat not far off. Such a state of affairs had been reached by 1955, so preparatory elections were held to start the independence process. The major

Honours and awards in 1954 included 1 DSO, 4 MC, 2 DCM and 6 MM.

political party, formed by the moderate Chinese and Malays, was known as the Alliance and stood for continued participation in the Commonwealth, with a broad-based and secular approach to affairs of state. Other political parties were fledgeling; fundamentalism played no part in the election which gave the Alliance 51 out of the 52 seats in the Legislative Council. The Chief Minister was Tenku Abdul Rahman. As the Alliance party also had majority control of the Executive Council it was obvious that this would all affect the future of Malayan affairs, operationally and politically.

The newly elected Alliance Government felt the need to take some initiative over ending the Emergency. On 9 September an amnesty was declared, granting what was virtually a free pardon to all CTs who had committed offences before that date or in ignorance of the amnesty declaration. Many millions of leaflets were dropped over the jungle and voice aircraft also played a large part in promulgating the news. All troops were withdrawn from the jungle by 7 September. Certain 'surrender areas' were declared in which there would be a ceasefire and no troops were to be sent to the jungle until further notice.

Those of us at ground level felt that the amnesty was a mistake; it was ill-conceived and had a touch of ingenuousness and complacency about it that boded ill. It gave us the impression that the new leaders did not fully understand the threat or the realities of communist revolutionary warfare. The talk at the time was that, with the British no longer part of the political scene for much longer, Malaya's own politicians would be able to solve the remaining problems politically now that militarily no major threat was posed.

Sure enough, the communists, with an eye for the main chance, utterly ignored the government's initiative and took the situation as being a golden opportunity to build up their supplies and, certainly in Johore, to increase their own offensive.

In mid-October troops were committed on operations in Johore and, later, in the rest of the country. Eventually, after many tortuous negotiations and with the promise of a free pass to go back unmolested, Chin Peng, the Secretary-General of the MCP, left his sanctuary in southern Thailand and met the Chief Minister at Baling, in the very north of Malaya. Chin Peng demanded official recognition; this was adamantly refused. To have had the MCP as a recognized political party was tantamount to the government conceding victory, although the terrorists were already on the verge of defeat.

The Emergency continued.

Sergeant Ramsor Rai, 1/6 GR, was leading a routine patrol during the amnesty when he came across an occupied enemy camp with ten CTs in it. Unusually, he only had one other man with him and, before he complied with the amnesty procedure of calling on the terrorists to surrender, he sent the other man back to fetch some reinforcements. As luck would have it only one man, a Bren gunner, was available, the rest of the men being away on another mission.

Not daunted, Ramsor stood up and called on the terrorists to surrender; they opened fire on the three Gurkhas before running away. Even so, the three soldiers managed to kill three enemy and would most likely have killed them all had it not been for the frustrating rule they had to comply with – although nobody would have been any the wiser had they not done so! The fact that the most wanted man in the Ipoh district was among the men who got away made many Gurkhas unhappy about the policy of 'Shouting before Shooting'.

The Adjutant, 1/7 GR, wrote: 'Operationally the last quarter of 1955 proved to be one of exasperation and despair in our thankless and patience-testing amnesty role . . . the wily communist terrorists roamed happily in our safe areas and made the best possible use of the quiet period to restock an up-to-then lean larder.'

Part of the Gurkhas' successes was because of bravery, discipline and good marksmanship, part from a good knowledge of jungle lore. Living undetected in a jungle camp was important. The three prerequisites were; not to be known about, to be able to react to an unexpected situation, and to have a modicum of comfort. Choosing a good camp site was not easy. It should not be in any obvious place, nor near enough to any village that it could be stumbled upon. It should be near water and have more than one route to make a quick exit yet only be approachable by a large force from one side.

I regarded a patrol as a mobile ambush, leaving as few tell-tale marks as possible. If, for instance, a leaf had to be used to cover a mark, the leaf to be used had to come from the nearest tree. Nothing that could be stepped over should be trodden on; nothing cut that could be broken and not to break where bending would suffice.

Tracking was an art in itself. There are so many points that can be looked for that can give a clue to someone else having moved through the area – although there were no visible boot marks or footprints – a sudden change in the colour of the foliage, or foliage bending against the grain, dampness in dry surroundings and dryness in damp, traces of mud, scuffed roots of trees, the bole of a tree 'wounded' with sap forming for no apparent reason, disturbed insect-life, broken spiders' webs, muddy water in a stream, birds flying towards the trackers, incautious animal movement and anything with a straight edge – nature very seldom produces straight edges and, unthinkingly, a person can pluck a leaf, fold it then drop it, thereby giving an important clue to those who know what to look for. Telling how long since anything had been cut was one method of gauging a time frame.

By now, also, those CT who had been in the jungle since the start of the Emergency were like animals in the way they could sense danger – on both sides we had learnt a whole lot in those seven years. As British units only did a three-year tour and the Gurkhas normally spent much more time in the jungle because there was not much opportunity to serve outside Malaya, British troops, with some noticeable exceptions, lacked a similar ability for prolonged periods of lying 'doggo', in concealment, tracking ability and various aspects of jungle lore. Examples of such skills were shown as soon as the amnesty restrictions were lifted.

Corporal Partapsing Rai, of Support Company, 1/7 GR, received orders to go and ambush an area where the local Special Branch had information that Goh Sia, one of the most notorious terrorists in the Segamat area of Johore, would be coming to pick up some food left for him. There was a large reward on Goh Sia's head; he was tough and cruel, he had led a platoon of the MPAJA against the Japanese during the war, he terrorized the local inhabitants and he boasted that only a silver bullet could kill him.

Partapsing and five riflemen had to go to an area of long grass, in the middle of an open rubber estate – this was the only area with any cover at all near the hidden food dump. The Gurkhas lay in the long grass, undetected, for three days and nights with no protection from the heat of the sun, the night mists, or the rain. Cooking was impossible and the soldiers could not leave the patch of long grass by day because of the rubber tappers. And even when they did leave their hiding-place at night, they had to enter it again in such a manner that no one would guess anyone was hiding there. It was later recorded by the regimental historian that it is doubtful if European troops could have maintained such a patient ambush for so long under such conditions. Having done exactly that myself, I know just how hard it is.

The Gurkhas lying in ambush were beginning to give up hope when, at around 0900 hours on the third day, Goh Sia suddenly appeared to collect the food. He was by himself and his carbine was slung over his shoulder. Rifleman Haikumsing Rai was the man who shot and killed him and there was much rejoicing among the local inhabitants when they heard the news.*

*There was also much rejoicing in Support Company when Corporal Partapsing Rai was awarded the MM.

All in all, communist terrorists were becoming harder and harder to pin down. Their numbers were whittled away, the Brigade recording 1,730 eliminations by the end of the year, with 1/10 GR reaching 300.

The policy of opening up forts in the very deep jungle gradually paid dividends. By the mid-1950s more and more CT finding their jungle cultivations at risk because of aerial recces and Security Force deep penetration, decided to surrender instead of struggling for survival in the remote areas. Heartened by this, the aborigines started to bring in information. One particular report concerned terrorist movement near Fort Brooke and Major (GCO) Harkasing Rai, MC, IDSM, MM, commanding 'C' Company, 1/6 GR, set out on 2 January 1956 to investigate it. About fifty CT were reported to be in the vicinity. Harkasing's men, having moved west, found temporary night stops with the enemy. The terrorists covered their tracks well and the Gurkhas lost them several times, having to cast around for 600 yards before picking them up again. The going was very slow, but, by 9 January, the Gurkhas were less than a day's journey behind.

At noon next day the leading scout spotted a hut in the dense jungle and signalled the information back, using the prescribed hand signals. As the Gurkhas started to move into position they were spotted by the sentry and fired at. They charged into a small camp, killing its only occupant, an aborigine, before comprehending that the fire directed against them was coming from a larger camp 200 yards ahead. This they also charged and killed three CTs, but by that time the rest of the enemy had withdrawn, most professionally, across a river and were firing accurately on the Gurkhas. As the soldiers tried to cross the river they were held up by one particular brave Chinese who, single-handed and armed with a Tommy gun, forced the Gurkhas to deploy and take up tactical fire positions instead of continuing with their advance, thus letting the rest of the enemy make good their escape. The Gurkhas chased the lone Chinese for over a thousand yards (one map square), exchanging shots with him but he managed to get away from them.

With contact lost a helicopter landing site was cleared near the enemy camp and the bodies were taken away. A search revealed documents that proved valuable. 'C' Company was also lifted out, only to return in early March. They were then in much more rugged terrain; they followed two-day old tracks from a valley floor to a knife-edge ridge, 3,000 feet higher. The tracks then split, moving both ways along the ridge, one set leading north, the other to the south. Major Harkasing

Honours and awards reflected the sparsity of guerrillas: 3 MC, 1 DCM and 10 MM only being won in 1955.

decided to pursue the south-bound trail, finding the countryside appallingly difficult, consisting mainly of steep, limestone cliffs, honey-combed with ravines, caves and steep waterfalls. The enemy had jettisoned its packs and so could move along the near-impossible terrain. The Gurkhas also had to move incredibly slowly and cautiously, keeping their eyes skinned for almost invisible tell-tale signs of where the enemy had gone.

The very next day a patrol saw a small, temporary camp with fifteen terrorists, so a man was sent back to call up Harkasing. He brought his company up, with only about ten minutes of daylight left – too late to take successful action. He ordered his men to lie where they were all night; no cooking, no smoking, no noise at all, as the enemy was within yards.

Next morning, before dawn, the Gurkhas started to surround the camp when, at first light, an enemy sentry challenged them. Everybody 'froze'. Minutes passed before the sentry relaxed, presuming he had made a mistake. It was full daylight then and the cordon was probably about half-way round the camp. The sentry challenged the Gurkhas again and fired a long burst, wounding two soldiers. The terrorists immediately evacuated their camp, splitting into groups of two and threes. There was not much that Harkasing could do; he signalled battalion headquarters, gave his report and suggested that the terrorists, without packs and therefore without food, should make for an area where food and help could be supplied by sympathizers. Other companies were deployed to the north, south and west, in the jungle and on the fringes, where further contacts were made in due course.

It later transpired that the terrorist group had a senior commander with it and was on the point of building a new, permanent camp when attacked by 'C' Company on 9 January. As a result of the Gurkhas' actions the gang had been so fragmented that, apart from suffering several casualties, it was never a threat to or an influence over the aborigines around Fort Brooke again.*

During this period all units that discovered a camp with enemy in it were forbidden to surround and attack it unless there were very good reasons for so doing, instead to have it bombed from the air. This procedure, called 'Smash Hit', evolved after one spectacular success – contrived, as we later learned, by Special Branch, and very nearly a complete flop – and involved marker balloons, filled by hot air made from adding water to some lumps of a particular chemical substance, being flown as near the target as possible as an added aid to the aircraft

*Major (GCO) Harkasing Rai was awarded a bar to his MC.

in case the man on the ground had been unable to read his map properly! Following the success of Captain Metcalf's classic 'fixing' in 1953, every Auster pilot had his eyes more than skinned when he flew over the jungle.

We were in an area where the map was useless as it showed large patches of white, marked 'unsurveyed'. While in an area to the south which was mapped, I personally (and unusually) had myself picked up tracks of the CT on three days. As the tracks led north, I moved the company north to continue the search. I had taken two men out on patrol early in the morning and had found nothing. The patrol on my left, however, had seen several pairs of black trousers hanging from a vine, drying. As the last patrol returned an Auster, in no way connected with us, flew overhead and circled once before flying off. Standing orders for the CT were to stand to if a plane flew overhead, evacuate the camp if it circled it. This, therefore, was obviously no time for laying on 'Smash Hit', speed being all-essential. I organized my understrength company so that the camp could be surrounded and there was a small assault group, which I was to lead. I allowed an hour for the cordon to get into position.

It had, most unusually, not rained for some days and the jungle floor was dry and crackly, instead of wet and noise-absorbing, so making stealthy movement extremely slow. I had hoped that the right-hand edge of the cordon would have closed in to where I could see it, up a small stream, by the time the hour was up. No sign. The NCO in charge, a sturdy footballer, was a recent arrival from the Signal Platoon and I am still of the opinion that his nerve failed him even if his compass work did not. I had to get into a position to see if I could spot him. I turned to my Bren gunner, Rifleman Ramansing Rai, and told him to cover me as I went forward, down into a dip, over the stream, which was the marker for the cordon, and up the bank towards the camp, which was on the lip of the high ground above the stream. 'Only fire when I give you the sign,' I said, as I went forward, followed to the rear and to one side by Sergeant Gyalje Sherpa.

As I climbed the far bank I could see no sign of the cordon, which had to be uncustomarily tight because of our low strength and the white map. I thought that if I could get almost to the top of the rise I'd see them. I crawled forward and, six yards from the top, craned my neck, peering around the trees. I saw nobody, but I had been observed. Ramansing, lying behind his machine-gun, had seen a bandit sentry, who must have heard me as I had had to negotiate the fallen branches and brushwood that had been pitched over the edge when the camp was being built. The sentry came to a tree at the edge of the camp and, as I craned my neck six yards below him, he brought his rifle into his shoulder and aimed.

I must have ducked out of sight too soon for him to have aimed properly. I inched myself forward a couple more yards and again craned my neck. Ramansing's fingers were itching as he saw me in mortal danger and, as the sentry fired, first at me and then at Sergeant Gyalje, Ramansing opened rapid fire. He saw the bandit hit; I saw Ramansing's bullets hitting the trees around me at waist height. I then saw some saplings shaking further up the hill and I was scared that it might be the cordon trying to get to the scene of the contact and, under the command of the inexperienced corporal, running into their own fire. I knew that if I stood up I was straight in the line of fire and that, if I continued to lie pinned down, I would be doing even less of my job than already was the case. I started yelling 'Cease fire!' and managed to get myself heard between bursts. When I stood up my knees felt as if they were made of water. It transpired that the CT had evacuated the camp very soon after the Auster's unscheduled circuit and the man left behind was also on his way out. It was no use indulging in mutual recrimination; hard though it was, I put it down to experience. I decided to follow my nose, so moved off in the direction I felt the bandits might have gone.

Two days later, with another two Gurkhas, we heard sawing and talking ahead of us. We crept back, contacted battalion HQ and, to the sound of the bandits making camp, managed to get the balloon flying. A message awaited me on my return to the set: 'Move back 4,000 yards. Bombing will come in at last light. Investigate first thing tomorrow morning.'

That evening five Lincoln bombers dropped many 11,000-pound bombs. We hardly slept a wink and, shortly after dawn, found a whole swathe of jungle flattened. Try hard though we did, we could find no evidence of any CT having been there at all. With the jungle flattened, the whole landscape had changed and lay in a thick coat of leaves. Bitterly disappointed we continued patrolling nearby and killed a courier soon after.

It was only after we returned that it emerged there had been no sign of the balloon when the first sortie flew in (had the CT found it, cut the string and left the area?) and that some of the bombs had been dropped unfuzed. I draw a veil over my subsequent interview with the Brigadier and the glacial conference I had to attend with the top air brass in Kuala Lumpur.

THE QUARRY BECOMES MORE ELUSIVE

Courier routes were on axes rather than along any particular paths and, by being in an area for some time one could get a 'feel' for them. There was one part of the jungle that cropped up in Intelligence reports as being the spot where couriers met. I thought that a search might be worthwhile and took some men in. We reached the area on the second evening and, before we made camp, I went on a recce. I found a particularly large tree, which I felt could be a landmark. Next morning I laid ambushes around it, having given strict orders that, if we were lucky enough and had a contact, the soldiers should shoot to wound, not kill.

And the surprising thing was that two couriers walked into our ambush that day. As firing broke out Corporal Parsuram Rai and I dashed to the scene with a small reserve. Somehow we outstripped the others and found ourselves in a small firefight – two against two. Parsuram deliberately shot the further of the two bandits in the leg so he couldn't go far or fast. The Chinese was a brave man and returned accurate fire as the corporal tried to get near enough to effect a capture, exposing himself each time he did so. However, by quick movement and a superb eye, Parsuram winged the CT in the arm, then went up to him, took his rifle from him and started to render first aid. By that time I had caught up with the other CT who had been wounded and, making sure he hadn't made a booby-trap of himself by concealing a primed grenade, had him under control. Parsuram had taken his man's rifle and came looking for me. His eyes were bloodshot, as Gurkhas' eyes can be when they set out to kill. I have often wondered why this happens and have yet to find an answer!

Carrying the two wounded men, we started on our way back. The man Parsuram had shot and wounded would not talk, nor did he want to be treated. He wanted to die, and he died that night. The other man had taken a liking to me and said he was going to become a civilian once he recovered from his wound. The interesting thing was that they were couriers and the tree that had caught my eye was the letter-box on the courier boundary. The letters we had recovered were of great interest to Special Branch.

Not as interesting as another lot we captured. We were in deep jungle and one morning I awoke with gut ache. I therefore countermanded the order I'd given the night before for an early start and decreed a 10 o'clock move after eating. I ordered double sentries out and, as they were being placed, a couple of bandits walked into us. There was some confusion as Gurkhas were in the line of fire and the smoke from the cordite hung over a stream where the shooting had taken place. We only killed one but captured both packs, which were full of magazines and some papers rolled into spills. The lurid covers of the magazines made me think they were all routine propaganda, badly produced from a CT printing-press. As they were bulky I nearly dumped them but decided not to, however uninteresting they were sure to be, not like those canny little spills of paper – or so I thought.

I photographed the dead man, had him buried, then moved off. It was a dreadful journey, but eventually we did get to the place where a helicopter came to evacuate a soldier called Dharmalal Rai, who had been taken ill, and I gave the pilot the bundle of documents.

It so happened that the spills of paper contained only low-grade information but there was something about the text in the magazines that intrigued Special Branch at district, circle and finally at state levels. Only at state level did they manage to decipher the code they felt was somewhere concealed in the otherwise straightforward text: this was that every fourth word made up another text that was too important to be published 'en clair' so to speak. Once the magazines were in sequence a remarkable discovery was made: a new policy from the central committee was being promulgated down to all branches, urging much more subversion than before and giving members of the Party not living in the jungle detailed instructions of urban targets, especially schools. Singapore was included. I gather that Singapore ignored the warning and there were incidents of insurrection in the schools and the university, with acid being thrown in people's faces and other atrocities that law-abiding folk could have done without. Indeed, Gurkhas were called out to help the Singapore Government contain the troubles in 1956 and 1957.

Mind you, none of us would have been any the wiser if I had thrown those wretched magazines away.

Later on in the year 1/6 GR was withdrawn from jungle operations to go to help control riots in Singapore, while 2/7 GR and 1/10 GR helped quell riots in Kowloon that started on 'Kalratri', the most important night of the most important of all Gurkha religious festival – 'Dashera'. Gurkhas are very phlegmatic about having to be deployed during such occasions, knowing that they would not have been told to leave barracks unless it were necessary. Days off will be given in lieu and a representative group of men will be left in camp to carry out the required religious rites. Naturally, the family men will be more dis-appointed than the single men in such an event.

Back in Malaya, sweating it out, the 1/2 GR diarist wrote, '. . . after the luckless period we have just been through, it is possible to gauge the staunchness and tenacity of the Gurkhas in their true perspective. Undoubtedly better trained than ever before they stand up to what can only be termed military failure to bring the communist terrorists to battle with constant enthusiasm and with an undiminished attention to detail that is beyond all praise. Their patience, coupled with the unflagging tempo of their efforts to destroy the enemy, be it by search, stalk or ambush, emerge, after eight continuous years, as the highlight of their post-war achievement . . .'

The Gurkha Engineers were deployed on building a metalled road (Ayer Hitam – Kemayan) fifteen and a half miles of which were in primary jungle. They reconstructed and bridged anothe road of six miles (Ulu Serting – Ayer Hitam). The Chief Minister of Malaya visited and the Minister of Transport opened the former on 10 September. A sidelight on operations the Gurkha Signals took part in are reflected in a vignette recorded by the regimental diarist, 'A corporal wireless operator was discussing the merits of various infantry units, their drill, discipline and prowess in the jungle . . . An NCO of the Divisional Defence Platoon politely challenged the corporal on his ability to judge these matters. The corporal retorted that, having served with The Green Howards, Gordon Highlanders, Fijians, two squadrons of the Royal Air Force Regiment, Somerset Light Infantry, a battery of the Royal Artillery, Rhodesian African Rifles, many Gurkha battalions, two Malay battalions, and having been on a trip to sea with the Royal Navy in HMS *Alert*, he felt capable, at least, of drawing comparisons . . . It reflects great credit on the ability of these young Gurkha NCOs that, during the seven years that the Regiment has been operational, not one man has been charged for an offence, other than for incorrect use of wireless procedure . . .'

Honours and awards in 1956 included 1 DSO, 4 MC, 3 DCM and 8 MM.

4
MALAYAN EMERGENCY: THE FINAL SLOG, 1956–1962

THE SMALLER THE HAYSTACK . . .

Nine years after the Emergency started the scene was very different. It was the year, 1957, that Malaya gained her independence and a hundred years since the Indian Mutiny when 2 GR won renown at the defence of Delhi and the Maharaja of Nepal personally led his own army of Gorkhas down to the Indian plains from the capital of his Himalayan kingdom, Kathmandu. There were far fewer contacts and an increase in surrenders – 120 between Independence on 31 August and the end of the year. The emphasis was still on food denial, which included checking at the gates of the New Villages that had been established during the final implementation of the Briggs Plan, begun in 1950. These checks were to prevent food being smuggled out to the rubber estates, many of which were now operating at full production, for the first time since 1941 in some cases, and gratitude for the work done by Gurkha units was expressed in the form of many presentations from the police, various liaison committees, estate managers and the local population.

Possibly because the Singapore Government had not paid attention to the new communist directive discovered in a chance contact on the mainland, there was considerable unrest leading to riots. 1/2 GR was called off operations and sent to help quell them. Just before that, they and their sister battalion had been engaged with the Special Branch in inducing communist terrorists to surrender and, as the 2/2 GR diarist put it, '. . . at the moment of writing, three companies of the battalion, three of the first battalion and two of the 1st South Wales Borderers are engaged on an operation whose target is one woman and four males! What will the old pensioners have to say about that?'

Food denial operations and checking gates at New Villages before the inmates were allowed out for the day's work were a commonplace. The diarist of 2/10 GR captured the flavour when he wrote, '. . . pre-dawn to locked and barbed village gates where arc lamps throw a sickly white light on to the straggly groups of men and women, buckets and bicycles gathering to go out and collect latex; the arrival of the police in an armoured vehicle, the search, of people by the police, of bicycles, tins and bottles by the soldiers, and finally the opening of the gates and the release of the flood, tins clanking, bicycles bounding over ruts in the road, coloured scarves flying in the pearl-grey half-light. And then the weary searching throughout the day, of all who pass. A distasteful and soul-destroying task, but one in which the Gurkha soldier's thoroughness, fairness and manners earn him the respect of all, and make the job worthwhile.'

Another sign of the times could be noted from the tasks of the Gurkha Engineers which, apart from roads and tracks being repaired and a high-level Bailey Bridge being constructed, included the dismantling of operational camps where companies had long been deployed and building jungle ranges so that an even higher standard of marksmanship could be obtained.

All in all it could be seen that the Government was winning with, by this time, more than half the country declared 'white'. These 'white areas' were not geographically connected, so their inclusion on a map would have shown a speckled mixture. No troops were needed in these 'white areas' so they could be concentrated against remaining pockets of hard-core resistance. The Security Forces relied more and more on the Special Branch for information. An example of this was provided by 'A' Company, 1/7 GR, under Captain (GCO) Nandaman Rai, who had been alerted to take action against up to twenty CT who were going to pick up some food one night barely 500 yards from the battalion's family lines, where there was an isolated hut.

It was arranged that an alarm system be set up between the hut and the CO's quarter. The hut contained an elderly couple, their son and his wife and baby. The son had put the alarm button near his baby's cot without his parents' knowledge. It was therefore the least suspicious place to go when the CT came to collect the food, as well as very easy to test out the system when required. It had been urged on the informer to wait until there was a large gang of terrorists in his house and not just a few, before he buzzed the alarm bell. It was also possible for the soldiers to carry out rehearsals without raising suspicions.

As was so often the case in operations such as this one, there was never any fixed time for the enemy to appear, only a wide bracket. Troops in this instance were on stand-by for 30 days, much longer than the CO had ever envisaged. However, when the alarm was eventually sounded, only five CT had come to the hut, not the expected twenty.

The Gurkhas moved to their ambush positions and opened fire as the enemy emerged from the hut. Two were killed outright, the rest were heard to escape. It was too dark to search the area so Nandaman waited till dawn, when an extensive search of the surrounding rubber and scrub for two and a half hours revealed nothing. It was decided to look at one last clump of bushes before calling off the search, and there three wounded CT, two men and one woman, were found.*

This incident was typical of many: troops had got used to being told that more of the enemy would come than ever did, it entailed a very long wait and the whole action was over in a few seconds with, in this case, something to show for all the planning at the end.

For a shorter wait, 'B' Company, 2/10 GR were luckier. They were also alerted by Special Branch information about a food lift by the local five-man branch members. This time the Gurkhas had to be inserted secretly inside the protective wire fence of a New Village the night before. They got into a small chicken coop which was within six feet of a house occupied by eleven people, including six children and the inevitable dogs that barked on the smallest provocation. Outside the wire a number of ambush parties were far enough away to allow the enemy into the village without being spotted and, on the sound of firing, were to close in as quickly as possible.

The group in the chicken coop, under Sergeant Damarbahadur Tamang, had been standing with its weapons at the ready for three hours when the door was suddenly opened and a double-barrel shotgun came within inches of Corporal Jitbahadur Gurung's naval. Jitbahadur had razor-sharp reactions and he killed two enemy and mortally wounded a third with his first burst of fire. These were the only three CT to enter the village.

The outer ambush parties had closed in within three minutes of hearing the firing. They waited for 90 minutes, when the district committee member who had been waiting outside the wire was seen and killed. The fifth member of the gang, who had been waiting back at base, moved to an area known to the battalion, where he was found and, after a 350-yard chase through some long grass, he was killed while burrowing into the undergrowth on all fours. The documents that were recovered showed that there had indeed been only those five in the branch, so the area was completely cleared of the communists.†

Ten days before Malaya achieved her independence, the last High Commissioner, Sir Donald MacGillivray, GCMG, MBE, made a speech to

---

*Captain (GCO) Nandaman Rai was awarded his third Mention-in-Despatches.
†Corporal Jitbahadur Gurung was awarded an immediate MM and Sergeant Damarbahadur Tamang an immediate Mention-in-Despatches.

the recruits who were passing out of the Recruit Training Depot. In it he said:

'. . . It is perhaps appropriate at this farewell parade that I should make some mention of the traditions of the Gurkhas as a soldier (sic). For more than 149 years of service they have fought in nearly every part of the world – from Europe to Japan – and invariably with the highest distinction . . . These traditions of the Gurkhas, built up over so many years, have been fully maintained against the communist terrorists since the first day of the Emergency. People are sometimes apt to forget that Gurkha battalions have been on operations in Malaya for over nine years with only short retraining periods by way of a break. At one time there were as many as eight Gurkha battalions and supporting Engineers and Signallers in action against the terrorists, and there have never been less than six battalions on operations at the same time. I know what a strain such continuous operations must have been on officers and men, and it is to their great credit that they have never failed to exert their utmost efforts in this most difficult of all campaigns. Gurkhas have accounted for nearly 1,800 terrorists and the Brigade has won some 225 awards for bravery and distinguished service. That is a very wonderful record of which all who have been associated with you cannot but fail to be proud.

It could not have been achieved unless the Gurkhas had displayed here in Malaya the same qualities that have made them famous in the past as soldiers and fighters: the highest standards of discipline, unswerving loyalty to friends, cheerfulness in adverse conditions, absolute impartiality and a stubborn and indomitable endurance. That the Gurkha still possesses these qualities in full measure has been shown not only on operations in the jungle but also in his day to day life in the towns and villages in Malaya where the friendliest relations have been maintained at all times with all communities. In peace and in war may these your traditions be long maintained.'

Despite there still being an estimated 2,000 CT left in the country, 500 of them in Johore, Malaya became independent as planned and, during the independence celebrations on 31 August, Tenku Abdul Rahman, who was then prime minister, said: '. . . Malaya has been blessed with a good administration forged and tempered to perfection by successive British administrators.'

Honours and awards in 1957 included 3 MC, 1 DCM and 4 MM.

In 1958, less for some units engaged on operations on the Malaya-Thai border, Gurkhas were used in the Emergency for the last time. It was a particularly sordid time for the army. 'Q' parties were formed to contact CT leaders in the jungle and arrange surrender terms, which finally ended the Emergency. Large rewards were offered for surrendering arms and ammunition, apart from the actual surrender for the leaders themselves. Terrorists who had been responsible for the deaths of Gurkha soldiers were being brought in by 2/2 GR 'Q' parties with the promise of vastly greater sums than the unfortunate widows concerned would ever see. One officer from a Gurkha battalion had to deal with the CT who had killed his father, the manager on a palm oil plantation.

. . . THE SMALLER THE NEEDLE

Battalions had time to reflect and record their feelings as the Emergency wound down. 1/2 GR were engaged on operations until 22 February, then 'after ten years of struggle in the jungle, disappointments, toil and sweat, with sometimes that satisfaction of victory, the battalion left operations and Johore, from the very same village which had been the first operational base when the Emergency started in 1948.' 2/2 GR were living under peacetime conditions but were still engaged on operations. '. . . The tedium of patrolling, however, was frequently interrupted at this time by Special Branch projects, usually of the ambush variety, based on information built up by planning, training and rehearsal to ensure success, and after a long period of tension waiting for the word "go" . . .'

1/10 GR, fresh from two years in Hong Kong, helped finish off the hard-core terrorists: '. . . four battalions embarked on weeks of intensive searching and ambushing . . . contacts were few. 1/7 GR killed a terrorist, then 1/10 GR killed another after a long chase, and gradually the CT began to crack. One surrender, then another, followed by a group and finally the remnants of a once-powerful, cruel and ruthless communist organization came slinking in to surrender. It was fitting that four Gurkha battalions should have been on the spot to see the end of ten years of communist terrorism in Johore State . . .' During this time 2/10 GR had one company on operations continuously for 58 days.

These battalions were, in fact, reporting on an intricate and highly successful master plan in the final elimination of the CT in the blackest state of them all, called Operation 'Tiger'. It was the brainchild of the man who had more experience of guerrilla warfare and Gurkhas than anyone else – Brigadier, later General Sir Walter Walker, commanding 99 Gurkha Brigade. Planning for Operation 'Tiger' had started in 1957. For the army this meant intense practice in jungle shooting on specially constructed jungle ranges and ambush techniques. All COs had to present their ideas for forthcoming operations at a two-day study period; supporting arms, notably the artillery and the Royal Air Force, had to be brought in for planning purposes. The Psychological Warfare Department launched a propaganda campaign and the Special Branch concentrated on its own particular aspects.

Operation 'Tiger' officially began on 1 January 1958. Phase One was for momentum to be built up, with increased pressure on the 96 suspected terrorists. The area they were thought to be in was about 1,800 square miles. Phase Two started on 15 April. 99 Brigade had four Gurkha battalions, with support from two companies of a British battalion. The target was the biggest known single terrorist unit in south Johore. Bombing and shelling for fifteen days, combined with an intense patrol programme, aimed to force the CT out of their jungle hideouts into ambushes. Ambushes became the troops' most demanding task; ten-day ambushes were to be regarded as the norm, with teams alternating every two hours. They were mostly sited on routes that informers said couriers especially took, but the time frame was always uncertain.

The longest such ambush, and probably the most demanding, was undertaken in Phase Two by 2/2 GR. Information had reached the Brigadier that a party of CT was due to move down a certain track sometime during the next month. 2/2 GR were therefore ordered to put an ambush on the suspected route. The best killing ground happened to be in swamp, so that is where the Gurkhas would have to be. After 27 days, the Gurkha CO approached Walker and appealed to him to lift the ambush as the appalling conditions must have taken the soldiers beyond the point of endurance for them to remain efficient. The Brigadier was not to be swayed. So the soldiers remained where they were but, on the very next day, three CT did walk into the ambush, two being killed outright, the other surrendering after his rifle was shot out of his hand. The Gurkhas were then allowed to return to base.

That one incident encapsulates all that the British have come to expect in the Gurkha on operations: unbelievable stamina, excellent marksmanship and superb fieldcraft. Remembering the standards of ten years before, trust in the Gurkhas, especially at regimental level, had been totally vindicated.

There were many other, less dramatic, ambushes that whittled away the CT organization gradually but irrevocably. That, combined with spectacular Special Branch 'footwork', was the only way of eliminating the enemy.

However, until the headquarter element of the CT organization had been destroyed, Operation 'Tiger' could not be counted as successful. It was particularly important that there should be success as events in

Johore had a great impact on Singapore, where elections were due before the end of the year. These elections would greatly influence the future shape of the Federation of Malaya and, then a remote possibility, of the larger political concept of uniting, with Singapore and the Borneo Territories, into a single unit of Malaysia. Operation 'Tiger' had to succeed – and it did. Special Branch played a very great part in the final eliminations but, on the ground, despite great contributions from the Army Air Corps and the Cheshire Regiment, it was the Gurkha element of 99 Gurkha Brigade that allowed all Johore to be declared 'white' before the end of the year.

As from 1 January 1959, the two untitled regiments were granted royal titles and became known as the 6th Queen Elizabeth's Own Gurkha Rifles and the 7th Duke of Edinburgh's Own Gurkha Rifles.

The official end of the Emergency was declared on 1 August 1960 and a contingent of the Brigade took part in the Federation Military Parade in Kuala Lumpur. At another ceremony, at Flagstaff House, Seremban, the Deputy Prime Minister, Tun Abdul Razak, presented a pair of specially mounted ceremonial 'krises' (Malay knives) on behalf of the Government of Malaya. Before making the presentation to the Major General Brigade of Gurkhas, he told all those present how much the people of Malaya admired the Gurkha, not only for his fighting ability – Gurkha units having accounted for over a quarter of all eliminations during the Emergency – but also for his bearing and behaviour off duty.

There was now time for thorough training in other aspects of soldiering which, despite the Hong Kong interlude during operations, had lapsed since 1948, so that the remaining weaknesses that had been unavoidable at the Brigade's inception at long last could now be eradicated less, perhaps, a high enough standard of proficiency in English below Queen's Gurkha Officer level.

The work of the battalion on the northern border was of particular interest in 1962. Twenty years after the legendary Spencer Chapman* was instrumental in helping to set up the MRLA in 1942, there was still a 'wanted list' of about 36 CT who were operating to the north of

Honours and awards in 1958 included 1 DSO and 4 MM, with 1 MM announced in 1959, bringing the Emergency total of these awards to 12 DSO, 53 MC, 27 DCM and 135 MM.
*Colonel F. Spencer Chapman, DSO, spent the war years working with the resistance against the Japanese. He describes his experiences in *The Jungle is Neutral*, Chatto and Windus, London, 1949.

Malaya, contiguous with Thailand. They were regarded by the Malayan Government as the rump of a once-powerful organization; they regarded themselves as the advance party of the next communist push from their sanctuary in Yala Province, Thailand. Spasmodic efforts had been made by the Security Forces all the while to get to grips with these remnants – Australians, New Zealanders, British, Malays and Gurkhas, to say nothing out of the 'Q'-type operations, involving Surrendered Enemy Personnel and a force of aboriginal Temiar, known as the 'Senoi Praaq', who roughly equated to the Home Guard – and none had had any success.

1/7 GR, back from a two-year tour in Hong Kong, were detailed to provide two companies at a time, based on the riverine town of Grik, in Perak. There the task was to try and win the 'hearts and minds' of the aborigines and acquire information about the CT. As far as could be ascertained, no more than three months ever elapsed without one of the three CT gangs keeping watch and ward over the area with its own group of Temiar* helping the gang make wide-ranging patrols in Malaya before returning to sanctuary in Thailand. In fact the Chinese were welcomed more than the Malays as there was a marked antipathy between aborigines and Malays, the latter thinking the former primitive and of low breeding, and the former thinking the latter little better than 'city slickers'. This clash made contact between the Security Forces and the CT ever harder than it might otherwise have been.

In December 1961 it was the turn of 'A' and 'D' Companies to move up from Ipoh, a hundred miles to the south of Grik. I was commanding 'D' Company and quickly set up good relations with the locals and equally quickly realized that nothing concrete would eventuate, the way operations were then being conducted. I obtained permission to take my company up to the Thai border and found out that the CT were using a certain area for their routes of entry and exit. We very nearly made contact with them.

After the month of operational duty was over I was told to stay in the area as, by then, I had formed a working rapport with the Temiar and could talk their language. I managed to get the chief man of the Temiar in Perak (who had been a weapon-carrying ally of the CT until a while back) to agree to give his son, brother and cousin, to act as a screeen for a small party of myself and ten Gurkhas, who would follow these three men wherever trails or information or plain hunch led.

Permission was granted by both military and police authorities for an extended period and we set off on a journey that had as little hope of success as any had had during the past fourteen years. For a start, no

*Temiar: one of ten or so aboriginal ethnic groups found in Malaya, mostly in the north of the country.

firm information about the CT had been furnished ever, all was rumour; no enemy had been seen for five years; we had to search an area of 1,200 square miles in thick, mountainous jungle; we could only eat what we carried or foraged, airdrops being forbidden by the Temiar headman as noise of aircraft circling an area was associated with troops on the ground – and secrecy was of paramount importance. Finally, to make our rations last as long as possible, only one quarter of the scale was taken and then not all of the commodities were carried. Our equipment weighed over 110 pounds for each man. The terrain was as rough as anywhere in Malaya. We had to walk over 50 miles to the east – and one mile in two hours was fast moving – over the ridge of high mountains that divide Malaya to Kelantan, where we were tricked out of our quarry, six and a half weeks later, by under 200 yards. We were withdrawn after 53 days; the doctor who examined us on our return to Ipoh noted that our condition was 'a classic example of starvation'. Our intake of food had been one kilogram every six and a half days.

Back in Ipoh the Special Branch, in consonance with the Federation Army, asked for me and some Gurkhas to return. This next phase lasted for 70 days, each man carrying not less than 128 pounds and living on between six and six and a half ounces of food each day. For 53 days and 52 nights we hid up in a small patch of jungle, the size of a tennis-court, while the Temiar whom I had won over did the patrolling to see when the CT next came down from Thailand, hoping that the route they took coincided with where we were hiding out.

After such a long wait, during which time it rained solidly from the sixth to the thirty-sixth day, I had to withdraw my force. No sooner had I gone, the CT appeared in the vicinity, carrying weapons captured in Vietnam. Their arrival was coincidental with our departure, not occasioned by it. One of the reasons why the area of operations concentrated where it did was because the headman nearest to it had been made headman by the communists as well as by the government.

On my return to Ipoh I was asked to return for a third time. The whole battalion was, by this time, deployed around where my small group had been. I was given a week or so to recover; we all needed fattening up.

On this last occasion, in an attempt to maintain security, the approach march was further, harder and higher than before. After getting into the target area and hiding for 30 days out of an expected 120 our presence became known and we had to come out into the open and live in the settlement of the twice-appointed headman. After a while the whole of the settlement allied themselves firmly behind me and had actually brought in information regarding the approach of some CT when 1/7 GR had to be pulled out of the jungle for redeployment as the result of a rebellion in Brunei.

The Malayan authorities were most impressed with the manner in which the Gurkhas had conducted themselves – as indeed were the Temiar – and I was told that both the British and the Malayan Prime Ministers were known to be kept informed of progress.

I was asked by the Malayan authorities if I thought that the endeavours we had made were successful. My answer was that, since 1942 no more than three months ever elapsed without the guerrillas visiting the Temiar, so if the CT were now to stay away for one year, surely this would count as a success. In the event the CT stayed away for six years, only to return after riots in Kuala Lumpur and Malacca in May 1969.

All this took place in 'peacetime'. As I was the first to admit, I could not have done it all with anyone other than Gurkhas; I was completely sustained by their wonderful perseverance, fortitude, good humour, uncomplaining determination and unfailing camaraderie, and all with not even one day's sickness. Even the CO of 22 SAS admitted that his men could never have done it – and no other soldiers in the British Army would stand better chance than they.*

*There were never more than 8 Gurkha battalions out of a maximum of 24. CT strengths were 4,000–5,000 in 1948, increasing to around 8,000 in 1952. At the height of the campaign, there were 40,000 regular soldiers, with aircraft, guns and naval craft, 70,000 police and 250,000 Home Guard, as well as technical and administrative services needed by the government. Of this total, the Brigade of Gurkhas numbered never more than 10,000 available for deployment, with less than 2,000 operational troops to start with.

5

THE BORNEO BATTLE, 1962–1966

During 1962 there was much talk about the uncertain füture of the Brigade of Gurkhas. This had become a source of anxiety and bewilderment to many, both in the Brigade and outside it. No decision had yet been made, but it had become obvious from various official and newspaper comments that some action was contemplated. However, before anything finite could emerge, all was overtaken by events happening in places that the planners had never given much thought to. On the world's third largest island, Borneo, first a rebellion in the tiny sultanate of Brunei occurred, then a war in the other two British territories of Sarawak and Sabah, the latter then called British North Borneo.

Britain's disentanglement from empire, and the resultant political pressures on territories that became independent, have often caused upheavals and bloodshed. In south-east Asia the tidiest way of arranging affairs was to form a new country, Malaysia, out of five separate neighbouring territories – Malaya, Singapore, Sarawak, Brunei and British North Borneo.

This clashed with another, equally expansive but less realistic idea from the President of Indonesia, Sukarno, to form a state to be called Maphilindo and made up of Malaya, the Philippines and Indonesia, which could rival any other power bloc in the world. Neither idea came to fruition as originally envisaged, but Malaysia did become an entity, never with Brunei, and with Singapore for only two years, whereas Maphilindo was stillborn. Nevertheless, in an effort to prevent Malaysia from happening at all, Sukarno waged war against it, the so-called Confrontation, which was preceded by a rebellion in Brunei.

The roots of the Brunei rebellion are obscure but there are two points to note: first that, with Indonesian connivance, a secret army was formed with a view to making all the British Borneo Territories, with Brunei at their head, satellite to Indonesia; and second that the British were taken completely by surprise.

It may not have been entirely coincidental that, around this time, there were strong rumours of an MRLA incursion from Thailand into Malaya, the Malayan railways were on strike and there was disruption in the postal services. In Singapore, the prime minister neatly rounded up over one hundred known agitators just before trouble on a disruptive scale was due to break out. The intention of those who masterminded the original scenario could have been to tie up troops on the mainland by the threat of trouble to the north and south, with resultant slowness of deployment exacerbated by transportation difficulties, thus not being in a position to reinforce Brunei at a crucial stage of the planned rebellion.

The name given by the Indonesians to Borneo is Kalimantan and the name of the secret army was the North Kalimantan National Army or, using the initials of the native language, the TNKU. It had an active strength of about 4,000 but not all were well armed.

REACTION ON A SHOESTRING

The first warning of rebellion came the day before it was launched and was quickly passed to the governments of all the three Borneo Territories, enabling certain precautions to be taken immediately to minimize the effects of the rebels to set up the state of Kalimantan Utara (North Kalimantan). The rebels launched their attacks at 0200 hours on 8 December 1962 against the police station in Brunei Town, the Sultan's palace and the prime minister's residence. Attacks were repulsed, but the rebels managed to capture the power-station, which they switched off, and to block the airfield. Elsewhere they captured a number of important places and took some Europeans hostage. Outside Brunei two towns in Sarawak, Limbang and Bangar, were also taken, otherwise nowhere else was affected.

During the day of the 8th much was done to restore the situation in Brunei, with the power-station recaptured and the airfield unblocked. Police inflicted casualties and made many arrests as they tried to restore order, but rumours of rebel reinforcements and the inability to enforce a curfew left an uneasy situation. Determined action by the rebels could have gained them success.

Across in Singapore 1/2 GR were alerted at 0200 hours on the 8th. The commitment was not theirs but the British battalion whose it was could not meet it, so the Gurkhas were totally surprised and completely unprepared; it was even thought, initially, to be an elaborate hoax. Nevertheless, at 1030 hours 'C' and 'D' Companies, under the second-in-command, left barracks and drove to the airport where they found that the Saturday holiday atmosphere resulted in their kicking their heels for some hours before they could take off for Brunei. By 2000 hours a headquarters had been established in the police station. Despite casualties to be taken and some fighting yet to be done, the rebellion had no chance of success from then on.

Patrols sent out into the town then and there met with rebels and confused fighting ensued around the government buildings. As well as a British officer being killed, casualties were sustained on both sides. Attempts to relieve Seria, where the Shell Oil Company is based, were called off after 'C' Company had fought its way towards it and had retaken Tutong as it did so.

The position in Brunei Town was consolidated the next day as were the vital oil installations and another airfield in the Luton-Miri area to the west. By then other units had arrived; the 1st Battalion, Queen's Own Highlanders completely took the rebels by surprise by a bold assault on Seria having landed on an unreconnoitred grass strip in Twin Pioneer aircraft and at Anduki in a Beverly aircraft. Although the rebels held the strip at Anduki the Highlanders overcame them, relieved Seria and rescued the hostages. Militarily it is most unsound to land aircraft on ground held by an enemy. To clear such a danger is the role of parachute troops if conditions warrant, and it was this operation that showed up the need to have a parachute unit always on hand. Rather than denude the Home Base of such troops, it was decided to raise a small parachute force from theatre resources and the Gurkha Independent Parachute Company was raised on 1 January 1963.

Limbang was retaken, in a direct frontal assault under heavy fire and with casualties, by 42 Commando, Royal Marines, just in time to save the hostages from execution. The 1st Royal Green Jackets moved in from the sea in HMS *Tiger* and relieved all the other towns in the south.

The TNKU had now ceased to exist as a fighting formation. The less venturesome members crept back to their villages, glad to be out of something they had never fully understood, while the hard core, becoming more of a nuisance than a threat, faded into the jungle.

By mid-January 1963, thanks to the initial flexibility, dash and determination of 1/2 GR and the bold follow-up action of the British troops, the situation had been stabilized; the three British and one Gurkha battalion set about hunting for the last remnants of the TNKU. Torrential rain set in which made the largest river in the area rise by 30 feet; 1/2 GR had to set about dangerous rescue work, eventually rehabilitating 3,000 people. By February 1/7 GR had relieved 1/2 GR and were later to coincide with 2/7 GR, who had come from Hong Kong. By the time 2/7 GR were fully operational there was only the very hard core of the TNKU left to eliminate. It was their bad luck that they happened to be in the area dominated by the Gurkhas.

The final flicker of rebellion was smothered on 18 May when a gang, led by the instigator of the rebellion himself, Yasim Affendi, with three others, were contacted in a swamp not far from Brunei Town. Rifleman Nainabahadur Rai saw them – he was in the cut-off line beyond where the rebels were presumed to be – at 70 yards' range. Nainabahadur did not open fire then for fear of hitting other Gurkhas who would have been in the line of fire, beyond the rebels. The leading rebel saw Nainabahadur from 30 yards and, pointing his pistol, he and his three colleagues charged at him. The Gurkha, now in the aim position standing by a rubber tree, waited until the rebels were only fifteen yards away before opening fire; his first bullet went straight through Yasim Affendi and hit the second in the chest, killing them both. The other two rebels took up positions and continued to fire at Nainabahadur who, cooly and deliberately, wounded them both then went forward and captured them. It was remarkable performance on the rifleman's part and earned him the first of two MMS. He was also nominated as 'Man of the Year'* by the British Army, the first Gurkha ever to be so honoured.

With the failure of the Brunei rebellion, Sukarno had to make a more direct move in his plan to prevent and, if necessary, destroy Malaysia. His main policy from the beginning was to divide the various entities and so break up the concept of unity and bring the five ingredients of Malaysia under a government subservient to Indonesia. Stage one was to separate the Borneo Territories from the proposed Malaysian federation, using military tactics based on guerrilla warfare theories expounded by Indonesia's Defence Minister, General Abdul Haris Nasution. Stage two, operating against Singapore and the Malayan peninsula, came later – and was a damp squib.

Nasution had published a book on the subject in 1953, based on the theories of Mao Zedon, but in the context of winning freedom from the Dutch. He seems to have paid less attention to the civilian element that needed to be won over than was the case in other theories. In brief the first phase would find the guerrillas too weak for anything except hit-and-run attacks on the enemy. During the second phase the enemy's lines-of-communication would be stretched and he would tend to isolate himself in fixed bases. Guerrillas would then consolidate by stepping up their attacks, while the regular army would prepare itself for the third and final phase. By then the enemy would be surrounded by an actively hostile population and would therefore be unable to continue

*Man of the Year: every year the British Council for Rehabilitation of the Disabled holds a luncheon to do honour to those who have distinguished themselves during the preceding year. In 1963 the theme was 'Courage and Achievement', and the Rt Hon Harold Macmillan, MP was nominated chief Man of the Year. Others nominated were two professors, a test pilot, a motor cycle racing star, a coach driver, a miner, a special constable and an engine driver, Mr Mills, of the Great Train Robbery. The services also nominated a man each. The Luncheon was held on 14 November 1963 at the Savoy Hotel. (*Kukri*, 1964, page 63) their campaign. Nasution would then claim victory. The probability of the enemy using the tactics of 'selling space for time' in terrain like Borneo never seems to have entered the brave General's head.

Confrontation, like the Malayan Emegency before it, was indeed a purely guerrilla campaign with the main differences, apart from Borneo being more rugged than Malaya, being that the Indonesian enemy was well-equipped, aggressive and willing to fight it out; and that the enemy in Malaya was an internal one, in Borneo, though, mainly external. Also, as crucial as any other factor, was that the Gurkha soldier of 1963 was not labouring under the crippling disadvantages that he was in 1948.

On the political front Sukarno combined threats with conciliatory gestures, alternating them with military pressure. He also underestimated the civilian resistance to Confrontation and the standard of the Security Forces, who, to a very large extent, consisted of the Brigade of Gurkhas and who were commanded and organized by officers of a calibre normally higher than had been seen, in either country, ever before.

Most of Borneo is a vast expanse of jungle and mountain. There are few roads and the numerous rivers and some jungle trails are the only means of travel between coast and hinterland, unless by air. The largest and most developed centres of population lie along the coast and, in 1963, were not joined by road. Between the coast and the mountainous border country, much of the terrain is so densely covered by tall trees that small transmitters were often used by the troops as a homing device for aircraft – so hard was it to locate them visually. One noted characteristic of Borneo, which is sparsely populated, is villages built under one roof, like one long house, hence the continual reference to 'longhouses'. I once came across four longhouses, all within half a mile of one another, all of which spoke different languages, and with no other inhabitations for over two days' walk in all directions.

The Sarawak border with Kalimantan, running from the west, rises rapidly to 3,000 feet and culminates in high and lonely mountains of up to 8,000 feet. The Sabah border continues at that height and gradually descends to 3,000 feet, the whole front being a natural watershed. Sections of relatively level ground are interspersed among the ranges and these are cultivated by the hill tribes who have settled there.

For administrative purposes, Sarawak was then broken into five divisions, numbered from 1 to 5, each with a resident as chief administrator, and each in turn subdivided into districts. The capital, Kuching, is in the 1st Division to the west of the country, which is narrower and much more cultivated that it is further east and so was much more sensitive to Indonesian pressure. The heaviest fighting took place in the west of the country.

Sabah was divided into four residencies, known as Interior, Tawau, West Coast and Sandakan, and it was only in the first two that any fighting took place. At the very eastern end the large timber plantations had much Indonesian labour and, indeed, the border runs through the middle of the island of Sebatik – an invitation to instability.

The coastline of Malaysian Borneo, including Brunei, stretches for 1,500 miles, while the land frontier with Indonesia is almost 1,000 miles long. The population is a conglomeration of many races: Malays, Ibans (the 'head-hunters'), Muruts, Kelabits, Kayans, Kenyans, Punans and many others – and Chinese, the largest immigrant population and potentially the gravest threat to internal peace and stability. Apart from the Chinese, the population was very pro-British (later, in the context of handing over to the mainland Malays, almost embarrassingly so): it was a traditional red feather, the call to arms, that was sent upriver to the upland tribes during the Brunei rebellion, to unite them against the new menace. The TNKU's retreat towards Indonesia was cut off by these people, hastily formed into a force that was the forerunner of the Border Scouts.

In the early hours of Friday, 12 April 1963, even before the Brunei rebellion had been finally wound up, 30 Indonesian raiders penetrated three miles into the 1st Division of Sarawak and attacked the police post at Tebedu, taking the small detachment completely by surprise. The raiders caused casualties and looted the bazaar.

At the same time as the nature of the external threat was being revealed, another danger, that of the internal menace, came to light. The Special Branch revealed just how well-prepared was the Clandestine Communist Organization (CCO) in west Sarawak. Large quantities of Chinese weapon-training pamphlets had been discovered. Training had also reached the stage when rehearsals for raids on police stations, for instance, had been reached.

The next day, 13 April, it was decided that early military reinforcements were urgently needed to assist the police in confiscating over 8,500 registered shotguns, mainly Chinese-owned. On 14 April 'C' Company, 2/10 GR was flown in from Singapore and the rest of the battalion followed soon after. By 25 April more than 8,500 shotguns had been handed over to the police in the 1st, 2nd and 3rd Divisions.

Of the two tasks, that on the border was the more pressing. Chiefly in west Sarawak ill-organized bands of raiders came from over the border and committed indiscriminate acts of terrorism and intimidation, which mostly cost them casualties. During the early stages of Confrontation the Indonesian Border Territorists (IBT), as the guerrillas were known, consisted mostly of 'volunteers', led by the cream of Sukarno's regular army. Training was sketchy, but the guerrillas all came from peasant stock and were inured to hard living.

The long, ill-defined, jungle-covered border had, in fact, many crossing-places which had been used in the normal course of events by the populace who had never paid much attention to it, regarding it as an unnecessary example of officialdom. Domination of the border was given top priority to the Security Forces; enemy attacks were aimed at isolated posts where it was hoped to capture arms and ammunition and, to counter this, platoon-sized bases were established in or near centres of population, with their own defence works and helicopter pads. A curfew was imposed.

One such enemy probe, near Ba Kelalan in the 4th Division, was foiled by the headman seeing strangers, entertaining them till 2/6 GR could be called in. The strangers, unarmed and in plain clothes, turned out to be raiders and they gave information about some others who were captured, so making a total of eleven.

Major General W. C. Walker, CB, CBE, DSO, by this time the Director of Borneo Operations, laid down five ingredients for success in Borneo: unified operations; timely and accurate information, requiring a first-class Intelligence organization; speed, mobility and flexibility; security of all bases wherever and whatever they might be (an airfield, a head-quarters, a patrol base, etc.); and domination of the jungle. However, another factor, equally if not more important, was the emphasis laid on 'hearts and minds'. The General emphasized that it was as much a battalion commander's task to win over the local people as it was to achieve results in actual combat. The old system, used with the aborigines in Malaya, of giving them basic 'goodies', was wrong for the Borneo Natives who would feel it against their dignity were they to be treated as grown-up children. The Ibans were particularly difficult people to work with if they felt they had been treated the wrong way. Infinite patience and human understanding were needed, as well as tact and courtesy; it was hard to remember that only the older Natives had even seen British soldiers before and none had seen Gurkhas. It was the responsibility of all ranks to establish good relations and luckily the character of British and Gurkha troops readily lent itself to conforming with local behaviour – much more than in the case of Malay troops. The odd time that relations did get out of hand led to sour situations.

Gradually the Security Forces started to get more information about enemy intentions. In the gathering of Intelligence there were three sources to be tapped: an increase in the Special Branch of the police; the employment of 22 SAS to provide early warnings from mobile observation posts – a task that the Gurkha Para were to do later; and a third, unique, force that was provided by the Natives of Borneo themselves, called the Border Scouts. These men had been given three weeks' basic training by soldiers of 22 SAS and the Gurkha Para, after which and until their own leaders were trained – something which did not happen for six months – Gurkha soldiers had to be their section commanders.

Spread along the frontier, sometimes with an army unit but often as satellite to a remote longhouse, using a language that did not come easily to him – if it came at all – the Gurkha found it lonely, uncomfortable, primitive and strange, to say nothing of the danger. His charges were frightened by the possibility of an armed enemy attack and were unused to Gurkha-type discipline. Results achieved and steadfastness shown by the very great majority of section commanders, for the most part unsung, were most gratifying – especially when it is remembered that in the sensitive 1st and 2nd Division, ordinary riflemen of the Gurkha Para were made into section commanders although they may not have been of NCO material themselves. This was in stark contrast to the start of the Malayan Emergency, when there was an acute NCO shortage. By 1963 all the '48 recruits of corporal and below had left the army and training for potential NCOs was systematic and successful.

There were still times when the literal turn of mind of the Gurkha rifleman showed itself to the man's disadvantage. One night in a Marine camp, a Marine corporal was giving orders to the Gurkha rifleman in charge of the Border Scouts and I overheard the following conversation:

'I want four hands on watch at 8 o'clock.'

There was a pause while this strange request was digested. Then the answer was given, 'My watch has two hands at 8 o'clock!'

At such times it was not an easy war at that level; nor at others. Gurkhas in the 2nd Division had to deal with Ibans; flamboyant, mercurial and sulky. An Iban could sulk for up to three days when he had been shown wrong in front of other Ibans. On one occasion the whole of one Iban Border Scout section surrounded their Gurkha section commander and said that they would not take any more orders from him and that they were going to cut off his head. The Gurkha, canny as ever, told them that they would have to get the local military commander's permission. They agreed to this, so they were fallen in and marched to the military camp a short distance away, having left one man in their own camp to act as sentry. On reaching the company office the Gurkha left his men outside and went into report to the Major, who happened to be his company commander in more normal times. The matter was explained and the Gurkha was given permission to bring his charges in.

The whole business was carried our smartly. The Ibans were marched in, 'right dressed', being told off when their drill was faulty, then stood to attention while the Gurkha saluted the Major. He then told him what the trouble was, in Gurkhali, which the Ibans did not understand. The Major spoke about as much Malay as did the Ibans and told them that they had to obey orders and his order was that they were not to decapitate their section commander but to do what he told them. They were then dismissed and the Gurkha marched them back to their camp, all much happer than before; the Gurkha because he had shown that military discipline prevailed; and the Ibans because they had impressed the Gurkha so much with their threat that he had had to take them in front of the 'Tuan Besai' – the Great Man.

The only man who was unhappy at not having 'proved his manhood' was the Iban sentry left behind who, perversely, was told by his comrades that as he had not joined in the mass censuring of the Gurkha, it would have to be his head instead. Once it was dark this man stole away from his camp and went to the main camp where he asked for sanctuary as his head was to be chopped off. He was suitably comforted and sent back to his section post where he was given a rocket by the Gurkha for being absent without leave. 'Oh,' came the answer, 'I had to go and tell the "Tuan Besai" that I thought you ought to be beheaded.'

Thus, in its convoluted Asian way, was one tiny problem defused.

I was made the Border Scout commander and seconded to the Sarawak Constabulary and later to the Sabah Police Force. It was unfortunate that I arrived after the initial formation of the Scouts as many of the early recruits were not the best type of men for the job and, instead of being 'the eyes and ears' of the Security Forces, wearing their normal attire of a loincloth or whatever and moving in areas where soldiers would not want to be seen, they were formed into military units and developed into poor militia. That made the Gurkhas' hard task even harder. I had gone to England to recover from my work with the aborigines and by the time I arrived in Borneo I found that the Scouts had already been deployed.

Supervision proved difficult as communications were so poor and sections were spread over hundreds of miles. There were obviously teething troubles, but the new force had to be a success. It was of paramount importance to the future of the country and the measure of their success was to the credit and enhancement of those Gurkhas who, in the early, formulative days, had greatness thrust upon them and accepted it all with never the flicker of an eyelid.

It appeared that Indonesian Confrontation would succeed if so much pressure was brought to bear on the border peoples that either they were absorbed by the opposition or forced to evacuate their border homelands. If the border peoples could be made to feel they were taking an active part in their own defence and that the government was behind them, Confrontation would probably fail; if not, Confrontation would probably succeed. The Border Scouts, beside being what their name implied, would so associate the border peoples with their own defence that their success could spell doom to Indonesian efforts; the converse was also true. I was told that it was up to me to make the organization work. I realized all too plainly the enormous responsibility given to me and I felt all too inadequate to cope with it. It is most certainly true to say that, without the Gurkha support in the initial stages, while training indigenous leaders and during the crucial changeover to a more fitting role, the Border Scouts would never have been the success that they undoubtedly were, nor played the essential part in defeating Confrontation that they did. Gurkha example, dedication and leadership proved indispensable.

In August 1963 the first deep incursion by the enemy took place. It was made by about 60 men with the aim of capturing the riverine town of Song, in the 3rd Division. Information about this incursion was first heard from an Iban who had been captured and, on escaping, alerted the Security Forces. The first contact was made some 30 miles from Song and ended indecisively; a patrol of 2/6 GR (who had two companies in Sarawak and the rest of the battalion in Tawau in Sabah) went to investigate, not realizing the size of the enemy force. A young British officer was killed and the follow-up action, vigorously applied, lasted a month. 1/2 GR were flown over from Singapore and took over as the two 2/6 GR companies were wanted back with their battalion. The captured Indonesians, on interrogation, revealed that they had been launched without maps, compasses or rations, relying on locals for guides and food. This showed that either the Indonesian assessment of the situation was wildly inaccurate or that their military planning and organization woefully bad. It was later thought that the raiders were used as an act of publicity and defiance to coincide with the United Nations fact-finding team that visited Sarawak in that month to ascertain whether Malaysia had popular support or not. In the event the creation of Malaysia was confirmed by the United Nations and came into being on 16 September 1963.

    Indonesian reaction to this proclamation was immediate and violent; the Indonesians refused to recognize Malaysia and, in Jakarta, mobs ransacked the British embassy. Along the frontier separating Sarawak and Sabah from Kalimantan, Indonesian regular forces and guerrillas

Right: Pasture for cattle is plenteous in the uplands. In spring, a mini-migration will take place, sometimes including all members of the family. A bracing climate, abundant milk, regular exercise, a frugal diet and self-reliancy, to say nothing of learning how to cope with monotony and a simple routine, all help to foster the characteristics for which Gurkha soldiers are so well known.

Right: At lower altitudes, arable farming is everywhere in evidence, clustered around villages or at some distance from the homestead. Problems of deforestation and soil erosion are worryingly serious. Amidst the terra cotta-coloured dwellings, a whitewashed house stands out in Dhamphus, near Pokhara, 125 miles west of Kathmandu.

Top left: Drill is the basis of discipline in that a man learns, corporately and individually, instant obedience to an order which later becomes an ingrained habit. This is always essential, sometimes vital, in situations demanding more than normal tenacity of purpose. Recruits learn drill at the Training Depot in Hong Kong.

Bottom left: Tactical situations at section and platoon level involve a knowledge, not only of tactics, but also of map reading, fieldcraft and weapon characteristics. Realism in training helps bridge the gap between that and the real thing. It is a commonplace throughout a soldier's service.

Above: During the Malayan Emergency, living in the jungle became second nature. Razor-sharp reflexes during movement through it or in ambush could give way to a more relaxed atmosphere during other periods. However, since life depended on a soldier's constant alertness, living for long periods in the jungle became a strain.

Below: Rubber plantations all had a monotonous similarity about them. They were important, not only for the financial welfare of Malaya, but also as places of contact between tappers and the terrorists. It would take about 30 years for a rubber sapling to become too old for profit.

Above: 3-inch mortars were often deployed against terrorists in the jungle, as pictured here in the Cameron Highlands, as was 25-pounder artillery. However, the terrorists only really feared the heavier medium (5.5-inch) shellfire and bombing. They also knew that no Security Forces would ever be in an area under fire.

Below: Road convoys were an essential part of the Malayan Emergency. Convoy discipline had to be tight or they would have become easy targets for ambushing, especially off the main roads. Each battalion had its own scout cars, while armoured cars were provided by British units.

Top right: The Gurkha paras were very proud of their red berets, which were normally handed out on the dropping zone after the final qualifying descent. Although a separate badge was mooted, it was turned down, to the Gurkhas' relief. 'Now people can see we're as good as the British paras,' was a common comment. Here the author is presenting a hat to Rifleman Sombahadur Thapa, 1/2 GR.

Bottom right: Gurkha Air Platoons became an indigenous part of Gurkha battalions in the middle 1960s, flying Sioux helicopters. Platoons were an admixture of British and Gurkha soldiers. Niceties of dress, both of the Gurkha Independent Parachute Company and 6 GR Air Platoon, as shown in this picture, are now 'collectors' items'.

Opposite page, top left: The traditional Gurkha felt hat, the utter impartiality, the immaculate bearing and unmistakeable air of military professionalism were all important elements in showing Greeks and Turks in Cyprus that the Gurkhas said what they meant, meant what they said and would brook no deviation from military rectitude.

Opposite page, top right: Traffic problems in any large city are enough to daunt the most seasoned driver. Apart from supplying transport for much of Hong Kong garrison's requirements, the Gurkha Transport Regiment runs a troop of Saracen armoured cars and has to plan, in detail, all aspects of military transportation in the territory. Here two Gurkhas are tying-up planning details.

Above: A far cry indeed from the semaphore flag-wagging that this man's father might have learned! Competent and reliable communications are the prerequisite of any army, and Gurkha technicians and tradesmen of the Queen's Gurkha Signals are more than equal to the daunting, unsung yet ever essential task of maintaining them.

Left: Up in the New Territories, the terrain is vastly different from the urban sprawl of Kowloon and Victoria, Hong Kong. Paddy fields and scrub, duck farms and marsh, and an open coast line all brought their own particular tactical problems during the Cultural Revolution and the periods dominated by illegal immigrants.

Left: Daubed with camouflage cream, a modern Gurkha recruit, near the end of his training, feels he has achieved much and is on the threshold of even more. Faced with challenges as yet unspecified, he now knows that he will be given every incentive and aid to fulfill his military commitments – yet, in the final analysis, it is he, the man, that counts.

Left: Soldiers the world over and from time immemorial have had a saying that, however expressed, means, 'You shouldn't have joined if you have'nt got a sense of humour'! Service with Gurkhas is enhanced by their ability to be uniformly pleasant, uncomplainingly philosophical and, as happy warriors, being blessed with a smile that 'says it all'.

began to build up their strengths for more and much-better organized cross-border raids.

The incursion towards Song marked a change in the pattern and scale of Indonesian activity and, a month later, a more serious raid occurred. It, too, took place in the 3rd Division, which was about the size of Wales, had a 382-mile stretch of border and was the military responsibility of 1/2 GR. It was wild, lonely, mountainous country, unmapped, sparcely inhabited and intersected with many fast-flowing rivers, often impossible to cross. Considerable distances separated headquarters from its company bases – it was almost 300 miles by river to the furthest sub-unit. Fortunately, with the helicopters of 845 Squadron, Royal Navy, in support, the journey was one of minutes rather than of days.

There was a Border Scout post of 21 scouts, with two Police Field Force radio operators and four Gurkhas, at a small village called Long Jawi. This was situated about 30 miles inside Sarawak and 50 miles from the nearest administrative centre, and company headquarters, at Belaga. Inhabited by Kayans and Kenyans, it represented the northernmost movement in a migratory movement from Kalimantan; the people therefore had their roots and focus of interests over in Indonesia, especially in a sister settlement, Long Nawang. Long Jawi was situated on the upper reaches of the 300-mile-long River Rejang, and consisted of one longhouse a hundred yards long, some grain storage huts and a school. The villagers maintained a constant barter trade with Long Nawang and had no real interest in anywhere else. Government propaganda posters concerning Malaysia, which were stuck on the walls of the longhouse, meant less than nothing to them.

Apart from the post at Long Jawi there was another downstream at Long Linau, a village much nearer to Belaga, also on the River Rejang. These two outposts maintained communications by radio with Belaga but conditions were tenuous and by Morse code only. A stand to at company headquarters was initiated every time either of the two outposts missed the daily call.

Captain J. J. Burlison, commanding the company based in Belaga, wanted to change some of his Gurkhas over and as two Border Scout officers, Captains J. A. F. Bailey and A. E. Berry, planned to pay a routine visit to Long Jawi also, the three British officers and three Gurkha soldiers went up the Rejang together by boat, calling in at Long Linau on the way and getting to Long Jawi on the afternoon of the third day, 25 September.

Next day the officers considered what might be done the better to defend the place against an attack and various measures were decided upon, some being put into effect at once. That evening, Captain Bailey explained to the assembled villagers, through an interpreter, what the

Gurkha plans were in the event of an attack on the settlement. What he did not know was that, at the back of the audience, was a reconnaissance patrol from an Indonesian unit, based on Long Nawang and hidden in the nearby jungle, which was planning to attack the place.

On the morning of 27 September the three British officers left with some of the Gurkhas. Corporal Tejbahadur Gurung, the commander of the Border Scouts at Long Jawi, moved his force, less the signallers, from within the longhouse where they had been to a newly prepared post on a hill a short distance away. At about 0530 hours on 28 September, by a stroke of incredibly good luck, the post was alerted by news that a large enemy force was about to attack. Tejbahadur stood his men to, then went down the hill to alert the radio operators.

The corporal left the signallers trying to establish contact with base, collected a case of hand-grenades and made his way back. The Indonesians suddenly attacked with a barrage of 60mm mortars and heavy and concentrated fire from medium and light machine-guns. Tejbahadur was thrown to the ground by the blast of an explosion, struggled to his feet and managed to reach a trench unharmed, but he had lost his case of grenades in the dark. The Indonesians then attacked the part of the longhouse where the signallers were and killed them all – less one policeman whose knee was shattered but who managed to crawl up the hillside under fierce covering fire from the defenders, which also broke up a dawn assault. Now there was no chance at all of alerting company headquarters to their plight.

The Border Scouts, never expecting to have to face such a situation and untrained for it anyway, began to slip away unobtrusively. They were seized by the Indonesians, disarmed and bound up. The situation for the Gurkhas was becoming untenable.

Tejbahadur was left with four soldiers: they took up the best positions to defend the hill, against what later was known to be some 150 raiders. By now it was full daylight and Rifleman Amarbahadur Thapa, the Bren gunner, could see that his fire was taking effect. Rifleman Kharkabahadur Gurung's aimed rifle shots caused the enemy casualties until his own thigh was torn open by a bullet; in another trench Rifleman Dhanbahadur Gurung was killed.

Incredibly the small band of soldiers held out for two hours but, by 0800 hours, Corporal Tejbahadur Gurung decided to withdraw. There were only three effective men left, two badly wounded Gurkhas and one Border Scout who was too frightened either to fight or to run away. One assault had already been beaten off but now ammunition was down to a few rounds each man and a further assault could not be repelled. Kharkabahadur begged to be left behind so the others could make their escape but he was ignored. The three Gurkhas and the Border Scout slowly dragged the two semi-conscious wounded men from the position without the raiders seeing and, after two agonizing hours, had crossed a stream and climbed deep into the virgin jungle above it. During this time the Indonesians remained quiet.

From where they were in the jungle, the Gurkhas could look down on where they had been. An hour later the Indonesians attacked their one-time position and, finding it deserted, presumed that the Gurkhas were not far away. They fired indiscriminately into the surrounding area for the rest of the day and, at dusk, first looted the hut then set fire to it.

With no food, no medical supplies and in pouring rain the Gurkhas spent a long and very miserable night. The wounded men were kept as warm as possible. Tejbahadur was anxious to reach Long Linau as soon as he could to alert his company. He decided to leave the wounded men behind so, having dressed their wounds with the last dressings, he hid them and set off with his two men and the Border Scout as guide.

Two days later, during which time they existed on roots, they reached the next longhouse downstream. There they were given food but they decided to sleep that night in the jungle. Next morning they borrowed a longboat and reached Long Linau, where they transmitted a message. Four days after the action Corporal Tejbahadur Gurung and his small group arrived in Belaga, exhausted, but with weapons spotlessly clean. They gave a first-hand account of what had taken place.*

At Long Jawi the Indonesians, flushed with victory, plundered the settlement before returning upstream to their base camp, taking several of the captured Border Scouts with them. Some of the Scouts had managed to slip away in the confusion and one arrived at Long Linau a day before Tejbahadur, with a garbled account of the attack. Another Scout threw himself out of an enemy longboat and, although bound hand and foot, did not drown and made his escape.

On the face of it, the Indonesians had dealt a telling blow, with the civilians' morale severely shaken and the Border Scouts decisively beaten. They had overlooked two factors, however: one, the CO of 1/2 GR, Lieutenant Colonel J. B. Clements, a shrewd old jungle hand, who had won two MCs in Burma, and two: the detachment of four Royal Navy helicopters under his tactical control, two at Sibu and two further downstream at Song. Clements studied the map and worked out the route the enemy would probably use for its escape over the border, and decided to send his men by helicopter to intercept them. To avoid alarming the Indonesians he asked the pilots not to fly their machines over the Indonesians' presumed route for the next week.

*Later Tejbahadur was awarded the MM.

On 1 October 11 Platoon, commanded by Lieutenant (QGO) Pasbahadur Gurung, was flown into the jungle several miles upstream from Long Jawi. The pad it aimed to land on had been staked by the Indonesians to prevent a helicopter landing. Luckily the place was not guarded and the Gurkhas were roped down in safety. The helicopters departed as they had arrived, contour flying to muffle their noise.

Shortly after landing Pasbahadur heard the chug of outboard engines in the distance and promptly laid an ambush on the river bank. By the time two longboats, packed with 26 armed Indonesians, came into view, the platoon was in position. Pasbahadur timed the springing of the ambush perfectly and the Gurkhas opened fire at point-blank range when the leading boat was at the far, upstream end. One boat sank at once, in midstream, the other ended up on some rocks on the far bank. However, as not one of the platoon was a strong enough swimmer to cross the swift-flowing river, the boat on the rocks could not be reached until the next day. It was thought few, if any, of the enemy had survived; later it was found that the boat contained one dead enemy soldier, a 60mm mortar and medium machine-gun ammition. Equipment and the two radio sets taken at Long Jawi were also recovered.*

A platoon had been put into Long Jawi and found the village had been ransacked and was deserted – the place smelt of death. The two wounded Gurkhas, who had somehow survived several wet days and nights of exposure in the jungle, saw the helicopters. More dead than alive, they managed to crawl down the hill, but on approaching the Gurkha position only narrowly escaped death by being shot at before they were recognized.

Meanwhile, in a separate development, the Border Scout who had jumped out of the Indonesian boat was able to give useful information: Clements had assumed that the main Indonesian camp was five miles upstream from Long Jawi, on the far bank of a tributary of the River Rejang. The platoon in the village was ordered to follow up on foot.

The broken countryside, the dense jungle and the almost incessant rain made the going hideously difficult. The platoon met one river that was impossible to cross and two helicopters had to be sent to ferry them over, roping them down on the far side. The Gurkhas reached upstream from where their CO had said the camp would be and there it was, but on the other side of the river, visible through the trees. Weighed down as they were, none of the soldiers could swim across the river. A British officer, Captain D. J. Willoughby and the one Border Scout guide, Bit Epa, were strong enough swimmers to undertake the journey. With the platoon ready to give covering fire, the two men swam across in their

*For this exemplary action Lieutenant (QGO) Pasbahadur Gurung was awarded the MC.

underclothes, armed with a knife each. The current swept them downstream but they managed to scramble ashore near the camp. They found the camp empty of the living – there were decomposing bodies of Border Scout captives who had been brutally murdered and some enemy graves.

The camp had been used as a staging-post. The Indonesians had arrived there on foot and then been ferried on downstream in five longboats. The follow-up platoon was replaced by fresh troops. By then, in Long Jawi, a Gurkha company had made a firm base with reserve troops and a ration supply.

By the end of October a few more of the raiders had been killed and some had died of starvation and wounds but the remainder had escaped back over the border. It was discovered that the enemy commander, a Major Muljono, had fought against the Japanese and the Dutch and had been to several military training establishments, including the British Jungle Warfare School in Johore! In 1967 he was executed during a drastic purge of communists in Indonesia.

Despite the Security Forces' amazingly quick and successful reaction and follow-up, local morale had taken a bad knock, which took some time to recover. Certainly Gurkha guts, fortitude and stamina did have a great effect on the minds of all the Natives who lived along the Rejang and, as the news spread, in many other places also. That, coupled with a revised role for the Border Scouts, prevented the Indonesian victory from having any long-term adverse effect.

The Long Jawi incursion proved to be a turning-point in Confrontation for three reasons: it changed the concept of the Security Forces from being a purely defensive one into one of attack; that, without the helicopter it would be impossible to control so vast an area against the Indonesians; and that, as they were then conceived, the Border Scouts were detrimentally ineffective against such an escalation of aggression.

There were never even one hundred helicopters in Borneo, compared with about 3,800 troop-carrying helicopters in South Vietnam. It was estimated that, with six helicopters per battalion, Confrontation might well have finished a year earlier than it eventually did.

As far as reslanting the Border Scouts was concerned, a great deal of work was required, not only in more realistically defining their role and their ability to carry it out, but also in the obvious requirement of speedily completing the training of indigenous leaders to command the scouts at every level. During the course of the next few months the whole force was correctly adjusted to become as it had originally been conceived; the help the Gurkhas gave for this to happen was, without any doubt, crucial and, without it, the scars of Long Jawi would never have healed.

Another incursion had, in fact, taken place before the Long Jawi affair overshadowed events. An enemy force in three groups and numbering about 150 made an incursion into the 2nd Division, where they hoped to capture the administrative town of Simmanggang. The terrain in that part of Sarawak is not as rough as in the 3rd Division and there is a road linking Kuching with Simmanggang, running close to the border. The area is more heavily populated. The Indonesians made contact with a Border Scout camp some miles down the road from Simmanggan where the Scouts reacted firmly – they and the company of 1/10 GR in the area soon chased the enemy back over the border, but not before one gang had ambushed a civilian bus, burning it and causing casualties.

All this time the CCO had been expanding its influence along the long unguarded coast, with infiltrators being brought in by boat. One group of six were identified by some Ibans and captured by Border Scouts. There was also activity elsewhere; for instance, a group of about 80 made an incursion into southern Sabah but, although troops of the Royal Leicesters waited for ten days in preparatory patrolling and ambushing, the Indonesians recrossed the border without firing a shot.

The last few hours of 1963 were bloodstained. At Kalabakan in the Tawau Residency of Sabah, troops of the Royal Malay Regiment were surprised by part of a force of 35 regulars and 128 volunteers, and suffered 8 killed, including the company commander, and 19 wounded. They had been unprepared in every way and put up no resistance. They were urged to counter-attack when the raiders started looting local bungalows and shops, but they declined. On the other hand, the local policemen, when attacked in their station which was prepared, put up a spirited defence, killing one and wounding four of the enemy.

So ended the first year of Confrontation, a year which began with the end of a rebellion and ended with the beginning of an undeclared war. At this time Major General Walker relinquished command of the Brigade of Gurkhas, though not his position as Director of Borneo Operations, and declared, 'It has been a great privilege to have served the Brigade as Major General and, more recently, to have had so many units of the Brigade under my operational command. They have all surpassed my expectations and I have no hesitation in restating my belief that the Brigade of Gurkhas is Second-to-None.'

To combat a deteriorating situation in Tawau it was not another Malay battalion that was detailed to go and sort things out, but 1/10 GR who were ordered, on 2 January 1964, with no prior notice, to fly in from their base in Malacca, in West Malaysia. In just under 24 hours a tactical headquarters and 'B' Company were deployed and the rest of the battalion was flown in just as fast as the air movement plan permitted.

On arrival the battalion found the area in chaos. Several more incursions were suspected but little information was available. Intelligence was negligible. An ad hoc tactical brigade headquarters was also quickly flown in from Singapore to coordinate the operations.

1/10 GR's immediate task was to secure Kalabakan and find the enemy. The operational area was immense, with large tracts of jungle that were being felled for timber and a multiplicity of tidal creeks and inlets, mud and swamp. Lieutenant Colonel E. J. S. Burnett, MBE, MC, had this to say about available Intelligence, from the point of view of battalion commander, 'All that I could find out that first evening in Kalabakan was that the enemy had raided a provision shop at [a village called] Brantian, and that the remains of a lot of chickens, cooked and eaten a short way up river from Kalabakan, had been found. I based all my initial plans on the single deduction that the raiders would be after more food before long. The hunch paid off.'

There then followed a series of engagements, one of which became the highlight of the whole operation. At about 1100 hours one day, 5 Platoon was working its way along a ridge about twelve miles north of Kalabakan. The platoon commander, Lieutenant (QGO) Indrajit Limbu, had only fifteen men with him at the time, as the remainder were struggling along in the rear carrying all the packs. Firing suddenly erupted from their front and, without hesitation, the platoon charged the enemy, displaying great courage. Two Gurkhas were killed in this charge but the platoon accounted for all nine of the enemy.*

That night the enemy attempted to break out of a two-company ambush cordon, at times trying to charge straight through the position, but they were driven back at every attempt. During this fighting one Gurkha and two enemy were killed and, three days later, three enemy were captured, then two more were killed. The battalion hunted the raiders remorselessly, every company taking its turn in eliminating the enemy. Helicopters shifted groups of Gurkhas into cut-off positions to seal the enemy's escape, boats navigated the creeks and inlets, taking troops to new and from old positions, foot patrols, in the more accessible areas, knitted a web around the Indonesians to prevent them from breaking contact. 'D' Company was sent into a large swamp area to the south – where drinking-water was a problem – to cut off any enemy who might attempt to escape using that route south to the frontier. By the end of January the battalion had killed twenty and captured thirteen enemy, and another thirteen had surrendered. The intensity of operations was more reminiscent of Burma than of Malaya.

*For their gallantry in this attack Lieutenant (QGO) Indrajit Limbu was awarded the MC and Lance Corporal Nandabahdaur Rai the MM.

By the end of February, in just under two months, 56 of the original 128 raiders had been accounted for. Of these 1/10 GR had killed 24 and captured eighteen. The battalion lost three men killed in action, another by drowning and one man by a tree crushing him to death. Two Gurkhas had been wounded. The Indonesians suffered their most decisive defeat up to that time.

By then the main battle was over and considerable redeployment and mopping up started, with the tally of kills, captures and surrenders continuing to rise.

The full extent of the planned incursion, when pieced together from prisoners' statements, displayed almost unbelievable confidence and boldness. It emerged that the attack on Kalabakan was the first stage of the move to Tawau and was designed primarily to replenish supplies. It also became clear that the enemy was a determined and tough lot, not afraid of moving or fighting at night and with heavier weapons than had so far been the case in Sarawak. Artillery support could be called from over the border.

The initial success of the Kalabakan raid, the killing and wounding of the Malays, redounded unfavourably on the Indonesians as it at once changed what had previously been proclaimed as an 'anti-imperialist' crusade into a war between Asians.

On 16 January 1964 the Secretary-General of the United Nations Organization appealed for an end to hostilities and Sukarno agreed to a truce to allow the foreign ministers of his country and Malaysia to meet for talks in Bangkok. The effective date for the ceasefire was 25 January and this uneasy truce brought to a close the first year of operations in Borneo. However, the peace talks were short-lived and with their failure the command of Confrontation passed completely to the Indonesian regular army.

By now all Gurkha battalions were taking it in turn to do their stint in Borneo – numerous were the clashes and many were the feats of bravery. 2/10 GR had some difficult battles to contend with: on one occasion the Indonesians controlled all road movement in the east of the 2nd Division from a knife-edged hilltop position. During the operation to dislodge them, guided missiles, SS11s, modified for firing from a helicopter, were used for the first time by the British Army. Five out of six missiles hit the target and the enemy withdrew. In another engagement lasting a month, 27 out of an invading force were eliminated. During the operation Lance Corporal Mandhoj Rai and one rifleman were ambushed by four of the enemy. Mandhoj calmly stepped out onto the track and shot three of them, the rifleman accounting for the fourth.

In yet another clash a seven-man patrol met about a hundred Indonesians at five yards range and extricated themselves safely. Not long afterwards eleven Gurkhas fought off 120 Indonesians in a 6-hour battle. The battalion diarist noted, 'The Gurkha soldier continues to burnish an already shining record of courage, endurance and patience. And let not those now on the sidelines imagine that operations in Eastern Malaysia are in any way similar to the 1948–60 Emergency. It has long been recognized by those taking part as being infinitely more arduous, dangerous and liable to escalation than any "cold war" action since Korea . . . the only unchanging factor is this 1964-type eastern warfare in the jungle which remains neutral, and even the jungle in Borneo is a tougher customer than its peninsula counterpart.'

After the Border Scout training and section-leading commitment ended in March, the Gurkha Para Company, still only a temporary unit, was made Brigade Reserve Company for a while. It then returned to the mainland to be reformed into a 'Patrol Company'. Its main role was, as a patrol company, to reconnoitre ahead of major units, interdictively or otherwise, so that suitable targets could be pinpointed for an attack at company level. For this it was split into sixteen five-man patrols. It also had an airborne role and a purely infantry rifle company role. Comprehensive tests were introduced to see if a man demonstrated the qualities of an extrovert to be a successful paratrooper, whilst ensuring he also possessed those of an introvert to maintain a high standard when working in a small group over a protracted period. Experience proved the efficacy of these tests, showing not only that compromising judgements by tempering them with leniency was an emotional luxury the company could not afford but that firm, objective judgements had to be made. Supermen were not required; so long as a man was keen, fit and intelligent, training, experience and leadership did the rest.

I later commanded the Gurkha Para Company for three and a half years and, although I was not concerned with the change in the unit's role as I was still the commandant of the Border Scouts, fully understood the rationale of having five-man patrols, unlike the four-man patrols operated by the Parachute Regiment, the Guards Independent Parachute Company and the squadrons of 22 SAS. The unit's fundamental task was to be able to capture an airhead and, for that, we had to have 128 Gurkhas. That number could not be reduced, nor could the type of radio required on patrol be supplied in any greater numbers than would support sixteen patrols, the control element at base, sets required on detachment and some spares. Tactically, we preferred one commander and four men (medical orderly, pioneers and radio operator:

all were linguists and commanders could manage all required skills) and, in emergencies – carrying a man on a stretcher, for instance – the fifth man was very useful. Finally, had we only used four men in each patrol, what would the others have done?

When patrol work started, men were in the jungle from 42 to 84 days. I cut that time down to two to three weeks. Much later on we were made into a long-term unit, as part of the Order of Battle of the British Army. I certainly found commanding the unit the most satisfying of all the many jobs I undertook. In Borneo the company's reputation for reliability and good work was slowly built up. It was once more shown that the hallmark of a good soldier was the ability and willingness to give of his best even though the audience was of the smallest. The men were no longer afraid of new ideas and realized that a high standard brought its own penalties of expectation.

WITH BOLDER RESOLVE

Cross-border operations, code-named 'Claret', were started by the British in 1964. They were very carefully controlled by the highest authority, namely the governments of Malaysia and the United Kingdom. Initially counter-bombardment was authorized, then the formation of killer squads for special 'pursuit' tasks and finally attacks in strength up to a depth initially of 5,000, later 10,000 metres, for specific operations against enemy positions were authorized – all part of the tactic of dominating the jungle.

The operations that followed certainly called for great courage and skill to overcome the tensions and problems of operating behind the enemy lines, hampered by severe constraints. Operations were to be confined to the limits of 105mm artillery range from guns located on helicopter pads just within the friendly side of the border, although it was often not possible to take any artillery pieces at all to some parts of the border. Sometimes 5.5 inch medium artillery also gave supporting fire. Aircraft were not allowed to overfly the border, except in a few cases of extreme urgency, and the guns could not be deployed across it.

One main concern of all commanders engaged on these operations was the portering of their casualties back to home ground. Without the use of helicopters, commanders were often faced with the tremendous task of manhandling wounded men through very rough country, continuously nagged by the danger of being engaged, on very unfavourable terms, by the enemy.

'Claret' operations had very strict 'Golden Rules' and were 'top secret'. For a short time only Gurkha battalions could be used for cross-border operations and no unit was to mount more than one raid at a time. Minimum force, preventative action and avoidance of escalation were the Director of Operations' cardinal aims – raids were not to be simply punitive. Without these aims and constraints, the border war would have turned into something very different, costly in lives as well as being beset with international problems. If the concept of 'Claret' had been any different, that is to say had the constraints already listed not been in force, political authority, from the very top, would never have been forthcoming.

An American General commented that only the British could have conceived 'Claret' operations and devised the masterly Golden Rules that governed them. Later he was kind enough to add that only well-disciplined troops such as Gurkhas, under experienced and capable leaders, could have won the successes that were obtained.

However good the pre-planning, the human element was always present and unpredictable. 15 Platoon, 'D' Company, 1/6 GR, com-manded by Captain (QGO) Damarbahadur Gurung, crossed the border into Kalimantan not far from Biawak in the 1st Division of Sarawak, there having been many reports of Indonesian preparations for activity against troops inside Sarawak. The Gurkhas moved slowly westwards looking for a site for a temporary base and a good ambush position, which was not easy as the area had houses scattered about in it and locals were constantly on the move. On 17 May an ambush was laid, covering a recently widened track along which it was hoped the enemy might move. Unfortunately two local women saw one of the base sentries and ran off screaming. When Damarbahadur was told what had happened, he very sensibly moved his positon. As luck would have it, no sooner had one been set up when a man, carrying a shotgun, walked right into it and had to be seized. As Damarbahadur was talking to him in what Malay language he could recall – at that level there was hardly any difference between Malay and Indonesian – another man, carrying an old muzzle-loader, approached, saw the position and ran off. Damarbahadur then told the captured man that his men were troops from Java, so there was nothing to be afraid of. He persuaded the man to go and tell the woman and the other man that there had been no need to take fright; the Gurkha officer also thought that this ruse might prevent news of this presence reaching the Indonesians. Even so he moved his position for the second time that day.

That evening he found a promising track junction to ambush and established a patrol base 400 yards away, with its north side well pro-tected by dense fern. Early on the 16th Damarbahadur moved into the ambush position with thirteen men, leaving the other eight men and the platoon sergeant in the base. He warned them that enemy probing would be more than likely so the base had to be alert and on its guard.

Unfortunately the sergeant did not site the men in the base correctly – they did not have interlocking arcs of fire nor did he check whether they could see any target if they adopted the prone position. It was never established whether it was the locals who told the Indonesians where the Gurkhas were or whether the enemy had seen the base camp itself, but at midday they approached from three sides. A sudden burst of machine-gunfire from the west killed one Gurkha and soon after there was shouting and a burst of fire from the south, killing the Bren gunner. He had just killed two of the enemy who were charging from the west. Then, from the northeast, a single man entered the base and grappled first with the sergeant and then with one of the riflemen. By that time Damarbahadur and his ambush group, who had the firing, were moving in an arc to come into the base from the northeast. On arrival they only found four corpses – two Gurkhas and two Indonesians, with the latter's weapons and identification marks removed. The attackers must have withdrawn, at least temporarily, but there was still some firing and Damarbahadur also decided to withdraw, south, that is to say away from Sarawak, then east, to the platoon 'fall-back' position. They had the radio set as well as nine extra packs, found abandoned in the base, to carry. When they reached the 'fall-back' position, picking up one man on the way, the platoon sergeant and four riflemen were already there. The one missing man appeared sometime later. Three men had not fired a single shot, indicating that they had been in positions that had been incorrectly sited, indicating that the platoon sergeant was clearly at fault. Apart from an Indonesian Border Terrorist, a Chinese captain and a Javanese corporal had been killed.*

In a National Resurrection Day speech in Jakarta on 20 May 1964, Sukarno had boasted that Malaysia would be crushed by the time 'the sun rises on 1 January 1965'. His attempts, however, later on in the year to open a second front in West Malaysia and to land commandos by sea and air were frustrated by 1/10 GR and ended in disaster – while, in Borneo, General Walker had demolished the first two stages of the guerrilla war. Sukarno had to revive the momentum of Confrontation and he ordered a considerable build-up of forces along the Borneo border, as well as in the forward island bases flanking Singapore and the southwest of the peninsula.

In June 1964 another attempt to find a peaceful solution to Confront-ation was made when a summit meeting was arranged in Tokyo between the Prime Minister of Malaysia, Sukarno and Macpagal, the

---

*Captain (QGO) Damarbahadur Gurung had shown skill and initiative and was later awarded the MC.

President of the Philippines. To clear the air for the meeting, independent Thai observers were sent to witness the withdrawal of Indonesian guerrillas into Kalimantan. While the summit was being arranged, however, over 30 border incidents occurred in East Malaysia.

The Tokyo summit 'truce' continued with several incidents. Parties of so-called guerrillas were seen leaving by Thai observers, but clearly these groups had been sent in only a short while before as they wore clean, new uniforms.

On 20 June the talks finally broke down. Within 24 hours Confrontation resumed, with 'Claret' operations now allowed to penetrate up to 10,000 metres. By then there were many more Indonesian regular soldiers in her front-line troops and, by the end of 1964, Indonesia stepped up her Confrontation campaign and trebled the strength of her regular garrisons in the border areas, particularly opposite Kuching and the 1st and 2nd Divisions generally. By this time there were many more helicopters available for the Security Forces and, with the introduction, later on, of radio sets with a re-broadcast facility (that is to say, the ability to install radio stations on prominent features, unscreened, to act as boosters), communications could be maintained for 24 hours with no interference. All this made for tighter control and speedier reaction.

1/7 GR found themselves based in Sibu, the administrative headquarters for the 3rd Division. Much of their task was against the CCO, who were being backed by Indonesian infiltration from the sea. The largest river in Borneo is the Rejang, so large is it that minesweepers can navigate many miles up it. Information was received from Special Branch that 26 Indonesians had landed on the coast with the aim of priming an insurrection that was to be fuelled by the CCO. Major D. O. O'Leary, MBE, MC, took 'A' Company headquarters and two platoons down river in two launches to take appropriate action.

Before they could get to their destination a Special Branch officer overtook them in a fast motorboat and took O'Leary back to assess some new information: this was that a local who had taken eight of the Indonesians, fully armed and carrying boxes of ammunition, onto a small island in the middle of the Rejang, called Lobe, now volunteered to lead the security forces back there.

The island was a difficult place to move about on, let alone attack, as it was little more than a large hummock of very smelly, very sticky, very black mud. In the first phase of action one rifleman was hit in the face by a bullet fired by a raider – once that phase was over, pinpointing where on the island the raiders were hiding, it was a question of getting to grips with them. Apart from both Indonesians and Gurkhas being covered with mud, all were continuously being devoured by clouds of insatiable mosquitoes.

O'Leary, a big jovial man and brave as a lion, personally got to grips with one man, knocking his hat off with a shot from fifteen feet away. The raider slipped in the mud and O'Leary, who had not been able to stand firmly when he shot at him, slithered forward to seize him before he could get away. The man shammed death, the bullet having glanced off his skull. He was disarmed, trussed up and taken away to the boats.

Apart from locating the enemy, there was a problem of keeping contact with the other platoon. The only way to communicate with 2 Platoon was by shouting, and each time O'Leary shouted he drew a burst of fire or had a grenade thrown at him. Eventually he came across 2 Platoon who were pinned down about 30 yards from where they thought the raiders were hiding.

While O'Leary was giving orders to 2 Platoon, Sergeant Shamsherbahadur Rai, the commander of 3 Platoon, was hit. He was found fifteen or so paces ahead of his platoon unable to move and in very great pain. O'Leary tried to crawl forward to help him but he too was pinned down. Placing two men to keep an eye on the wounded sergeant, O'Leary resumed his search and, half an hour later, thought he saw where the enemy were – in a small depression. He called on them in Malay to surrender; they tried to trick the Gurkhas into believing that that is what they would do. As the Gurkhas moved forward one of the enemy dashed out, only to be shot. In the hollow were a badly wounded raider and some dead ones.

Back at 2 Platoon O'Leary found that a rifleman had tried to crawl forward to rescue the wounded sergeant but had been hit, the bullet grazing his spine. At that moment two helicopters arrived overhead, having been sent by battalion headquarters on their first receiving news of the battle. Both wounded Gurkhas were evacuated to the government hospital at Sibu, then a helicopter returned to evacuate the two wounded raiders. Meanwhile a seventh Indonesian surrendered without a fight, the eighth also surrendering to locals three days later after swimming across the river.

The remainder of the Indonesians, harassed by the Gurkhas and police, were all caught after a nine-day chase; they were then in a launch that did not stop when challenged, having been chased by a faster vessel.*

Two days after 1/10 GR's return to Malacca from Kalabakan, the Indonesians escalated the level of Confrontation by invading mainland Malaysia, landing some hundred raiders, marines and parachutists, on the southwest coast, north of Pontian, on 17 August. Malaysian and Singaporean infantry successfully dealt with this raid — many of the

*Major O'Leary was awarded a bar to his MC.

invaders were killed or captured and the survivors, far from getting support they had expected from local Malays, were dispersed and harried in a lengthy jungle search before finally being eliminated.

Two weeks after the sea-landing, the Indonesians landed nearly a hundred parachute troops in north Johore, from two C-130 Hercules aircraft. 6 Royal Malay Regiment contacted them, killing six and capturing seven in the first four days. However, rioting broke out in Singapore and it was decided that the Malays should be sent there in haste, so 1/10 GR, hardly three weeks into their 'rest and retraining' programme, was ordered to Labis, the scene of the parachute drop.

The battalion yet again demonstrated its ability to react to the unforeseen at a time it was off balance. It was taken by road to Labis, an area of mountainous jungle, with rubber and palm oil estates between the jungle and the main north-south road. Information was sparse and extremely inaccurate: one villager reported that 25 enemy had been seen digging on a hill near a village. Trenches were even then three feet deep and medium mortars had also been seen. The area was cordoned off and an assault was put in at first light on 7 September. However, nothing was found at all as the Indonesians had never been there – the only casualty was one dead owl.

The original estimation had been that up to 40 Indonesians had dropped since the Malays had contacted those in the first drop. 1/10 GR wasted no more time and went into the thick jungle, moving east from the original dropping area. Success came quickly and on 9 September 'C' Company contacted three raiders – Rifleman Lalbahadur Gurung killed two of them as they charged at him from point-blank range and the third was killed some hours later by Lance Corporal Tejbahadur Rai.

This success was typical of Gurkha ingenuity. Both Tejbahadur and Sergeant Manbahadur Tamang could see a dark object in the long grass ahead of them. They knew that the Indonesian they were after was somewhere in that area. Manbahadur signalled silently to Tejbahadur, the battalion champion shot, to take aim. He then picked up a rock and threw it about 20 yards to one side of the dark object. It immediately revealed itself as the head of the raider as he looked in the direction of the noise the rock made when it landed. He was killed instantly.

There had, in fact, been two drops, fifteen miles apart. From aerial reconnaissance the pattern of the parachutes on the jungle canopy and the bearing that all the captured enemy had on their compasses, an accurate assessment could be made of the direction in which to search for those still unaccounted for. Skilled debriefing of those captured allowed a nominal roll to be made of the force. It was not difficult for 1/10 GR to know how many more Indonesians there were still at large.

Casualties were taken by the Gurkhas, including one British officer killed. By 25 September the last effective enemy had been eliminated and the battalion returned to its base on 6 October.

Ninety-six enemy were dropped and 90 were either killed or captured. 1/10 GR had accounted for 51 of them. The speed with which the battalion had responded and the extremely competent manner in which the operation was conducted at all levels was most impressive and clinically efficient.

As the regimental historian wrote, 'It was one of 1/10 GR's finest hours.' And, as a postscript, on 29 October, the unit was called out once again to deal with a seaborne landing by the Indonesians, with 52 of the invaders being captured in 36 hours.

By the beginning of 1965, cross-border operations became more sophisticated – potential targets tougher and harder to reach, terrain more difficult to use to advantage, fire plans tighter and more complex and engagements with the enemy more likely. The Director of Operations had a fine balance to maintain between the minimum force needed to achieve domination of the jungle, so discourage the Indonesians from making predatory incursions into Borneo on the one hand, while, on the other, not allowing the necessary punch required for this to provoke reaction on a worldwide propaganda basis by the Indonesian Government who felt it was time to start squealing. To the outside world, even those in it who had an interest in the way that Confrontation was proceeding, it was only the Indonesians who were crossing the border.

A Company, 1/6 GR, under Major C. J. Scott, a man with a nice sense of humour and an eye for meticulous detail, was given a target: the Indonesian troops billeted in a riverine village about 3,000 yards across the border. Civilian casualties were always sedulously to be avoided for very obvious reasons. A river ambush of Indonesian troops was hoped for but, as there had been several successful ambushes on river traffic in the recent months, the Indonesians had got wise to this threat and would clear the river bank with foot patrols before any convoy was dispatched. It was for that reason that the siting of such an ambush was much harder than it otherwise would have been.

The whole company was used for this particular operation; five and a half days' rations were carried and, with the required ammunition and the constant need for extreme caution in movement, meant that it took two days to cover the distance from its base in Sarawak to the target area. 105mm and 5.5inch artillery were both in support.

The third day was spent in careful reconnaissance – two likely tracks were found, one alongside the river and one that was more or less parallel with it about 400 yards away. The village and the Indonesian soldiers were about 500 yards distant. The company was laid out with 2 Platoon on the river track, 1 Platoon on the inner track and 3 Platoon were another 500 yards further back, on a small rise. Company headquarters and the gunner Forward Observation Officer (FOO) were sited between 1 and 3 Platoons. The immediate task of the FOO was 'silent registration', that is to say, working out the exact location of each probable gunner target, pinpointing it on a map and sending it back to the guns so that, in the event of fire being needed on that particular target, it could come straight down with minimum delay. It was not often that the opening rounds were exactly on target, but corrections could very quickly be made, spoken into the radio, to bring the next salvo onto the target. In this instance, there were two guns at the disposal of the Gurkhas.

The whole company, concentrated in the base area around 3 Platoon's position, spent a quiet night and, after a brew of tea or a drink of self-heating soup, troops left for their ambush positions. The ambush was ready by 0630 hours. However, nothing happened, except that two civilians in a boat were seen all day, normally an innocent enough sight on a river with a village nearby. The ambush was lifted at 1730 hours and the Gurkhas went back to the base, 900 yards from the river.

Next morning troops were in position by 0630 hours and two hours later the same two boatmen of the previous day came downstream. This time, instead of being placid as they had been, they were singing until they drew level with the ambush, when they became silent. They drifted past the ambush zone and when they reached the lower end, they started singing again. The platoon commander of 2 Platoon did not report this as it did not then occur to him that it was, in fact, a signal to some Indonesian troops of the extent of the ambush which they must have spotted.

Half an hour later 1 Platoon, who were on the track that was parallel to the river, saw an Indonesian soldier coming towards them. It was quickly realized that he was the leading scout of a larger group and was searching the ground on both sides of the track as he moved cautiously along, rifle at the ready. It is always at such a moment that discipline and fire control play an all-important part in springing an ambush, as it is imperative that as many troops as possible should be in the killing area when fire is opened. In this incident only five men were in the killing area when fire was opened and they were well spaced out. Four of them were hit, three fatally, with one getting away. The fifth man was fortunate in that, by a stroke of his good luck, he was not fired upon at all.

The enemy then charged the position but were driven off; they then opened up with small arms fire, luckily inaccurate. The gunner called for artillery support and his original calculations were so accurate that the first round fell within a hundred yards from where the assessment had been made, thus allowing the Gurkhas to evacuate their positions. Unfortunately there was a snag – radio contact with 2 Platoon was lost and this delayed the withdrawal. There was also a wounded man to be evacuated, which called for a quick move but, without definite information of the state and whereabouts of 2 Platoon, the move was delayed.

Eventually two hours later a move became imperative. Fear of an ambush on tracks back to Sarawak meant an uncomfortably slow move on a compass bearing across country. As the going was hampered by recent rain, and by having to pass through old cultivations that had overgrown, carriage of the wounded man was difficult and painful. A request for a helicopter was turned down until the company was on the Malaysian side of the border. After one more night on Indonesian soil and the three-hour walk the next day, the Gurkhas crossed the border, a helicopter coming to take away the wounded man.

Scott was more than relieved to find that the missing platoon had reached base before he had, although he of course wanted to know how it was that contact had been lost for such a long time. The answer lay in a combination of the fog of war, human frailties and plain bad luck.

Not all Indonesia's tactics were straightforward, conventional moves on the border. On 28 June 1965 a policy of infiltrating guerrillas by sea to terrorize civilians in the rear areas of Sarawak was initiated. This followed the pattern of terrorism perpetrated during the critical years of the Malayan Emergency. Regulars and volunteers moved to known areas of strong CCO influence and carried out acts of violence and sabotage.

On 2 September 1965, Support Company of 2/2 GR crossed the border of the 1st Division and penetrated 10,000 yards inside Kalimantan to ambush a river that was being used for Indonesian troop movement. In this they were helped by an exceptionally skilled member of 22 SAS, Company Sergeant Major L. Smith. The FOO was Captain J. Masters of the Royal New Zealand Artillery.

The level of the river was so low that the company commander, Captain C. J. Bullock – a man whose character exemplified what all Gurkhas respond to – sited his ambush on a parallel track but kept the river under observation. The company firm base was 650 yards from the river. Two enemy boats did use the river, but so silent was their approach that the lookouts did not have time to alert troops to move down to the water's edge.

The next day Bullock reversed the procedure and ambushed the river, keeping only two groups on the track, one at each end. Behind them was a check-point, where the FOO, CSM Hariparsad Gurung, a signaller and a medical orderly remained – back at the base were the redoubtable Smith and 24 Gurkhas.

As it so happened, more than a hundred enemy came down the track and Rifleman Ramparsad Pun, the Bren gunner, waited until the leading scout was ten yards away and there were 25 Indonesians in the killing ground before opening fire. Four enemy were killed and many wounded in the Gurkha's first burst.

The Indonesians reacted instantly, with heavy machine-gun and mortar fire, counter-attacking the numerically weaker Gurkhas. A savage firefight developed during which another twelve enemy were killed. A Claymore mine was detonated by Lance Corporal Birbahadur Pun, killing and wounding several more, but this in no way restrained the Indonesians who pressed on hard and bravely. There were some savage head-on encounters, Gurkha steadiness proving to be decisive.

As the enemy then tried to encircle the Gurkhas, Bullock wanted to call down artillery fire but Masters' radio remained silent so Bullock himself went to make contact. He very narrowly missed being killed by two enemy who, in the gloom of the jungle, he had mistaken for Masters and Hariparsad. As they were about to shoot him down, they were killed by Rifleman Hariparsad Gurung who had felt that the company commander needed escorting and, unbeknown to Bullock, had quietly followed up behind and seen what danger the British officer was in.

Another Indonesian attack followed and it was time for the Gurkhas to withdraw. There was considerable confusion and only individual Gurkha marksmanship, steadiness and courage, in many little isolated incidents, prevented a disaster and allowed a clean break to be made.

However, at the critical moment, the group at the check-point were found to be missing. Bullock with two Gurkhas went back for them. Calling softly, a large enemy force was alerted and set on them and it was only superb shooting by Lance Corporal Reshambahadur Thapa that held the enemy back long enough for the search party to retire intact.

Back with the others, Bullock found it was Masters, Hariparsad and the signaller who were missing, but they had been seen moving off after the withdrawal to that point had been completed.

On the move back to the firm base the Gurkhas were harassed by heavy Indonesian mortar fire, but without the FOO fire could not be brought down to neutralize it. CSM Smith, most professionally, had realized that there was something wrong and had worked out a complete fire plan himself and passed it over to the guns on his radio net so, when the Gurkhas did reach the firm base, effective defensive fire was immediately brought to bear. A clean break over the border was thus ensured.

The signaller, covered in blood, had already arrived in Sawawak when Bullock and his men got back. He had been jumped on by two Indonesians whom he had killed, one of them falling on him, covering him with blood. The Gurkha, unharmed, had managed to make his lone escape, through the surrounding enemy, without map or compass, over 10,000 yards of hostile territory.

Masters and Hariparsad, however, had become separated from the rest of the force and were suddenly surrounded by the enemy. Hariparsad was hit twice in his leg. The enemy closed in but Masters, with complete disregard to his own safety, opened fire, wounding two. The Indonesians were temporarily distracted by the fire from some of the other Gurkhas and Masters lifted the wounded Gurkha and carried him to where he thought the remainder of the company were. Unfortunately he missed his way and did not re-establish contact.

All that day, in the intense heat, he carried the wounded man over his shoulder as he made his tortuous way back to the border. He was constantly held back or tripped up by the undergrowth. At one place he found himself up to his thighs in an oozing, filthy swamp. It had been a nightmare journey. In the soft mud he was able to ease his aching back by dragging Hariparsad inch by inch until he felt he was strong enough to carry him over his shoulder once more. By 1930 hours he decided he could go no further. He had, unbelievably, managed to bring the wounded Gurkha through 6,000 yards of thick jungle and swamp.

Next morning, soon after he had moved off again, he realized that he could no longer carry the Gurkha. He explained that he would go for help and left his second water bottle and the remainder of his hard tack before setting off, so at least Hariparsad could assuage his thirst and hunger. By that afternoon, more dead than alive and utterly weary, Masters reached his gun position in the Gurkha camp in Sarawak.

Bullock took immediate action. Tired as they all were, a wounded man's safety was paramount so, straightaway, with 20 men, Masters, Smith and a doctor went to look for Hariparsad. It took until late the next day to find him, all tracks very nearly obliterated by heavy rain. The doctor, seeing the loss of blood and the onset of gangrene, considered that immediate evacuation by helicopter was vital.

The despatch of the helicopter – against all orders into Indonesian territory – the evacuation by winch, in heavy rain and at night, with Hariparsad being lashed onto a stretcher, the superb flying, were all outstanding examples of skill, devotion to duty and dedication, without which Hariparsad would not have recovered to the extent that he could walk without a limp.

Captain Masters was made an honorary life member of the 2nd Gurkha Rifles; as the CO said, 'We will none of us forget what he did.'*

In November 1965, 2/10 GR, on a 'Claret' operation opposite the 1st Division of Sarawak, stormed a strong Indonesian position on a razor-backed ridge killing at least 24 for the loss of three Gurkhas. In this assault Lance Corporal Rambahadur Limbu fought with a bravery that was so consistent and inspired that it earned him the Victoria Cross. However, so tight were the rules governing such cross-border operations that, even though he was sent to London the following year to be decorated by the Queen, the location of the battle was not reported until three years later.

The best way of telling the story of this action is by quoting the citation that appeared in *The London Gazette* of 22 April 1966, even though the place mentioned is not the actual site of the battle:

'On 21 November 1965, in the BAU District of SARAWAK, Lance Corporal Limbu was with his Company when they discovered and attacked a strong enemy force located in the Border Area. The enemy were strongly entrenched in Platoon strength, on top of a sheer hill the only approach to which was along a knife edge allowing only three men to move abreast. Leading his support group in the van of the attack he could see the nearest trench and in it a sentry manning a machine-gun. Determined to gain first blood he inched himself forward until, still ten yards from his enemy, he was seen and the sentry opened fire, immediately wounding a man to his right. Rushing forward he reached the enemy trench in seconds and killed the sentry, thereby gaining for the attacking force a first but firm foothold on the objective. The enemy were now fully alerted and, from their position in depth, concentrated their fire onto the area of the trench held alone by Lance Corporal Rambahadur Limbu.

Appreciating that he could not carry out his task of supporting his platoon from this position he courageously left the comparative safety of his trench and, with a complete disregard for the hail of fire being directed at him, he got together and led his fire group to a better position some yards ahead. He now attempted to indicate his intentions to his platoon commander by shouting and hand signals, but failing to do so in the deafening noise of exploding grenades and continuous automatic fire he again moved out into the open and reported personally, despite the extreme danger of being hit by the fire not only from the enemy but by his own comrades.

*Captain Masters was awarded an immediate MC. Lance Corporal Birbahadur Pun the DCM, Rifleman Ramparsad Pun the MM and later, in connection with other feats of gallantry, Captain Bullock and CSM Smith the MC.

It was at the moment of reporting that he saw both men of his own group seriously wounded. Knowing that their only hope of survival was immediate first aid and that evacuation from their very exposed position so close to the enemy was vital he immediately commenced the first of three supremely gallant attempts to rescue his comrades. Using what little ground cover he could find he crawled forward, and in full view of at least two enemy machine-gun posts who concentrated their fire on him and which, at this stage of the battle, could not be effectively subdued by the rest of his platoon. For three full minutes he continued to move forward but when almost able to touch the nearest casualty he was driven back by the accurate and intense weight of fire covering his line of approach. After a pause he again started to crawl forward but he soon realized that only speed would give him the cover which the ground could not. Rushing forward he hurled himself on the ground beside one of the wounded and calling for support from two LMGs which had now come up to his right in support, he picked up the man and carried him to safety out of the line of fire. Without hesitation he immediately returned to the top of the hill determined to complete his self-imposed task of saving those for whom he felt personally responsible. It was now clear from the increased weight of fire being concentrated on the approaches to and in the vicinity of the remaining casualty the enemy were doing all they could to prevent any further attempts at rescue. However, despite this, Lance Corporal Rambahadur again moved out into the open for his final attempt. In a series of short forward rushes and once being pinned down for some minutes by the intense and accurate automatic fire which could be seen striking the ground all round him he eventually reached the wounded man. Picking him up and unable to seek cover he carried him back as fast as he could through a hail of enemy bullets. It had taken twenty minutes to complete this gallant action and the events leading up to it. For all but a few seconds this young NCO had been moving alone in full view of the enemy and under the continuous aimed fire of their automatic weapons. That he was able to achieve what he did against such overwhelming odds without being hit is miraculous. His outstanding personal bravery, selfless conduct, complete contempt of the enemy and determination to save the lives of the men of his fire group set an incomparable example and inspired all who saw him.

Finally rejoining his section on the left flank of the attack Lance Corporal Rambahadur was able to recover the LMG abandoned by the wounded and with it won his revenge, initially giving support during the later stage of the prolonged assault and finally being responsible for killing four more enemy as they attempted to escape across the border. The hour-long battle which had throughout been fought at point-blank range and with the utmost ferocity by both sides was finally won. At least twenty-four enemy are known to have died at a cost to the attacking force of three killed and two wounded. In scale and in achievement this engagement stands out as one of the first importance and there is no doubt that, but for the inspired conduct and example set by Lance Corporal Rambahadur at the most vital stage of the battle, much less would have been achieved and greater casualties caused.

He displayed heroism, self-sacrifice and a devotion to duty and to his men of the very highest order. His actions on this day reached a zenith of determination and premeditated valour which must count amongst the most notable on record and is deserving of the greatest admiration and the highest praise.'

The regimental history comments that the citation well described the physical victory but it could not do justice to the unique psychological pressure created by operating 4,000 yards inside enemy territory in a garrison complex sited for mutual support and covered by artillery and mortars; pressures that were magnified two-fold at a stroke as soon as casualties were suffered at the very outset of the action. Indeed the evacuation of the casualties made it necessary to stay on the captured position half an hour longer than prudence alone would have dictated.

The award by Her Majesty the Queen of the Victoria Cross to Lance Corporal Rambahadur Limbu was the highlight of the year. This award not only brought well-deserved fame to a very brave soldier and honour to his battalion and regiment; it also crystalized the toil and sacrifice of the Brigade as a whole. It brought into sharp perspective the burden borne so well and so long by the Gurkha soldier in the heat and toil of battle over the previous eighteen years in south-east Asia.

The extent of the involvement of the Brigade of Gurkhas over the eighteen years from 1948 to 1965 can be gauged by the number of casualties suffered:

	British officers	Queen's Gurkha officers	Gurkha other ranks
Killed in action	13	10	189
Wounded in action	10	21	361

Details of the twelve other VCs being won by Gurkhas, this being the thirteenth, are: 1915, France; 1918, Suez Canal; 1943, one in Tripolitania, North Africa, one in Burma; 1944, four in Burma and two in Italy; and 1945, two more in Burma.

A further pointer is shown by the awards won by the Brigade of Gurkhas between 1948 and 1965: 1 VC, 15 DSO, 33 OBE, 113 MBE, 81 MC, 32 DCM, 158 MM, 45 BEM and some Brunei government awards also.

The year 1965 was also the 150th anniversary of the enlistment of Gurkhas under the British Crown. Over the century and a half since then, the reputation of the Gurkha as a fighting man had spread far and wide. The renown won over those years had and has been upheld by generation after generation coming down from the Hills of Nepal to do battle with Britain's enemies. This renown, won on the battlefields of the world, has still been maintained by the modern Gurkha soldier, despite the unfavourable beginning there was to service within the British Army. The British officers of the Brigade realized then, and still do, with pride and humility, the honour they have had in serving and leading men who are among the finest soldiers in the world.

The British Army Gurkhas had known only eighteen months of peace in eighteen years. For the remainder of that time units of the Brigade had been on active service. And, in 1965, the Indonesian enemy were fighting with a tenacity and skill that had not been seen since the Second World War.

The battalion diarist of 2/2 GR had this to say, '. . . notwithstanding, the battles fought over the last twelve months, with all their limitations of manoeuvre caused by the existence of the invisible line of the border between Sarawak and Indonesia and the further limitations imposed by shortages of equipment appropriate to this type of warfare, have proved as difficult and arduous as any of former times. The same qualities of steadfastness and courage that have always been required of riflemen have been displayed on many occasions, together with those of initiative and low cunning – an unfailing requirement of a successful guerrilla. For this is the way the Borneo campaign is being fought. The guerrilla is being beaten on ground favourable to him by guerrilla tactics, the only difference being in the quality of the troops putting those guerrilla precepts into practice . . .'

THE BOGEY FADES AWAY

I remember my first 'Claret' operation with the Gurkha Para in a way that one remembers all one's firsts – the first day in the army, the first time one is shot at, the first time one shoots at and kills someone, the first parachute jump. It would never find its way into any history book as there was nothing sensational about it. It was a small recce, just to see if Indonesian troops had been in a sector south of the Interior Residency of Sabah. It was, you might say, the 'last piece of blue sky in the jigsaw puzzle', as your Intelligence analysts like to have it.

There were ten of us and, once over the border, we were going to split into two groups. We were not allowed more than 3,000 yards' penetration into Kalimantan, which was enough to see if a certain patch of country was being used by the Indonesians or not.

We were airlifted in and dumped on a small sandbank and waved the pilot farewell. The border ran through a feature a mile or so ahead of us at some 4,000 feet above sea level and my plan was to climb it and then select a spur that ran down to the target area. The maps were not very accurate in that area but did give the main features.

When we were ready we set off; at that low level the jungle was dark, damp and clammy. We moved slowly and cautiously, eyes skinned for tell-tale signs. The climb was stiff and we were soon sweating. The higher we climbed the cooler it became and the more shrill the cicadas.

At about 2 o'clock we neared the top of the mountain. It was, by then, appreciably cooler and the vegetation was changing – trees shorter and thinner, more spaced out so there was more light. At the very top the change was dramatic. We were in moss jungle, always a sign of a high rainfall at altitude and the plants, especially the orchids, were alpine. Even the birds were of different species. It was so pleasant that we longed to make the most of the coolness. But as the Gurkhas know, one definition of civilization is to bring the cool of the hill top to the valleys and the water of the valleys to the hill tops. Water – we had to be on our way.

The psychological difference in stepping over a line on the map into enemy territory is like lowering one's voice to a whisper as one enters a church, even on a weekday. I decided which spur to follow and we started our downhill journey, quickly losing that lovely freshness in the air.

We carefully hid ourselves and our tracks that first night, so losing a little of the sense of being an intruder, and continued south early on the morrow. As you can imagine, the limited range of vision in the jungle means that the ears have to do more work than normal and many places remain unsearched. We had branched off the ridge line that we had started on when it bent away east as we needed to continue south. Now we were on a narrower one with steep slopes on either side – not an easy place to get off in a hurry. We came to a bit that was slightly broader and flatter than before. Was it our imagination that some of the lower fronds were thinner than expected?

Whatever it was we all felt an increased alertness, a rise in tension and instinctively we took up all-round fire positions. But there was nothing really to make us behave as we did and after listening intently for several minutes we looked at each other a bit sheepishly and got up.

But there was something that had struck us but which none of us could immediately identify among the small rocky outcrop, the trees, the leaves on the jungle floor, the bushes, the faint smell of rotting vegetation, the patches of sunlight filtering through the upper branches and the ever-present, infinitely varied but all-pervasive green.

There was nothing heroic about the discovery. At first sight all seemed natural but, on moving from one side of the ridge to the other, four otherwise normal saplings, about twenty yards down the ridge from us, suddenly appeared to be the four corners of a square – and nature does not like straight lines.

They easily came out of the ground – they had been cut elsewhere, brought to the comparative flat of that part of the downward ridge then 'planted' so that people could fix a square of plastic to keep them dry as they covered themselves at night, having kept watch to their front, where we had stopped to look – their killing ground.

Even though camouflaged, the weapon-post should have been easy to spot; such sloppy work showed that the troops who had been there were probably not, therefore, the Indonesian Marine Commandos (KKO) nor the Indonesian Para Commandos (RPKAD), but lower-grade men.

And by looking at where the saplings had been cut and the state of the scars we guessed that they had stayed in the area a day or so and left it, maybe about the time we were getting out of our helicopter.

Subsequently other evidence proved us right – the 'little piece of blue sky' on the jigsaw was, in fact, clouded over . . .but the next piece was a closer run thing. There were twenty of us this time, four patrols' worth, and we went across to Kalimantan from Sarawak to see if a path that ran parallel to the border was used by the Indonesians as an easier route from a base they had in the vicinity to points opposite the border where there were military camps that they had been attacking. If that were the case, it could be a good target for the Gurkha battalion across the border from where the Indonesians would launch any attack. The mission was to go for a couple of days in four directions then meet up again to set up a combined ambush. There were about 400 to 500 Indonesians in their base, which was some three miles down the track to the west and we thought that they might hear of us, come careering along the track and we would set off some of the deadly Claymore mines we had brought with us. These mines were concave-shaped, with thin plastic containers, often mounted on tripods, that were full of little bits of metal that spread out on detonation and made mincemeat of anyone in the way.

The patrol I was with was to move east, along the axis of the track, away from the enemy camp. The map survey of that area was dismally poor and the path we found was big enough for us to presume that that was the one we wanted. Looking back on it I suppose there could well have been two or even more tracks, although the map did only show the one.

However, before we all separated, and as bad luck would have it, we bumped into a civilian who was coming from the direction of the enemy camp. It was one of those difficult occasions when there was no easy, best solution. We found we had a common language so we could communicate and eventually we decided that he should continue on his way, which was the way my patrol was to move. He was in a hurry and we let him go; we also decided to curtail our activities and meet up that evening and not the next day as had been the original plan. Before the civilian left us he mentioned the one longhouse in the area where Indonesians sometimes went.

Off we went and my path disappeared into the dried-up bed of a stream. It took some time to find it again and there were no tracks of where the civilian had said he would be going. Come the time to return and, somehow or other, we must have got onto a different path because we never met up with the others and, after a while, found ourselves almost in the vegetable patch of the one longhouse we had been told about.

It was getting latish and movement was channelled up a rise by a blanket of thick, matted fern. The countryside had once been cultivated and we were out of the jungle. I thought to myself what a marvellous killing ground this would make as the thick bracken completely restricted movement yet gave any ambush troops a very good field of fire. At the top of the knoll was a tree and, as I passed it, I turned round and saw that something had been carved at the base, just the height of a man lying in ambush. It read, quite simply, RPKAD, and had the previous day's date. By then we all admitted that we were lost, certainly our position was difficult to pinpoint on the map but equally certainly we were not only nearer the enemy than was the ambush party but also, were we to return, we could well walk into it.

We found somewhere to hide. Luckily we had a radio with us and, making a stab at our position, I sent a message to the others telling them where to meet up with us the next day by, if possible, 0800 hours. We were getting anxious when, by 1000 hours, there was still no sign of the others. Dawn revealed we had chosen the one clump of trees in a wide prairie-like expanse with hundreds of water-buffalo roaming about.

'Why don't you make a monkey call?' asked one of the Gurkhas. 'The others will hear it if they're not very far away.'

Cuckoo noises were better and my mind flashed back eighteen years to 1948 when I'd learnt that there were no cuckoos in Malaya. Even though the biggest cuckoo in Kalimantan was to be me, I'd try it – and twenty minutes later, to our intense relief, it worked. The others had been half a mile away but, thinking that is what I would do, had sat down and waited for the call!

We quickly moved to the nearest bit of jungle and decided that, before we went back to Sarawak, we would have a look at that longhouse. It didn't take long to get to and we advanced towards it tactically, ready for a showdown but found only a few old folk there. We were invited to enter and sit down. This I decided would be all right for a few minutes – the 'hearts and minds' aspect – and we were given bananas and warmed-up ground nuts. One old crone greatly amused the Gurkhas by coming up to me and stroking my face.

Not wanting to outstay our welcome we moved back to our base and, on the way out the next day, passed through an area where 1/2 GR had had a battle some months before. This was the first time, so it turned out, that the site had been revisited by Security Forces, so we had a good look round, making notes on such things as the debris we found and a large, well-maintained helicopter landing pad. After making a quick sketch map we upped and pulled out fast – we were still quite some way from the border.

Late that afternoon we made camp on a ridge in thick jungle, above the scene of the battle and, as we were having our evening meal, the sky reverberated and rattled as the largest troop-carrying helicopter the Indonesians had – a Russian job we knew as the 'Hook' that could carry a score or more of fully-laden troops – and its fighter escort made their way to the landing site. From the change in the noise of the engine – the two steamrollers had stopped their rhumba and were now waltzing sedately – we presumed that troops were being disgorged for a recce and a follow-up; certainly a few minutes later the chopper was once more airborne and the two planes flew away.

We did not have any contact with the Indonesian soldiers and, on being debriefed at Brigade HQ, I was told that that was the first recorded occasion that the Hook helicopter had been within 10,000 yards of the border for quite a long time.

My little group had been ready to do battle but, when the two aircraft flew away and it was obvious that no contact would be made, the Gurkha who was next to me put down his weapon, looked at me impishly and said, 'And there goes your MC!' And, of course, he was quite right.

On 27 February 1966, carrying ten days' rations, 'D' Company, 1/10 GR, under Major C. J. Pike, a small, lithe man, with an eye for spoor, a nose for hunting and a cold, steady nerve, moved over the border into Kalimantan to ascertain whether there were any enemy using a certain river near the border to resupply his forward troops prior to their attacking units in Sarawak. By midday on 1 March three firm bases had been established and for the next three days a detailed reconnaissance of the area was undertaken, no easy task because of swamp, thick fern, long grass and jungle, to say nothing of enemy patrols and normal civilian movement in and around the area. By 4 March firm details of the enemy had been established. Plans were then drawn up.

From first light on 4 March, 11 Platoon watched the river for enemy movement. The rest of the company moved their base and, working their way through a swamp that was wet enough not to show traces, came onto some dry ground 300 yards from the river. The undergrowth was thick fern, often less than head height, and the men tunnelled out a firm base underneath. All this having to be done stealthily took time and it was not until noon on 5 March that all three platoons were in their ambush positions.

An hour later a landing craft-type vessel carrying 35 enemy moved downstream towards 11 Platoon, who engaged it at ten to fifteen yards' range with two machine-guns, Number 94 Energa grenades and all the platoon small arms. The result was devastating. Lance Corporal Jagatbahadur Rai, the machine-gunner, fired a 200-round belt down into the midst of the troops sitting in the boat, reloaded and ran along the bank firing from the hip as he went. The 94 grenadier registered two hits at point-blank range. As the boat passed out of the ambush it leant over on one side. No sound from it was heard – complete silence.

Almost immediately enemy fire was returned from the opposite bank and 11 Platoon was ordered to withdraw. 10 and 12 Platoons stayed where they were. After waiting four nail-biting hours the Gurkhas' patience and Pike's tactics paid off as, at 1705 hours, two boats, one with an outboard engine towing the other, containing nine Indonesians, approached 12 Platoon, who opened fire at twenty yards' range, killing all the enemy and sinking both boats. Again fire was opened on the Gurkhas and 12 Platoon was ordered to withdraw to company headquarters; when no threat materialized they were sent back into their ambush position until 2100 hours, when they were withdrawn.

During the early hours of 6 March continuous enemy movement up and down the river was heard. As it could have meant the enemy gaining the north bank where the Gurkhas were, it was decided to move out immediately. In darkness the company crept through the swamp and out into primary jungle by first light, picked up 11 Platoon at the firm base to the rear and all of them headed fast for the border, which was crossed that afternoon.

Recalling the ambush, Lieutenant Colonel R. W. L. McAlister, OBE, the CO, wrote, 'For sheet impudent daring, cold courage and determination, to extract maximum results from what was planned as a reconnaissance, this operation of Pike's was, in my view, unique. And yet with daring, went immaculate planning and briefing and, in tactical execution, a faultless attention to detail. Pike had the company on balance from start to fiinish. The result, not less than 37 killed, was the highest number of casualties inflicted on the Indonesians in one action in the whole of Confrontation . . .'

One other action Major Pike's company was engaged in saw another thirteen Indonesians killed for the loss of two Gurkhas.*

In June of that year reports began to be heard that a man called Sumbi, a person feared by the local people, was training about one hundred volunteers in jungle warfare, over in Kalimantan, and boasting that, one day, he and his men would cross the border and march to Brunei Bay and thereafter sabotage the Shell oil installation in Seria. The rumours persisted. Then, on 23 July, a report reached Ba Kelalan in the 5th Division of Sarawak, that Sumbi with some 50 men, had moved out of Long Bawang, in Kalimantan, for 'an unknown destination'.

The battalion opposite Sumbi's probable crossing-point was 1/7 GR. It was thought that Sumbi would try and infiltrate between Ba Kelalan and Long Semado, over a lonely, high and cold, jungle-covered ridge. Patrols were sent out to try and locate any movement. In front of these battalion patrols were patrols of the Gurkha Para. Two men of one patrol, Corporal Singbahadur Gurung and Rifleman Dharmalal Rai, were out on 29 July, early in the morning, on a reconnaissance near the border. Dharmalal saw something on the jungle floor glint. He took no notice of it – many things with a speck of dew on them glint in the morning sun, but, on their way back, approaching from the other direction, he spotted it again. Curious, because had it been dew it would have dried out long before, he examined it. It turned out to be a small piece of foil, smelling of coffee. Coffee was not a feature of Gurkha rations; British troops might, for all he knew, have coffee in theirs, but there were no British troops within miles. It therefore had to be Indonesians, but there were no tracks.

The two Gurkhas cast around a while and did discover tracks of two or three men – but the tracks were of British Army jungle boots, making as through from the border northwards into Sarawak, so the two men decided to return to the three others and follow the jungle boots. This they did.

*Major Pike was awarded the DSO and Lance Corporal Jaqatbahadur Rai the MM.

There followed an extraordinarily patient and expert piece of tracking. From midday on 29 July through to the 31st, these five men slowly and inexorably tracked the footprints. For two nights they did not make camp or cook anything, fearing that the noise and the smell might give them away. It is very cold at night in the Borneo uplands.

On the third day their patience was rewarded – they found not only the three pairs of jungle boots but sacking – to tie round the feet so as not to leave any distinguishable marks – for over 45 people. How right they were not to have relaxed their precautions. Having established that their quarry had indeed continued northwards only a short time before, they opened their set and gave a full report to their tactical commander, the CO of 1/7 GR, and to Para Company headquarters.

Initially the report was scarcely believed by 1/7 GR so, to make doubly certain, the Gurkha Para patrol was sent to backtrack the footprints to ensure that they had come from over the border and that this group therefore had to be Sumbi's.

From then on 1/7 GR took over the tracking of Sumbi and his gang and, from the first contact until the final incident when Sumbi was captured on 3 September, which was after the official end of Confrontation, many troops were deployed, including a company of 2/6 GR, three platoons of Police Field Force, a platoon of Border Scouts and five more patrols of Gurkha Para. It was a very complicated and well-planned follow-up; tracks were found, followed up, then lost, then found again – numerous times. The country was extremely rugged and radio communications became difficult to maintain, so control was never easy. Some of the raiders were captured, some surrendered and some died of starvation. By dint of tight planning, clever debriefing and flexible deployment, success was achieved, all but four men being accounted for. The threat to Brunei's oil supplies was no more.

Towards the end of the chase the country was viler than it had been; after two weeks of cliff hanging, river crossing and slow tracking, 24 enemy were eliminated. 1/7 GR could account for 46 eliminations. The officer who eventually captured Sumbi at the very top of a precipitous feature, Major A. M. Jenkins (who would be the first to admit that even he was not originally designed for quite such a tough haul) was awarded the MC. His Gurkha Captain who was with him was aggrieved to learn that he, the QGO, had only been awarded a 'C' grading on a jungle warfare course at the British Army Jungle Warfare School yet Sumbi, who had also been a student there as a lieutenant in the Indonesian Army, had been awarded a 'B' grading!

When, on 7 December, *The Times* published an account of the Sumbi incursion, it was headlined 'Courage of the Gurkhas Foiled Saboteurs' and it continued 'Details of one of the most brilliant actions in the history of Gurkhas have just been released . . .' and went on to describe Rifleman Dharmalal Rai's meticulous attention to detail as he sniffed the tinfoil that smelt of coffee . . .

In October 1965 a communist coup to seize control of the government in Indonesia had been foiled within five hours by General Nasution. Sukarno's powers were then curtailed. By the middle of February 1966, after some political in-fighting, Sukarno tried once again to join hands with Mao Zedong, the doughty chairman of the Chinese Communist Party. The idea was to defy the world by setting up a world body to rival the United Nations Organization, to be known as the Conference of the New Emerging Forces (CONEFO). However, the idea never took on and, by early March, the situation became intolerable for the Javanese and mobs went on the rampage in Jakarta.

Following that, a full-scale purge of the Communist Party of Indonesia (PKI), was launched in an effort to destroy the Party by eliminating its members. The resultant killings have never been accurately established but estimates of the death toll certainly reached at least 30,000.

Then, on 23 May 1966, an Indonesian goodwill mission went to Kuala Lumpur with a message of peace and, after considerable discussion and not a little face-saving, Confrontation officially ended at noon on 11 August 1966.

The Indonesia-Malaysia Agreement of that date contains only three short substantive clauses: public opinion in Sabah and Sarawak to be tested by elections; diplomatic relations to be restored; hostile acts to cease.

Thus Confrontation ended, 'not with a bang but a whimper'. Without British support the outcome would either have been very different or very much more protracted. The bulk of the British Army forces was the Brigade of Gurkhas, who again proved the superlative qualities of the Gurkha soldier when properly trained, properly equipped and properly led, plus always that especial flair that the Gurkha so modestly has in abundance – of pulling the stops out when others have thought they had been pulled out as far as they could be pulled.

After Confrontation was officially over, everyone in Malaysia – Sarawak and Sabah – had to stay in camp, waiting for orders for the peacetime pull-out. We, in the Gurkha Para Company, were not in Malaysia, but in Brunei, so these cease-fire orders did not apply, so we were still operational. The Brunei Government wanted to know if the last four of Sumbi's gang had, in fact, infiltrated into Brunei or had died in the Sarawak jungle. In an area of wild country that could have been anything from 500 to 2,500 square miles, the odds against finding four men were infinitely remote. Nevertheless a patrol was sent to the border of Brunei and Sarawak, a ridge of hilly jungle, to see what it could pick up. One of the soldiers, Rifleman Jamansing Rai, needed evacuating and, pressure of other duties off, I flew in to take his place.

Corporal Chandrabahadur Rai put me as number 4 in his patrol and off we went along the border ridge. The jungle was dark and damp. It had been raining. We travelled slowly, keeping our eyes skinned. And then I saw it – a leaf, one of myriads in all that vast expanse of jungle, caught my eye in that it had an unnatural crease making its outline straight. Nature abhors anything straight; this leaf was not the product of nature. Man must have created it, yet we were the only people in the area. There was just a chance that it was Sumbi's last four men; one of them might even be a 'leaf doodler' – one who picks at leaves and sticks, plays around with them without realizing it, then discards them. I called Chandrabahadur's attention to it and we cast around even more thoroughly.

Our search revealed more suspicious signs, moving away from our area into the area of the Royal Brunei Malay Regiment's area on our flank. A message was sent to them, alerting them as to the possibility of trespassers.

I got a message the next night from the CO, an old friend of mine who had spent all his life till then with Gurkhas. 'Why', I was asked, 'are you frightening my soldiers by pretending to be a ghost?'

Working, as we were, on key (Morse code) prevented me from sending a fitting retort. All I could do was to send a 'Wilco, Out' and leave it at that until I emerged from the jungle and went and saw my friend.

This I did; the Brunei soldiers knew that I was on the flank. The day we found the leaf they had sent a party to get water from a stream in order to cook their evening meal. Approaching a thick bush a voice, speaking in English, ordered them to stop, turn round and go away. This they had done and, on reflection, reported that a ghost had spoken to them, otherwise how could a voice, disembodied and unexpected, be anything else?

Their CO knew better but, still unconvinced that the evidence we had found was correct, presumed that I had tracked the prints of some local Ibans into his company's area and, out of sheer impishness, pretended I was ethereal.

In fact four men did emerge from the jungle, from the direction where we had been patrolling and, almost dead from starvation, went to an Iban longhouse in the valley below and asked for food. As they were eating, the soldiers were fetched and captured them. They indeed were the last of Sumbi's gang and, at their interrogation, one of them did admit that he did have a habit of plucking leaves, folding them and then discarding them.

Without in any way belittling the efforts of the many other dedicated stalwarts involved in Confrontation – and there were many – it does not take much imagination to see how very different it all would have been, whether it was straight fighting or the raising, training and leading the Border Scouts (to say nothing of training their leaders), but for the blood, toil, sweat and, probably, tears of the Brigade of Gurkhas (who were awarded 1 vc, 5 dso, 15 obe, 12 mbe, 36 mc, 3 dcm, 41 mm, 4 bem and 90 Mention-in-Despatches during the campaign). The standards achieved by every unit in the Brigade could hardly have been higher and would have been reflected in a greater total of awards had there not been a fixed quota.*

At the end of Confrontation, in the House of Commons, the Secretary of State for Defence, the Rt Hon. Denis Healey, mp had this to say about it, 'In the history books it will be recorded as one of the most efficient uses of military force in the history of the world.' He also paid tribute to the men of the British and Commonwealth nations who fought in Malaysia:

'. . . the campaign had been a model of inter-Service co-operation; all three Services have worked as one. We should pay tribute to all those, from the highest to the lowest rank, who have served alongside the forces of our Commonwealth partners and who have made so signal a contribution to the settlement that has been achieved. I should like to add a special tribute to the Gurkhas.'

*The ratio of Gurkhas to British troops was about 2:1. Peak strengths of the Security Forces in Borneo were 17,000 Commonwealth troops in-country, with a further 10,000 immediately available. Service casualties were 114 killed, 118 wounded, while civilian casualties were 36 killed, 53 wounded and 4 captured. Minimum enemy casualties were 590 killed, 222 wounded and 771 captured.

6
THE GURKHA

THE GURKHA HOMELAND

Nepal, an impoverished Asian third-world country, carries a mystique that few other countries do. This is because it is where the world-famous Gurkha soldiers come from. The Himalayas form the northern border and, until the early 1950s, it was forbidden territory. Indeed, fewer than 130 Europeans had visited the capital, Kathmandu, between 1796 and when the country did finally start to open up, during which time they were either representatives of British officialdom, or (as in my case) there at the invitation of the Nepalese ruler. Nowadays very many more than that number enter Nepal daily as tourists, showing that the fascination of the unknown and the unusual still exerts a strong attraction. Many Nepalese, in Kathmandu and along the tourist trails, still regard the hordes of 'low-budget, new-world' back-packers with a mixture of suspicion, insatiable curiosity and incredulity, bewildered by their diverse similarity, yet often falling victim to the 'quick-buck' syndrome. For many of these tourists, as well as for such people as aid workers and research scholars, it can be a disturbing experience to be in a land where life off the few roads is hard, and still moves at the same unhurried pace as it always has, that of a man walking. It would be a useful exercise for such visitors to imagine how their own country of origin would have coped if it, too, had jumped from a period before the industrial revolution into the age of 'mod cons' in one generation.

Nepal's Hindu king, the only such monarch in the world, is held to be semi-divine and his country is a Hindu, not a secular, state. Its laws, customs and way of life are slanted towards the centuries-old caste system and all that such a system involves. Buddhism and Islam are both recognized officially and Nepal has never had a religious war throughout its long history, showing a refreshing tolerance in such matters. Hinduism with its inbred fatalism, flourishing in a countryside of infinite variety and untold contrasts – the southern border is about 300 feet above sea level and, in the north, the highest parts are not far off 30,000 feet – has produced a rigidity that has held the country together despite the diversity of its population, in mountainous terrain, and very poor communications. Away from the roads, man is the main beast of burden and the method of agriculture is as it was centuries ago. Nepal has as high a proportion of its population working on the land as anywhere else in the world, remorselessly tying the great majority of its citizens to a life of toil, hardship, privation, drudgery and weariness as subsistence farmers with little reward and little surplus.

With scarcely any flat land, planting areas have been hacked out of the hillsides into ridged terraces. Apart from the gradual and steady impoverishment of the soil, landslides undo the results of incredibly hard endeavour as the hillsides crumble and disappear into the valleys below. As deforestation and soil erosion spread, in ratio to an expanding population, such essentials as water, kindling, and fodder for cattle become harder and harder to find. So ominous are conditions that, in the mid-1970s, a special United Nations committee on such problems said that the middle reaches of Nepal – the 'Gurkha heartland' – would be the world's next desert. The horrific events of famine in Africa, highlighted in the mid-1980s, point to the enormous human tragedy that occurs when the balance of nature is upset beyond the point of no return.

It would be wrong, however, to give the impression that life in Nepal is untenable, despite all the danger signs, but it is a continual struggle for the vast majority of its peasant population, most of whom spend their entire lives fighting the elements and warding off demands for what they regard as excessive costs and rising prices. As long as 'existing' rather than 'living' is its lot, no community can ever enhance itself to the extent that its rulers and friends, to say nothing of the community itself, desire.

Besides many ethnic groups who have their own languages and cultures, not only does Nepal happen to be a 'blue-print' country for international aid but also it has a unique geopolitical spectrum, resulting from being landlocked between India and China. It has never been a vassal of either, and historically, nearly 200 years of independent diplomatic relations with Britain have seen a genuine mellowing and warming of those original prickly and suspicious attitudes, which reflected a small nation's wariness and unease of a powerful, distant, strong and, sometimes, devious government thousands of miles away – a government that held sway in neighbouring India, acquiring territory as though it were going out of fashion. The bonds of time and trust have fused to make the present relationship between Britain and Nepal very close and cordial – as witnessed in the Royal visit to Nepal in 1986 – having withstood periods of change and new political idiom that have caused upheavals in many other parts of the globe. This state of affairs intrigues many, causes resentment to a few and brings benefits to both

London and Kathmandu, besides adding a measure of stability and balance to this corner of Asia. The clue to all this is to be found in the one word 'Gurkha'.

As I have previously stated, the people of Nepal can be divided into Mongolian and Aryan and it is almost entirely Mongolians who become 'Gurkhas' – British Army soldiers. In broad terms these are Thakurs, Gurungs, Magars, Puns and Tamangs from the west who serve in 2 GR and 6 GR, with Limbus, Rais, Sunwars, Tamangs, a few Gurungs and the occasional Sherpa from the east in 7 GR and 10 GR. The three corps units, namely The Queen's Gurkha Engineers, the Queen's Gurkha Signals and the Gurkha Transport Regiment, have equal western and eastern representation. There is minuscule representation of Aryan Nepalese as some Chhetris (associated with the Rajputs of India) are enlisted in all regiments, with one Brahmin priest in each major unit. Apart from these men who come from a comparatively small area of Nepal, no others are enlisted for 'general duties', although enlistment as clerks is open to all and sundry.

To many westerners all Gurkhas look alike and, deflatingly for such people, many westerners look the same to the Gurkhas! One reason for seeing Gurkhas as one and the same must be because their uniform tends to blur distinctions; the other main cause is that those men the British Army enlists conform to a mould that reflects only a small part of the populace.

It is probably the result of a feudal regime (officially terminated in February 1951) and the Hindu caste system that cause the difficulties of getting off the treadmill of endemic poverty and an indifference to the suffering of others – as one's personal miseries are so severe – that engenders the paradoxical situation of many Nepalese being prone to trust foreigners more than other Nepalese, which is surprising when it is remembered for how long Nepal was a closed country. In the case of the good relationships with the British, the aspect of being 'time-hallowed' is one of the elements of the bedrock of mutual trust, being true for the highest echelons of society and for those living in the traditional recruiting areas; also, neither nation interferes in, nor tries to influence the affairs of the other.

The Gurkha who is enlisted has never known an easy life, unless he is one of those very few who have spent more than one tour with his parents in the unit family lines, where he will have enjoyed the same benefits as his parents. Sadly for such lads, although well taught in British Army schools and so probably speaking more than passable English, the inherent chemistry engendered by an upbringing in the hills is missing to such an extent that only the natural leaders among them make good if they are enlisted, although the education they will have received is useful when technicians and specialists are being recruited. These young men are often less acquisitive than are their compatriots in Nepal and many seem duller by comparison. After six months back home, however, they are better able to equate to the typical hill lad who has not 'had it so good', and who is brought up on old soldiers' tales of prowess, the magic of service overseas, and the opportunities available in a stimulating, well-paid job with a pension at the end – the British Army is often all he ever sets his heart on. From his early childhood he will have become used to roughing it, of going hungry, of sharing whatever there is with the rest of his family, of being by himself for long periods of time when looking after some goats, becoming hardy and self-reliant. He will have had to forage for fodder in dangerous places on steep slopes and up trees, often risking his life. The area of search is large, the load collected heavy – all this and much more is the basis of being a good rifleman in the years to come as it has been for generations past. As a member of a rice-growing community a young Gurkha will have learnt early on in life the need for corporate discipline if the full benefit of toil and resources is to be obtained. Strict observance of family customs, religious rites and group traditions, fortified by a respect for parents in particular and seniority in general, added to an active dislike of appearing foolish and a positive repugnance of others' detraction – all form the matrix that has proved so successful in producing some of the world's finest soldiers who have stood the test of time. The combination of British officers, who, too, are embedded in tradition yet are forward-looking, with the Gurkha soldiers can be superb. Nevertheless, mere reliance on past achievements is no panacea for future success. Strengths must be made stronger and weaknesses eliminated, as in every non-profit making organization that wants to 'remain in business'.

It is interesting to try and compare the Gurkha of 1948 and of today to see if the opening up of the country to foreign influence, the development in the political framework of Nepal, the influence of the welfare-state Briton who is now his officer rather than one of the 'old school', the spread of education, the communist-inspired 'cold war' in Asia and the general awareness of the super-power/third-world syndrome have had any appreciable effect on the modern Gurkha. The answer is a qualified affirmative of an undramatic nature. Men are now more aware of the need to approach modern problems with a more flexible mind, more aware that some of the inviolable social values (such as arranged marriages) may have to be questioned and that, with the spread of education and the greater mobility in the country, the old pattern of ethnic solidarity is being disturbed to an extent that could not have been imagined in 1948. As examples of this, the standard of the language used by Radio Nepal would have baffled practically everyone twenty years ago, while new educational standards to be enforced have resulted in village communities being joined by teachers from other areas of the country and of different ethnic groups, thus loosening the age-old tempo, mores and ideas of rural life. It is not being hinted that all this is 'good' or 'bad', 'better' or 'worse', only different, with, as yet, unknown long-term results. Fundamentally, the basic conditions in the hills have not changed. Maybe, taking a 'generation' of solidery to be fifteen years (a rifleman's pensionable service), the 38 years of British Army Gurkha life is too short a period to change the basic strengths of the Gurkha – stamina, acceptance of hard conditions, an ability to improvise, resilience to adversity, combined with an adherence to discipline that allows the maintenance of high morale, which I personally define as 'the ability and willingness to give of one's best when the audience is of the smallest', in other words 'to go those last few yards' either when the soldier finds himself tired, cold, hungry, outnumbered, frightened, lonely, perhaps wounded, and far from base, or when in the midst of battle.

The British Army Gurkhas' ability to accept change, to react to the unexpected, to maintain standards is still a constant that delights the military purist; for instance, the five-man patrols of the Gurkha Independent Parachute Company would be at the height of their operational efficiency on dangerous missions over the Borneo/Indonesian border and would return to their base camp in Brunei to relax and retrain before the next operation with none of the drunken traumas so often associated with off-duty soldiery. This vividly demonstrates the quality of being able to adhere to the highest standards on both sides of the soldier's coin – operational and peacetime excellence. But, as ever, it needs leadership of the highest quality to ensure that standards are maintained and improved, and that goes for far more than the Brigade of Gurkhas!

Gurkhas are not, however, supermen, and their critics would point out various aspects of the Gurkhas that are displeasing: a slowness in responding to technical requirements, so necessitating a much longer training period than their British counterparts, poor English language standards in an army that has no time for 'foreign' languages and a lack of imagination and initiative, to the extent that time-cherished routine is more to a platoon commander's liking than fresh thought. There is truth in all of this and the cause, basically, lies in the man's cultural background. The opportunities of improving his basic lifestyle are so insecure that, unless something is seen to be of real importance, it is not considered worthwhile risking that which has been already achieved by deviating from known and approved paths. The charge of being slow in the uptake is also real to the extent that being incorporated in such a complex and demanding organization as the army is so different from an uncomplicated pastoral life that it takes time to get used to. When orders are to be obeyed to the letter and when they are to be interpreted is a problem not confined to Gurkhas. Thought process is different, as is seen from the structure of Nepali and its pronunciation placing the tongue and the lips in ways unfamiliar to those of us who speak English as a first language. Many a British officer has said 'talk' instead of 'tomorrow', 'wise' and not 'road' and 'put one's kit in order' and not 'stretch one's legs'. The time taken to digest an unreal situation and determine which alternative is meant is one cause of a Gurkha's 'slowness'.

A point missed by many people is that Gurkhas do not come from all over Nepal and that serving British Gurkhas only account for some 8,000 men in a population of about fifteen million. In Nepal only those 'martial classes' within the recruiting areas become passionately concerned over recruitment, with the vast majority of Nepalese either not knowing or not caring about this facet of the British connection. It is not an 'issue' – until foreign, hostile propaganda uses it to try to embarrass the governments of Nepal and the United Kingdom, as was the case in 1982 during the Falklands crisis.

To the 'cultivator on the hillside' service in the British Army is still the greatest attraction that there is. It is seen as the one method for advancement of self and family, a repayment of debts, of acquiring enough money to educate the children and to build a house in an area where there will be electricity and running water. Failure to join dashes a man's hopes of 'making good' as, apart from joining the Indian Army where basic pay rates pertain – conditions and terms of service are so different that the Indian Army will not enlist the son of a British Army soldier – only 'education' can offer a step on the ladder to improvement. This can take the form of, say, a degree in commerce, teaching or engineering, all fine as far as they go, but they do not go very far and are comparatively expensive. No, it is the British Army that draws potential recruits to it, without let or hindrance from officialdom, showing that the long-standing friendship between Nepal and Britain exerts its time-honoured influence more than any other – that relationship is unique.

RECRUITMENT

The whole process of recruiting is most carefully controlled and the main problem is not whether enough suitable material can be found, but that there is always too much to have to choose from. However good the recruits are and however high the standard is, the ratio of promotion remains constant. This can result in some soldiers being recruited who are potential commanders but who, through the law of averages, can never earn promotion, although the man himself may well realize that, were he to be promoted, he would probably be a good commander. But that is the luck of the draw and, although Gurkhas will not have heard the words 'many are called but few are chosen', they all know the sentiment.

Policy for recruitment initially stems from the Ministry of Defence in London and is processed by the Major General, Brigade of Gurkhas and his staff, who moved from Malaysia to Hong Kong in 1969, and then 'fine tuned' – making up for wastages of men going on pension and discharge – by the record office, which moved to Hong Kong from Singapore in 1970. The exact figure for each recruiting season is worked out and promulgated to the British Army organization in Nepal, whose other responsibilities are, basically, movement, the paying of pensions and certain welfare aspects. The Brigadier, in his camp at Dharan in the east of the country, has two deputy recruiting officers, the one in the east co-located with the headquarters in Dharan and the one in the west in a smaller camp in Pokhara, about 125 miles west of Kathmandu. These deputies, known as DROs, have a staff comprising four or five retired QGOs, known as Area Retired Officers (ARO), and up to 40 recruiters, locally known as 'galla walas', who are ex-service Warrant Officers and NCOs. AROs live in the camps, the recruiters live at home. The pattern of work varies only slightly between the east and the west; in both cases the recruiters have to report in to the camp for early and detailed briefing, as the 'time and space' problem is one that defies normal conventions.

The traditional recruiting areas, for much of the past 175 years, certainly until the late 1950s, were very much in the hands of the recruiters as no British officer was allowed into Nepal. Very strong family and clan relationships determined that only certain areas were tapped, with a nice balance being kept between sufficient men to answer the call to arms and ensuring that farming and the home did not suffer. The requirement was evenly spread along the middle of Nepal, leaving the areas adjacent to Kathmandu for the Nepalese Army, a facet that no longer pertains so rigidly as it did. During the Second World War a total of 114,971 men were recruited, an average of over 19,000 a year, with the great majority of them coming from Nepal rather than from the various Gurkha colonies in India, which provided most of the clerks and some of the specialists. The British Army requirement, since 1948, has been far more modest – once numbers had been made up by 1949 – never exceeding 2,100 in one year for a 15,204 ceiling. It might be thought that the requirements of the modern Indian Army, with maybe eight times the Gurkha strength (with, admittedly, many coming from India itself) would clash with British interests, but this does not seem to be the case. Unlike the British Army, which has its recruiting and pension-paying organizations on Nepalese soil, India only has arrangements for the latter. Being contiguous with Nepal, and having large pockets of Indian-domiciled Gurkhas, all recruiting for the Indian Army is done on Indian soil. Indian Army recruiters do go into Nepal, but nowhere on the scale that numbers of Gurkhas in the Indian Army would suggest and the impartiality of selection found in the British system is lacking. Many sons or brothers are taken down to India by a man returning from leave or by a pensioner; the sons of British Army Gurkhas are not recruited by the Indian Army but the British Army has no corresponding constraints. It is the raw material that matters.

As the popularity of the British Army spread in the 1950s and 1960s, so increased the amount of men wanting to join, until it became a great problem to know how properly to limit numbers of aspirants trying their luck. Such were the pressures on the recruiters, including some by powerful and unscrupulous people, that a crisis point was reached, resulting in the recruiter system being suspended and lads going to the two depots 'under their own steam'. Such was the confusion of thousands of young men landing up near the camps that the extra numbers needing to be fed and accommodated could not be managed and the local authorities asked that the system be discontinued. By then, though, it was hard to hit on a solution that could cope with the limited numbers required – in part due to fewer men being enlisted – and the hopes of those from villages and communities outside the traditional recruiting areas who had seen others from the same origins try their luck and succeed. A mixture of the 'own steam' and recruiter-inducted systems led, in the east, to a death, and, in the west, to some ugly scenes, to say nothing of increased pressure on the recruiting staffs. In 1978 the system was changed again, bringing a measure of stability that had neither been seen before nor ever imagined.

In brief, the number of recruiters was almost doubled, spreading over a much larger area than before. I, as the western DRO, had two-fifths of the country as my bailiwick, though not all that area is concerned with recruiting. They were selected by a filter board and I would then arrange for a Brahmin priest to make them swear a solemn oath that, if broken, had an efficacy for seven generations – not that they necessarily needed such unusual treatment, but it made a very good answer to any formidable personality demanding that a favoured son be processed when otherwise this would not have been the case with a below-standard lad. After briefing on what was required, physically and administratively, they would be sent away with the timetable for the next stage of the selection process, namely 'hill selection'. It has to be stressed that it is not a question of picking up a telephone, as none exists, nor of sending letters, as the system is slow beyond belief even when mail does reach its destination. As the area that the recruiter has to cover is vast, to say nothing of the farming activities that occupy him during the six months of recruitment, it can be readily understood that firm dates have to be given from the very start. Some of the hopefuls travel a couple of days to see the recruiter at his home, often arriving without any means of support and with only the clothes they are dressed in. Others are seen during a tour programme that is already known about, as the recruiter will have made an earlier round of his parish to give that news. In all it is reckoned that each recruiter has to cull from around the 2,000 mark to about 60 and the hard-pressed ex-warrant officer and NCO will say that this job, with no *Manual of Military Law* or *Queen's Regulations* to back him up, is by far the hardest he has ever had to perform for British money.

Hill selection had to cull the recruiters' 60 plus total of lads down to ten – an awesome task. Basic tests were given, both physical and mental, and a record made so that the chances of a chosen lad being switched before reaching camp were nullified. All this meant that about 400 young men were brought in for final selection, at a ratio of something slightly over two to one.

I would personally welcome all the hopefuls for making the effort to serve the British, almost as soon as they had settled in. It was stressed that, apart from medical failures – details of which would be passed on to the individuals concerned – the words 'pass' and 'fail' were forbidden. For the lad concerned, to have reached that stage was, in itself, no mean feat; all that remained was for an order of merit to be produced and, to qualify for acceptance, it was up to each individual to prove that he was better than the next man. A warning against cheating was given and only one or two of the more brazen, who could very well have shown other unwelcome characteristics as recruiting proceeded, were ejected for this. Second chances at all the tests would also be given which was a great help for both recruiters and recruited in the long run.

This period of about two weeks was one of very hard work and great tension as a formidable programme had to be adhered to. When, for instance, the extra medical officers, school masters or physical training experts were frustrated from arriving on time because of a delayed flight or a landslide blocking the road, the 'shuffling and dealing again' became a highly skilled art. It was equally indefensible not to give each aspirant as much chance of showing himself in as good a light as possible as it was unfair to the British Army not to get the very best material possible, with due regard to the enormous effort involved.

From a personal point of view I found that the most demanding activity of all was the interviews with the potential recruits. I well remember how, at the very first interview I undertook – and there were 660 young men to be processed that time – I felt overwhelmed at the task – at 80 interviews a day, weekends included, it was a formidable proposition, lasting for more than eight days. At ten minutes each, without any pauses for such things as meals or a break, that meant more than thirteen hours a day and, of course, having to draw out some of the more diffident men meant that, in fact, interviews could be longer. To repeat myself 600 times (allowing for 60 medical failures) over a nine-day period and remain sane was a mental task of great magnitude, yet without talking to each man myself meant that the overall basic standard could not be properly adjudged, with those rejected men who had not had an interview with me feeling that they had not had a fair chance of enlistment. I had to decide which questions over a ten-minute period would give a representative picture of the man and allow him to show his true mettle, so that I could make the all-important decisions of who to accept and who to reject.

It was a cold day and a small, electric fire was in my office. A young Gurung came in, full of confidence, but shivering. He looked around then came up to me and said, 'Cousin, this is a big room for one man!' I realized that to 'pull rank' would be counter-productive as the young man was being entirely natural and, with such a friendly remark, to have snubbed him would have merely meant that he would have retired into his shell, and would be difficult to draw out again. 'You're cold,' I said. 'Warm your hands by this fire for a moment while I sort out my paper-work.' He went over to the fire, held out his hands and grinned. On the spur of the moment I asked him an old Nepali riddle: 'Which is the superior, fire or water?' Another impish grin, 'Right now, it is fire, but I've known times when it was water!'

And then the idea struck me – I suppose the eggheads would call it lateral thinking but I started to ask a number of similar questions that had no fixed answer (rather shamefacedly, even after all these years, do I make them public!). The idea crystalized after the next questions, 'Which do you value more, the eyes or the mouth?' '. . . the eyes or the nose?' Western readers may well be excused if they think that I had been in the east too long, but ask them I did and it was the answers that fascinated me. To the first question it was 'the eyes' because one could still eat and watch out for any enemy. The response to the second question delighted me, 'The ears, because one can always breath through one's mouth if one has a cold, but one can't wear spectacles if there are no ears to fasten them on to.'

I realized, with a thrill, that the lad was thinking out his answers, was reacting constructively to an unexpected situation and was using his brain. I knew I was on the right track and had to think out less ludicrous questions. Over the next few hours I improved and perfected a set of questions about farming, making baskets, schooling, social pressures, Dame Fortune, religion and all, mostly, in rhyming couplets. This method proved most effective as it allowed me an insight as to a candidate's mental process, his personality and his potential; it kept the man at ease because he was intrigued, interested and willing to show off his knowledge. Relations never became strained and, as I learnt much later, acted as a bond between us, whether the potential recruit was successful or not – and it had the additional merit of keeping me alert all day! But one of the great advantages was that, as there was no stock answer, there could be no rehearsal beforehand nor could there be any passing on of what to say, although that was unlikely.

I learnt later that my interview was considered as the easiest part of the potential recruit's ordeal as I allowed even the most bewildered to give a 'proper' answer and that, once out of my office, the man nearly always completely forgot just exactly what had been asked. And, instead of becoming drowned in boredom, I learnt a lot myself. My time as DRO coincided with a small expansion of the Brigade of Gurkhas and I enlisted half of the serving western content of the Brigade in the five and a half years I was in the post. The final results from the Training Depot, showing a remarkably high standard, vindicated my adopting such a system. Other tests included a stiff medical examination and stamina, physical, scholastic and mental agility tests. Many of those being processed would not have spoken to a European before, while some might never have seen one.

One difficulty that the young Gurkha aspirant has is the disbelief that a British officer can know more about Nepalese humanity, certainly in a Gurkha context, than the potential recruit knows – a man who has not been brought up under hard conditions is more likely to crack when, on active service, he finds himself cold, tired, wet, hungry, afraid, far from base and possibly outnumbered by the enemy. Will he give of his best although his audience is of the smallest? Will he go those last few yards? By the time the officer concerned with the final selection of recruiting is considered suitable for this task, he will most likely have experienced all these feelings himself and may even have seen men crack under strain, so he will know what to look for, although exact or even adequate description of what to look for is very difficult.

A fair question is what makes it possible for a British officer to judge all these characteristics in a Gurkha? As a young officer joining his unit, he will set out to learn as much as he can about all aspects of his men in the knowledge that he is ignorant. Because of an initial language difficulty he realizes the limitations of his knowledge – whereas an officer in a British unit takes his knowledge of his men far more for granted and so does not realize the limitations of his ignorance. 'The spectator sees more of the game than does the referee' is an apt analogy. Many years of service with Gurkhas gives the British officer as good a background as any, helped by visiting Nepal, and experience playing a very great part. Of course mistakes are made during initial assessment and, even when, in the great majority of cases mistakes are not made, men change as they develop. However, it must not be forgotten that the Deputy Recruiting Officers are not asked to spot future Gurkha officers. Their task is to see if a potential recruit is of the required calibre who will not, if enlisted, sully the fair name of Nepal or the reputation of the Brigade of Gurkhas, and assess his potential among his peers.

The final order of merit might take up to twelve hours to finalize; there were always those who were obvious selections, just as there were also those who were clearly weaker than the others. The difficulty was always found in those places last to be filled and among whom those selected would, in most cases, never rise to lance corporal. Which factors had been gleaned from the tests and the interviews that pointed to a man accepting a humbler but important job when those enlisted after him were to be his commanders? Here I found that the hungry, under-privileged lad from an unhappy home, would be the best choice, one who would do fifteen years' service as a private soldier gladly, welcome the benefits during service and the pension it brought at the end, believing that anything must be better than to return to the conditions left behind at home. Filling these last few vacancies always took much more time than for the others.

Apart from rejection on medical grounds, no reason was ever given to an unsuccessful man. Objectively, it is easy to tell a person that he is under weight or that he is too short for enlistment but, subjectively, it is very hard to explain that there is something about a man that irks, that there is a flaw in his character or a streak of dross in his temperament – and even harder for the man to accept that such a judgement is accurate or can in any way be substantiated. None the less, once the traumas of the final announcement were over, those rejected left the camp in a philosophical frame of mind, having drawn their allowance to take them home. A few men wept, others put a brave face on it all, others were quietly resigned, but all knew that the system, lengthy and unwieldy, was essentially as fair as it could possibly be and that the staff, both Gurkha and British, had shown that all efforts had been appreciated. Only the wilfully perverse few, with an in-built belief of a semi-divine right of selective presentation, would allege to the contrary.

The new recruits are put into uniform very soon after the final announcement has been made and given a short-back-and-sides haircut, so making them unrecognizable to all but their closest friends. They are given sufficient training for a formal parade to be held at which they take an oath of allegiance to Her Majesty Queen Elizabeth II. Meanwhile documentation is undertaken – clothing, financial, medical, personal and legal – and, some two weeks after that has started and allowing enough time for immunization to accord with international requirements, men are moved to Kathmandu, by road from the west and by air from the east. The adventure begins! Many of them will not have seen their capital city before and will be overwhelmed by its size. They will be overwhelmed even more by the size of the aeroplane that flies them to Hong Kong, but nothing will quite rival the cultural shock that greets them as they emerge at about 6 o'clock in the morning at Kai Tak airport. Nothing could prepare them for this; life would never be quite the same again.

A few days for mental and physical acclimatization are needed before training of the recruits, in the New Territories, begins in earnest. The syllabus is based on what the British recruit will undergo, with added requirements for the cultural difference, the lower standard of education, together with the essential factor of English having to be learnt – and learnt fast. Other subjects taught include drill, skill at arms and range work, field firing, fieldcraft, minor tactics, physical training, swimming, first aid, basic nuclear, biological and chemical warfare with, later on, platoon weapons, internal security work and a basic radio user proficiency, to say nothing of such indispensable matters as discipline and knowledge about the Brigade of Gurkhas and its regiments, which comes from lectures given outside parade hours.

Allocation to regiments is no longer made by the DROs but by the Commandant of the Training Depot. Based on results achieved during training, aptitudes shown and the requirement for a balanced representation in all units, a man is posted to a regiment, 'cap badged' as the jargon has it. It is only then that training for the three corps units can begin. Technologically, Gurkhas have produced a high enough average standard to satisfy requirements, but it does take time, careful planning and much hard work. Only a few, however, easily take to the concept of a concept. It is fair to say that the more 'technical' a Gurkha becomes, the further he moves from the traditional 'Hill Gurkha' mould.

The Gurkha has found himself, for the first time in his life, in a position where his activities, his training, his welfare, his comfort, his problems, his very livelihood are the concern of a dedicated band of highly motivated, talented individuals whose cause is service, not self-interest, and whose bedrock of faith is trust. He finds himself in a traditional but forward-looking society with a stricter code of conduct than he has ever experienced before, where patrimony, partiality and the familiarity that breeds contempt or provides for subtle pressures to be exerted on an individual are all absent. There still exists a disillusioned, very small, but sadly vociferous minority who like to believe the contrary, have a self-inspired, semi-divine right of selective reporting to suit their personal failures. When a Gurkha does fail, it will be because of unkind fate – never because of himself. A good Gurkha is superb – the opposite is also true.

His British officers recognize that all men in the British Army are rational, aware individuals, with any amount of potential, and they are determined to develop this potential as much as circumstances permit. And the man responds. He is now someone in his own right and his opportunities for advancement depend on himself, on his own showing, his own ability, his own performance and not on the whim of another; this is heady wine.

REGIMENTAL LIFE

Regimental life in a Gurkha unit is a totally absorbing round-the-clock way of life in an extended yet tightly knit family. Taking the rough with the smooth becomes a habit. Routine plays the greatest part of a man's life, with training and ceremony ever alternating for immediate concentration. Certainly, in the infantry, training can at best only be the dress rehearsal; if it all goes wrong on the day few people get a second chance. Active service is not the normal lot of the regular soldier and, while the Brigade of Gurkhas has indeed had more than its fair share of operations, contact with the enemy is a rare occurrence. But whatever other ingredients go to make up regimental life, without discipline, the regiment is no better than a rabble.

Discipline is something that many folk have a tendency to shy away from, smacking as it can of 'bull' and bullying. Discipline should be looked upon as 'training or conditions imposed for the improvement of physical powers and self-control'.

And how does the Gurkha see his British Officer? Certainly, as a type, the British officer is regarded as a quick-reacting, fair-minded, dedicated, impartial professional whose breadth of vision lets him rise above all matters except 'professional integrity'. He cannot judge a man on anything but merit, efficiency, guts, behaviour, endeavour, temperament and results. It cannot matter to him who, of the traditional martial classes, comes to serve, provided that he is of the correct stock, from the correct mould and has potential. Nor does it matter who gets promotion so long as it is the best man who gets it. Add to all that the knowledge embedded, almost, in tradition if not in folklore, that the British officer is above everything except Service and therefore can be implicitly trusted in all matters, from correcting examination papers to making the correct tactical plans for going into battle. Flattery and backbiting play no part in his life, while petty-mindedness does not colour his judgements. His compassion and sincerity are marvelled at, while his attention to detail and meticulous planning are of such a high standard that the Gurkha sees it as little short of magic.

In a regimental context, British to Gurkha and Gurkha to British, sentiment and myth cloud, albeit only a little, the unromantic truth that both are, in fact, fallible but both, also, are normally utterly sincere and work on reciprocal trust. Gurkhas are intensely human people with strengths and weaknesses like everyone else. As the Gurkha's strengths are the ones the British Army needs and his weaknesses not so intrusive as to be an encumbrance or a liability, it may well be that the extraordinarily successful results of the Gurkha presence in the British Army stem from his strengths and weaknesses being nicely balanced with the British soldier's weaknesses and strengths – the Gurkha soldier and his British counterpart complement one another to an amazing degree.

One facet of discipline is self-discipline, without which morale will falter. It is during maximum stress that all the training and discipline absorbed over the years until they are second nature pay great dividends. This is where the Gurkha stands supreme but he does need leadership of a high order and, above all, he needs to feel that those set in authority over him have done and are doing all they can at their level. The rest is Fate.

In such a corporately minded, closely bonded, and traditionally knit group as a regiment, if even one of its members disgraces its name, all feel the shame. Thus it is that the strength of the Brigade of Gurkhas – and strong it is – lies in the warp and weft of its fashioning, the steady and unspectacular application of the dull, uninspiring but important tasks to be done properly, without which the foundations for successful action in an emergency would not be strong enough to bear the burden of its consequences. That the Gurkha has stood the test of time is self-evident; that he will continue thus is a tenet of British faith. So when it comes to a situation where the strength of the Brigade has to be drastically cut, with men being sent on redundancy, it can be seen that the problem has far wider implications than would appear to anyone who has not the detailed background knowledge of what, in fact, Gurkha service in the British Army means to the individual Gurkha. It may not come as a surprise that there has always been a small handful of British Army brass and civil servants who would find it 'tidier' not to have Gurkhas in the British Army. The hard-faced planner of policy has to ask the question 'What are we in business for?' Despite the very powerful friends the Brigade is blessed with, stark realities have to be faced and difficult policies have to be adhered to. It is the job of the regimental officer to try and make the traumatic change to a Gurkha's life as easy and painless as possible – and it is never easy or painless.

On 7 December 1966 it was announced in the House of Commons that, with the ending of Confrontation, the strength of the Brigade of Gurkhas would be reduced from 15,204 to 10,000 by the end of 1969. There was to be a gradual reduction in the strength of all units, with the amalgamation of 10 GR in 1968 and 6 GR in 1969. The three Corps units would each lose one of their three squadrons. 17 Gurkha Infantry Division was to disband as were all Gurkha Infantry Brigades, except for the one in Hong Kong – 48.

Compensation terms were agreed for all those who were retired or discharged prematurely and were based on a Gurkha soldier's career structure. Once a Gurkha has passed out of the Training Depot he can expect, under normal circumstances, to serve until he qualifies for a pension although he is only signed on for 4 years in the first instance, then again at the 7, 10, 12 and 15 year points and thereafter a year at a time until he reaches 24 years' service as a regimental sergeant major. The minimum time to qualify for a service pension is 15 years. If a man has saved wisely during his service, that money, terminal grant and the pension all give him a good chance of not falling back below the poverty line on his return to the Hills. Joining the army at 18 years of age, he will only be 33 years old when he returns home, with, probably, more than half his life ahead of him. The longest serving Gurkhas are the officers, when retirement after 32 years' service is the lot of the most senior.

The rank system is virtually the same as for the rest of the British Army, but with one unusual and significant difference, which is residual from the old Indian Army days when native officers, holding the viceroy's commission as opposed to the sovereign's, filled the ranks more normally filled by subaltern officers in the British Army. This system stemmed from the fundamental tenet that there had to be a conduit between the higher echeloned British officers and the rank and file, and who better to fill this need than tried and trusty men from those very ranks? Continuity in the unit was also ensured and a paucity of young British officers over the years lent weight to the efficacy of this system – still used in the Indian Army and also in the Royal Nepal Army.

When Gurkhas became part of the British Army this category of officer was retained, becoming known as King's Gurkha Officer, or

KGO for short. The three ranks concerned were Lieutenant (KGO), which is the rank of the platoon commander, Captain (KGO), the company second-in-command, and the one Major (KGO) in each major unit, the CO's right-hand man and a person of great influence. These ranks are now called Queen's Gurkha Officers and are known colloquially as Gurkha Lieutenant, Gurkha Captain and Gurkha Major. They are addressed by their rank with the word 'saheb'. In seniority these officers come between a Warrant Officer Class I and a 2nd Lieutenant.

A few particularly well-qualified Gurkhas are commissioned in the same way as are their British counterparts. Some of these Gurkhas undergo the full officer training course at Sandhurst, while others receive their commission from the ranks. Depending on the type of commission he qualifies for, again like his British counterparts, a Gurkha can either serve until he is 55 years old or on a shorter engagement. An officer from Sandhurst may qualify for advanced staff training and command of a major unit as a lieutenant colonel, which indeed has happened. In theory and practice there are no constraints on how high a Gurkha may rise, except those of selective competition and recommendation.

Redundancies for those 'fully' commissioned are always in line with any overall British Army policy that affects everybody and is planned army-wide. For all other Gurkhas in the Brigade different rules and guidelines pertain.

The compensation terms were the best that could have been negotiated at the time. It was most unfortunate and entirely unforeseen that the oil crisis and inflation would hit everybody soon afterwards, thus making the amounts seem, in retrospect, a pittance.

Everybody selected for redundancy was given six months' notice and all received resettlement training in Nepal. The difficult and heartbreaking task of selecting men for retirement (those who had already qualified for a pension) and discharge (those whose service had not yet so qualified them) started as soon as the terms were announced. No one underestimated the sadness of losing stalwart soldiers and well-loved Gurkha friends nor of the disappearance of fine fighting units.

Plans for redundancy were detailed, time-consuming and complicated. Nevertheless one fundamental point made by the Major General Brigade of Gurkhas was that each unit, at whatever stage it was in shedding men, had to be ready and balanced for any operational emergency at any time. This was a very wise decision as it turned out. The 10,000 target reduction had barely started when news came that there would be a second phase of the rundown to 6,000. This meant that 7 GR had to plan to amalgamate in 1970 and 2 GR in 1971. The Gurkha

Independent Parachute Company was disbanded in 1971. In the event the target strength of the Brigade rested at around 6,600 and 2 GR remained as two battalions. Even so, as redundancy was 'across the board', the equivalent of a platoon of men left units every six weeks for some years. By the end of 1971, when rundown had finished, units had lost over 70 per cent of those who were serving when the process started.

It is not part of this story to go into details of the strenuous and, at times, bitter in-fighting behind the scenes that went on for some time to prevent the whole Brigade being disbanded. The eventual announcement did not come as a shock as there had been so much speculation beforehand, and it was a relief to have hard and fast details at long last. On top of all that, the 'East of Suez' policy meant that all units had to plan to leave Singapore and Malaysia, where the Brigade of Gurkhas headquarters and record office were. The Brigade concentrated in Hong Kong, with one battalion in Brunei and one in the United Kingdom.

It speaks volumes for all those at 'soldier level' that the rundown was accomplished so comparatively smoothly. It must also be remembered that the events that unfolded in Hong Kong as soon as the soldiers left Borneo had to be countered by units that were in the throes of planning and implementing the rundown.

7

THE ALL-WEATHER WARRIORS: HONG KONG, CYPRUS AND THE SOUTH ATLANTIC, 1967–1982

HONG KONG – THE CULTURAL REVOLUTION

Almost as soon as Confrontation ended in a whimper, it was followed by another confrontation that started with a bang. This was in Hong Kong, Britain's toe-hold in southern China. The Great Proletarian Cultural Revolution in the People's Republic of China, to give it its full name, of 1965–8, which caused so much turbulence and misery in that vast country when gangs of youths calling themselves 'Red Guards' and who were fortified by the famous 'Little Red Book' of Chairman Mao's thoughts, spilled over into British territory. British Hong Kong, with a teeming populace, is comprised of Hong Kong island and the mainland of Kowloon, as well as many islands, some barren and others with many inhabitants, along with the New Territories that were leased, in 1898 for 99 years. There are a number of new towns, some large, with dense high-rise buildings, light industries and a young, volatile population. For the previous eleven years there had been two, if not three, Gurkha battalions near the border; the British battalion had its barracks at Stanley, on the southern shore of Hong Kong island.

Over the years the British have changed the face of Hong Kong. In 1841 it was a barren, almost waterless island. The Chinese had never been able to do anything with the place and laughed up their sleeves at the willingness and stupidity of the 'Red-Haired Devils' – as they termed all Europeans – in taking the island and the worse of the bargain known as the Treaty of Nanking. Modern Hong Kong is something that, even in their wildest dreams (or nightmares) no one of those days could ever have started to conceive.

The land boundary between China and Hong Kong, marked by the narrow Sham Chun river, is a seventeen-mile strip of land and freedom of movement for farmers living on the Chinese side of the border to cross over and farm, even owning land, on the British side is guaranteed by the treaty. The frontier is crossed in four places: by the railway line from Kowloon to Canton at Lo Wu, the only international crossing-point; a Bailey Bridge a little farther east at Man Kam To, across which farmers from China daily bring produce for sale in Hong Kong and to work their fields on the British side; Ta Ku Ling, where there is a foot-bridge for farmers; and Sha Tau Kok, on the eastern end, a fishing village where the border runs down the main street. Royal Hong Kong Police posts are located close to the frontier at all the important points and the police were solely responsible for protection and security of the border zone, with the military situated unprovocatively some way back. Until April 1967 the police had seemed to cope very well with any situation that arose; regular and militia troops of the People's Liberation Army were openly visible in positions right down to their side of the river, so the initiative was clearly theirs. Some of the farmers who crossed over each day were, in fact, militia in plain clothes.

There had been grumbling discontent for some time in the colony (which was the correct name to give it then) and it was not difficult for the rabble-rousers to find some local industrial dispute to become a rallying-point for major industrial action and disruption. Of all incongruous things, it was where plastic flowers were being made that was chosen as the powder keg – and Labour Day, 1 May 1967, was the obvious occasion to launch a campaign of violence and hate against Authority. The elements were not kind to the forces of law and order – it can get extremely hot in Hong Kong around that time of year and the concrete jungle heats up fit to make anyone wilt. 1967 was an excep-tionally bad year for water, and so strictly did its use have to be con-trolled that taps were allowed on for only four hours every fourth day.

May and June were months of labour and industrial unrest in Kowloon and Hong Kong with rioting, a 'poster campaign' and work stoppages going on. From the way the communists behaved it seemed that they were trying to split the Security Forces between the metro-politan area – Hong Kong, Kowloon and some of the large industrial towns, which are all in the south of the territory – and the frontier. There were ugly scenes, first in the one sphere then in the other, with the intention of making the police and the troops commit some rash act that could 'justify' massive retaliation by the Chinese Army that, to use a phrase of the time, was 'eyeball-to-eyeball' with the British forces.

On 24 June two Land Rovers and their police escort were surrounded by a hostile crowd in the frontier area. The police abandoned their vehicles and sought protection in a police post. By the time reinforce-ments came on the scene, the abandoned transport had been gutted. There were so many other incidents of a like nature that it was decided to send for reinforcements. There were three Gurkha battalions in 48 Gurkha Infantry Brigade then – 1/6 GR, 1/7 GR and 1/10 GR. On 26 June, 2/7 GR were called off an extended jungle exercise in Malaysia in the small hours to go and reinforce the Hong Kong garrison for four weeks. They were ordered to take 'light scales' of kit. This was fine for a short spell but the battalion did not return to its base near Malacca until early December – four months later. By then there was a continuous commitment for a Gurkha presence on the border. But in those early days no one had the slightest idea that matters would either be so serious or drag on for so long. Meanwhile, in the urban areas, troops were subjected to much vocal propaganda by the Chinese, but it almost certainly had the reverse effect from what had been hoped for. The Gurkhas had always found the Malays and the Malayan Chinese friendly and could get on well with them; not so with the Hong Kong Chinese. In no way was there any empathy between the two races – even if the content of the propaganda and the accent in which it was delivered had been intelligible, the Gurkhas would not have taken any interest in it at all. Their patience was sorely tried by other methods – children throwing stones was one that became commonplace.

After the initial troubles of rioting, of union premises and ware-houses, known as 'godowns', being used by left-wing fanatics to store weapons, inflammatory posters, and many acts of disruption, had been tackled by the police with Gurkha backing, all three battalions were on continuous stand-by. For instance, in 1/10 GR, the men virtually lived by their vehicles, weapons to hand, ammunition in pouches and magazines, and detonators close by grenades. Many were the practices, both by day and night, so that an emergency could be dealt with as efficiently as possible.

It was not until 8 July that trouble on the border broke out so badly that the police could no longer contain it. Some policemen were marching down the road from Sha Tau Kok to take over duties at the frontier post when they were fired on from the British side of the border. At least two policemen were killed and five wounded.

'A' and 'D' Companies of 1/10 GR were rushed forward but they were allowed to go only to the main police station, as the government was ultra sensitive about letting troops go to the actual border. After a wait of two hours the order was given to the CO, Lieutenant Colonel R. W. L. McAlister, OBE – one of the most 'unflappable' of commanders one could wish to have – to clear British territory of armed invaders. By then the intruders' sniping had increased and their automatic fire from medium machine-guns (MMG) was thrumming against the building in which the beleaguered police had taken refuge, the Rural Committee building, causing further casualties.

The CO gave out his orders and the move towards the frontier started. 'D' Company was ordered to move to three small hill features to the left; the remainder, escorted by a troop of armoured vehicles of the Life Guards, moved along the axis of the main road. There was no cover.

Part of the strictest of orders CO 1/10 GR had received was that there was to be 'no shooting of any kind unless life was truly in danger'. The intruders were firing on the advancing column of Gurkhas with at least one MMG and, in the spirit of the strict injunction about not opening fire, there was little that the Gurkhas could do but to go to ground. After five minutes the firing ceased and the soldiers resumed their advance. Ninety minutes later, at 1700 hours, the Gurkhas were in Sha Tau Kok, having seen off the invaders. The Gurkhas had sustained no casualties except for one soldier who had a split finger, caused when his weapon was shot from his grasp.

For the men on the ground it was tense. The invaders turned out to be militiamen and they were still spoiling for a fight, standing only 50 yards away, side-by-side with between 150 and 200 soldiers of the Chinese Army proper. After spending an uneasy night 1/10 GR was relieved by 1/7 GR, one of whose officers had said about the situation in Kowloon, 'If one man trips on his rifle and looses off a round accidentally, we could be facing a war.' How much more did that apply up on the border!

1/7 GR found an eerie atmosphere. All the civilians had left the village and Chinese soldiers were manning machine-guns on the roofs of some of the houses. Essential services were not working properly and Red Guards tried to shoot out the street lights on the British side of the border with air guns and catapults, and throughout, intense and sticky heat jangling nerves and shortening tempers. From that time on, two companies would be in the Sha Tau Kok position with one company on stand-by – instant readiness all 24 hours of the day and night – and the fourth resting, but in reserve. For all commanders it was a nerve-racking business, especially at junior level, where nastiness first manifested itself. Men had to ask themselves – what to do and when to do it?

Following what happened to 1/10 GR, their next serious task came only four days later, on 12 July 1967, when two companies were called out after midnight, this time to go to Lo Wu railway bridge. The following day all police stations were occupied by the rest of the battalion. Frontier posts were also taken over, some manned only by Gurkhas, others having joint military/police control.

Internal security operations are never easy, in fact nearly always the reverse. On an international frontier it was infinitely more acute as there were no hard and fast rules about what to do, when, on the other side of it, armed rioters were spoiling for a fight. Great was the provocation and great was the temptation to settle the score by opening fire. The doctrine of 'minimum force' is intrinsic to British Army internal security work and was observed, using all the tact, patience and calmness possible at every level. 1/10 GR was in a most invidious position because everything it did to react to the provocations from over the border became an international incident. The sight of the Chinese Army fully dressed for battle, running to their previously prepared stand-to positions had a sobering effect on all commanders' conduct, yet to do nothing at all was taken by the Chinese army as a sign of weakness and, as there was nothing then that could be done, the Chinese escalated their actions.

In Lo Wu the small boys who threw stones and bottles at the troops were replaced by youths who started to destroy the Immigration Department office, using bricks and rocks. These groups would advance across the bridge – the far end being in China – and attack British property at point-blank range. On 3 August Lo Wu became so violent that the Gurkhas had to react more than before – Major B. M. Niven and his company used tear-gas for the first time in the border 'confrontation'. The bridge had to be cleared three times, the situation becoming more tense and more delicate each time.

Around the Man Kam To bridge there had been a rash of propaganda posters plastered on the police station on the British side of the border. The villagers lived on the Chinese side of the border but, since before the British ever went to China, they had been working their fields south of the Sham Chun river, paying little or no attention to the border. They had always been well-behaved and there had been no trouble till then. They crossed the small bridge, as traders and farmers, without let or hindrance. However, heavily infiltrated by militiamen dressed as locals, the temper of the crowd changed dramatically. On 5 August, angered by the removal during the night of some of the posters that they had affixed on the walls of the police station on British territory, they sprang a sneak attack on the small police post and disarmed the policemen. Matters were prevented from becoming any nastier by Lieutenant (QGO) Dhanraj Rai, who calmly parleyed with the villagers. While this was happening, the company commander, Major C. J. Pike, DSO, the CO, the Brigade Commander, the District Officer and some senior police officers were on the scene. After more parleying the matter was settled amicably.

A wire fence was then erected to protect the police from the daily 'poster' attacks against its station walls. On 11 August the traders mounted a protest against this and again the CO and the District Officer (Mr Trevor Bedford) were called for. Escorted by a platoon of 'C' Company, they parleyed with the villagers for eight hours, over the border fence. During this time the Gurkha Engineers were erecting a fence that all hoped would be more 'suitable' to the villagers. This did not, in fact, please them and, at about 2300 hours, the villagers broke through the wire and seized first the District Officer, then the CO. Shooting was out of the question and gas was useless, with everybody intermingled. The two Britons were closely threatened with meathooks, knives and axes as the Chinese drew up petitions for the two men to sign, as well as being asked to accede to other 'demands'. Attempts to help the two men were useless and soon three Gurkhas were just as powerless.

Two platoons were moved into positions while two other British officers planned the release of the Colonel and the District officer as best they could. Niven – a wiry, tireless, indomitable Scot – went to the bridge itself with an interpreter to try and sort out what was by then an ugly and menacing situation. At the same time, orders came from the Brigadier to have the whole business settled by dawn, an order that the traders and farmers from over the frontier were unmoved by! The danger was that the villagers should attempt to abduct the two Britons and the three Gurkhas over the bridge into China proper. Parley and patience won the day – or more correctly the night – and, just before dawn, the Chinese accepted a fairly harmless document in return for the release of all five captives.

By 'keeping their cool' during every phase of this unpleasant episode, 1/10 GR had resolved a nasty situation without bloodshed. It had been the aim of the Chinese troublemakers, by insult and provocation, to get the Gurkhas to open fire and so create a situation on the frontier that would be an embarrassment in itself as well as helping the urban ruffians, who were also engaged in a fierce outbreak of lawlessness and crime.

As a punishment for the humiliating treatment given to McAlister and Bedford, the Hong Kong Government ordered all gates on the frontier to be closed. At Ta Ku Ling, 'B' Company, 1/6 GR, under Major R. H. Duncan, carried out this task, and the villagers' reaction was one of instant anger. As the mounds of pigs and vegetables intended for Hong Kong piled up, the villagers infiltrated through the numerous holes in the boundary fence and attacked a platoon of 'B' Company with anything that came to hand – including stones, staves and pickaxes. Gas grenades proved ineffective in the open air and the platoon did not want to escalate matters by opening fire. There was no choice but to take shelter in the police post. By the time they eventually got there a number of men, including Duncan and his Gurkha officer, had been badly bruised by brickbats. It was clear to Duncan that, unless the gate was opened again, the situation would become untenable. After repeated demands for this to happen the Hong Kong Government, several hours later, did agree to this. By then the local militia, dressed like farmers, had joined the thronging villagers and their efforts at enraging the crowd further were proving successful.

To show the villagers that the military on the British side had no aggressive intentions, Duncan – sincere, calculating and deliberate – decided to open the gate himself. He was unarmed to emphasize the point and, accompanied by his runner with a small police squad on call, went to the gate and duly opened it. He was immediately surrounded by the angry crowd who refused to let him return without signing a state-ment apologizing for the gate's closure, for carrying out provocative acts and that he, Duncan, would behave himself properly in future – a demeaning proviso that made his Scots blood boil.

It took a combined military/police patrol to extricate Duncan, the Gurkhas with him and the police who, by then, had gone to his aid and had also been seized. Regrettably some of the police were badly hurt, with the mob also suffering casualties. A platoon commander had to use his kukri to prevent his weapon from being snatched. Later the Chinese spent much time searching for something in the area and it was presumed by the Gurkhas that they were looking for a hand or some fingers.

All these episodes caused a rethink of border policies. A 'cordon sanitaire' was needed and a large wall was built. The Immigration Department at Lo Wu was protected behind a massive cement wall with in-built gun ports. The hill top at Man Kam To was occupied, so leaving a no-man's-land between the Gurkhas and the agricultural compound below. The police post was bulldozed, but before the dozer could arrive tension had mounted to breaking-point. To cool the situation 'booby-traps' made of bottled water with string 'fuzes' were hung from the wire barricade – the ruse worked. Sand-bagged section posts were built; wire and other defence stores were utilized.

On the communist side of the border the People's Liberation Army worked itself into a frenzy as they dug deeper trenches and prepared for something more militant. Rumours of 'Struggle Committees' and 'Suicide Squads' filtered over the border. Trading came to a complete stop, goods piled up, vegetables started to rot and pigs to get hungry, with the farmers unable to cross the border and work their land or reap their crops; tension become electric.

On 24 August the storm broke simultaneously at Lo Wu and Man Kam To. At about 1600 hours both crossing-places were rushed by locals. At Lo Wu this meant that there was a battle at ten yards' range. The use of tear-gas was ineffective as, apart from the wind being in the wrong direction, the attackers had taken to wearing dampened face masks and to smother the grenades thrown at them, hurling them into the river below. While the smoke of the phospherous grenades billowed away too, the heavier, burning element did have an adverse effect on the intruders. The battle raged nonstop for three and a half hours with the

Chinese firing medium machine-guns over the heads of the Gurkhas from only 250 yards from the border line. The Gurkhas fired no bullets at all.

At Man Kam To, Niven fought a similar action. Newly arrived 2nd Lieutenant Nima Wangdi Lama and the old hand, Lieutenant (QGO) Dhanraj Rai commanded their platoons in a four-hour battle. The Gurkhas threw grenades nonstop as the rioters attempted to remove the barrier. Some Chinese wore 1914–18 pattern respirators, many had grappling hooks and many piled the goods trolleys with hay to shield themselves as they all tried to knock the barrier over the bridge, using other trolleys as battering-rams. The Gurkhas set the hay-laden trolleys on fire and the attackers were eventually driven back.

The very next day Lo Wu erupted again. This time there were fewer rioters but they made up for lack of numbers by throwing Molotov cocktails and fragmentation grenades. As Chinese bullets were fired over the police station, Lieutenant P. Reid, the Intelligence Officer, reported on the conduct of the battle to battalion headquarters, so letting the commanders on the ground pay full attention to what they were doing. Despite some anxious moments, it was the Chinese who could not sustain their efforts sufficiently to prevail against the Gurkhas and so broke off contact. The situation remained very tense. The Chinese were reinforced with more troops, who prepared more trenches, rehearsed their stand-to drills and practised grenade throwing. The Gurkhas remained unflinchingly firm. However, further aggression was forestalled as all frontier gates reopened, taking the Chinese completely by surprise. They now no longer had a 'just cause' to continue defying the Hong Kong Government so could not whip up sufficient enthusiasm to continue their insurrection. The Gurkhas therefore had won the day without having fired that fateful shot, which the Chinese had so hoped for, but had hoped in vain.

Although the troubles were not yet over, the peak period had passed. The last major event was the abduction of Inspector F. Knight, of the Royal Hong Kong Police Force, into China. This again led to the closing of Man Kam To bridge, but this time with a formidable barrier of steel and sandbags. Two police constables had also strayed over the border and, until negotiations for their release were effected, trade again came to a standstill. Inspector Knight managed to escape, the policemen were returned and tension gradually eased.

In the urban areas the communists also failed in their campaign for victory, a campaign that involved maiming and killing as well as many other atrocities. The Red Guards and their fellow countrymen had failed and, while new tactics were being thought out, many of the rowdies went underground, thus cooling things off. In both areas escalation was avoided; so too was the shooting war, which could have been so damaging.

A high wire obstacle, called 'Snake Fence', was built about 1,000 yards back from the Sham Chun river line to allow space, well enough away from Chinese army posts for them not to be provoked and to give just a little depth for manoeuvre if necessary. It was also intended to help control any large influx of illegal immigrants, although, at the time it was erected, no one had any notion how big a part this aspect was to play in the lives of the Gurkhas in later years. The Gurkha Engineers took the major part in building and maintaining Snake Fence. Apart from that, defensive strong points were dug and well wired in at all key points. These were to be constantly manned by the Gurkhas in the years ahead. So, for a while, the situation stabilized and the Cultural Revolution blew itself out.

Although maybe 1/10 GR's experiences were the most dramatic of all the Gurkha battalions', the role the others played was in no way less important for final peace. In fact, when any unit has a series of minor irritants, it is often harder to overcome the inevitable drain on emotional resources than when something dramatic happens. A typical example of the low-grade irritant with high-grade potential for trouble is quoted from the regimental history of 7 GR: eight Chinese youths, pretending to play basketball, edged their way closer and closer to two sentries of 1/7 GR. They then rushed at the riflemen but were stopped in their tracks when the Gurkhas drew their kukris and stood firm. The youths saw that they could not provoke the Gurkhas so, tiring of their 'game', merely spat vituperation at the soldiers and left.

Concerning the Hong Kong situation of that time and the part the Gurkhas played, Walker, by now General Sir Walter, KCB, CBE, DSO, Colonel of the 7th Gurkha Rifles, wrote a Special Regimental Order after visiting them and, while it was intended for 7 GR, it is equally applicable to all the Gurkha units that were deployed in aid of the Hong Kong Government, maintaining law and order. The General wrote:

'. . . in Hong Kong, the deliberate provocation and confrontation of Communist China were defeated by your superb coolness and strength, by your resolute behaviour and high discipline, by your renowned soldierly qualities and the superiority of your tactical skill. You showed once again that, when it comes to doing a tough job with minimum force, you have no equal. No praise can be too high of the manner in which you have acquitted yourselves in extremely difficult circumstances.

You have filled an arduous duty with great distinction and in your long and proud service under the British Crown, you have once more earned the high respect from your comrades in the British Army and the gratitude of the British nation.'

Indeed, it is true to say that events in Hong Kong had showed the Gurkhas to be without par and indispensable in such a situation. In December 1970 the Major General Brigade of Gurkhas announced that the rundown would halt and that the Brigade had an indefinite future. A year prior, few people would have believed such an announcement possible. The halting of the rundown was therefore of great significance. Details of the new Order of Battle were announced: five battalions – meaning that the planned amalgamation of 2 GR would not therefore happen – of which three would be stationed in Hong Kong, one in Brunei and one in the United Kingdom, initially 7 GR, at Church Crookham, not far from London; the three Corps regiments, each at two squadron strength; and a smaller training depot.

The final withdrawal of the Brigade from Malaysia was when the Gurkha Para disbanded, on 31 October 1971, after being employed at the Jungle Warfare School near Johore Bahru in a demonstration-cum-exercise enemy role. 414 Gurkha officers and men and 1,055 dependants who have died since the end of the Second World War lie buried in West Malaysia and Singapore and a further 69 Gurkha officers and men who have no known grave are commemorated in the Terendak (Malacca) military cemetery.

In 1973 the last British toe-hold in India was finally handed over when the transit camp left Barrackpore, outside Calcutta, and moved to Kathmandu.

CYPRUS

The occasion that again brought Gurkhas into world headlines was the move of 10 GR, then in England, to Cyprus. The predictable cries, still heard, against sending Gurkhas anywhere mildly contentious were happily left unheeded and it would not be boastful to state that the Gurkhas carried out the tasks given to them in the admirable manner normally associated with their name.

Cyprus is an island in the eastern end of the Mediterranean Sea. Its population is a mixed one, 80 per cent Greek and the remaining 20 per cent Turkish. Both races think of themselves as Greek or Turkish, not as Cypriot. Modern Cyprus can be said to have started with the Russo-Turkish War of 1877. The Turkish Sultan asked the British if they would 'occupy and administer' the island. This was ratified by the Convention of 1878. The British regarded Cyprus as 'the key to western Asia', by controlling the Suez Canal – which was opened that same year – and thus the route to India. The Indian Government was invited to garrison the island and to pay for the military presence. Thus it was that 1/2 GR were in the original garrison, landing at Larnaca in 1878. The British occupation aroused considerable interest and resentment among the other European powers. Gurkhas were also stationed on the island during both world wars.

Cyprus is 'a scene of that continual conflict between east and west, which is always to be reinterpreted but never ignored'.* As a result of the Greeks wanting 'Union with Greece' – Enosis – there was much anti-British activity in the 1950s and, in 1958, the Turks intervened. Independence, within the Commonwealth, came in 1959, then, after much international negotiating, the United Nations took a hand in relieving the British in keeping the peace. On 4 March 1964 UNFICYP (United Nations Force in Cyprus) was formed 'to use its best efforts to prevent a recurrence of fighting . . . [and] . . . to contribute to the maintenance and restoration of order and a return to normal conditions'.*

By the Treaty concerning the Establishment of the Republic of Cyprus in 1960, two British Sovereign Base Areas (BSBA)** were set up at Akrotiri in the west and Dhekelia in the east, amounting to 99 square miles of territory. Dhekelia has three enclaves, two villages and the power-station, with the major enclave at the communications centre of Ayios Nikolaos, which is adjacent to Famagusta.

Hostilities between the two communities broke out again on 21 December 1963 and lasted until August 1964. The British intervened. In 1974, as a result of the largest opposition group, supported by the renewed Enosis party (the Eoka-B organization), and the launching of a coup by the Greek National Guard against the President, Archbishop Makarios, the Greek National Guard attacked all the Turkish communities in Cyprus. The Turkish Cypriots' resistance, in the main enclave in the old walled city of Famagusta in the south and Nicosia to the north, was heroic, and continued until the Turkish regular army invaded the island from mainland Turkey to relieve them. This was 'Stage 1'. No solution to the Turkish-Greek problem has yet been found.

10 GR, in the United Kingdom, were put on 72-hours' notice to move to Cyprus, at the end of July 1974, as a result of the deteriorating situation there. Their advance party flew there on 6 August, landing at Akrotiri, then going to Dhekelia, in the Eastern Sovereign Base Area (ESBA). The departure of the main body was accelerated: at 1900 hours

*Hilaire Belloc, quoted by H. D. Purcell, in *Cyprus*. Ernest Benn Ltd, London, 1969.
**The BSBAs attracted Cypriot labour and contained a British expatriate population that was richer and spent more freely than elsewhere in the island. The affluence generated often exceeded the Cypriot Government's economy so, despite nationalist noises against them, the BSBAs' status was unchallenged.

on Saturday, 10 August, the Ministry of Defence phoned the battalion to say that they had to be ready to fly by noon the very next day. Within a 24-hour period, 600 men, 37 Land Rovers, 31 trailers, 2 water-trailers, all support weapons and 50,000 pounds of freight were in Cyprus – all over a weekend!

For the first week after their arrival a ceasefire held, then broke down as the Turks began 'Stage 2' of their invasion. The Turkish Army advanced on the coastal town of Famagusta, and the ESBA and Larnaca were imperilled. The lesser important of the two bases, the western (WSBA), was not as severely threatened. Thousands of refugees poured into the eastern base. The battalion manned road-blocks, searched vehicles, put out mobile confidence patrols to let the various ethnic communities see who, in fact, 10 GR were, distinguished by the traditional Gurkha felt hat, and how they operated. The Gurkha hat was worn not only to distinguish them from among the many other nationalities of UNFICYP but also as the Turks remembered, with great respect, 1/6 GR similarly dressed at Gallipoli in 1915 and 2/7 GR at Kut-el-Amara in 1916. All this was an attempt to restore shattered confidence and calm the fear-ridden minds of the refugees. Every rifleman had to give traffic signals in Greek and Turkish – not all that easy for anyone to remember which was which, but a comforting gesture of familiarity when done properly.

In the face of the Turkish advance on Famagusta, the Greek National Guard was expected to withdraw into the apex of land south of Famagusta and east of Dhekelia, known as 'The Triangle'. 'A' and 'C' Companies were deployed to meet them, disarm then, escort them through the Sovereign Base and then return their weapons to them on the far side. All this was far from easy – in the middle of the night when it happened, there were 60 vehicles and some 800 very nervous Greek Cypriots who had no intention of surrendering their weapons. 10 GR's aim was to be absolutely neutral and to safeguard the sovereignty of the base, within which only the battalion of Gurkhas was allowed to carry weapons.

Refugees had to be administered. The Gurkha soldiers were excellent in this role and had a most tranquil and reassuring effect on them. In all, some 25,000 refugees had to be catered for. Initially the work involved planning and setting up communal kitchens, food lines, living areas, roads and paths. The camp run by the Gurkhas was called Athna Forest and was to be recognized as the best organized, the happiest and the most efficient centre on the island. It was run democratically by the refugees themselves and by a very small band of dedicated volunteers under a British major, a Gurkha warrant officer and a Gurkha cook corporal. Only occasionally did the pro- and anti-Makarios factions spoil the calm and peace of the camp. Later the battalion was only responsible for the security of the camp, and not the running of it.

During the battle of Famagusta Turkish tanks got lost at night, ran out of fuel near the ESBA and had to be refuelled by the battalion, reorientated, and then sent packing outside the Base Area. Greek Cypriot fighters would climb up on these lost tanks expecting a lift so that they could go and fight the Turks, only to leap off and disappear into the night at top speed when the helmeted tank commander spoke to them in Turkish. Next day Major B. M. Niven, MBE, had to land his helicopter in front of a lost advancing Turkish column to point out to them where the boundary stones were.

There was then a ceasefire and the Gurkhas patrolled, manned snap check-points and searched for and confiscated any weapons found. The Turkish Army was now in sight of the ESBA boundary and were digging in. Their map reading was not always correct and to help them recognize the boundary, the Pioneer Platoon set out with a lot of boundary posts, a drill and cement to fix them into the ground.

Strengthening road-blocks with sandbagged positions, chicken wire, knife-rests and vehicle ramps became imperative as the Turks were still in a threatening posture and near enough to try their luck at capturing the Base Area. Support Company went to Famagusta to move out tons of baggage, boxes, furniture, food and supplies – all the paraphernalia of the British Army's peacetime requirements.

As the situation became more stable the emergency reinforcements to the island were withdrawn to the United Kingdom and 10 GR became the sole infantry battalion in the eastern sector. Their Operations Room became the control centre for the entire eastern Base Area. One company was sent to Ayios Nikolaos to garrison it, one company did duties in Dhekelia, another did all the fatigues and the fourth was held in reserve. The Reconnaissance Platoon, using radars, tracked goats and Turks, catching and eating the former and merely capturing the latter.

There was always the threat of a Turkish 'Stage 3' when they might come further south into Larnaca and the Base Area to take away the Turkish refugees. There were several alerts and tense moments as the battalion braced itself for more trouble and a further avalanche of refugees were the Turks to make such a move.

The battalion met and made friends with the Swedish and Austrian members of UNFICYP. General Prem Chand of the Indian Army, the ex-1 GR Head of UNFICYP, was presented. The battalions also held many meetings with Greek Cypriot local administrators to solve problems that new boundaries created and also with the Turks to sort out any flash-points or sources of friction.

As the regimental diarist wrote, 'Several armies have now seen our Gurkha Hats and our men were obeyed and respected wherever they went. All respected their calmness, efficiency, industry and politeness.'

At the start of 1975 there was a major confrontation at Ayios Nikolaos when Mr Clerides, the Greek Cypriot Acting President (of Cyprus) arrived, unannounced, to visit some refugees. His arrival coincided with the arrival of a company of Turkish troops who seized some Greek shepherds on the Sovereign Base Area boundary close by. A large and angry crowd of over a thousand Greeks formed up on the boundary and proceeded to throw stones and shout abuse at the Turks, who promptly took up positions and threatened to open fire. 'B' Company, deployed on the border, succeeded in separating Greeks from Turks. Their rapid and skilful deployment stabilized this potentially very dangerous situation. Mr Clerides was persuaded to depart, negotiations were opened under the auspices of the United Nations and ultimately the situation was normalized with the release of the captured Greeks.

That same month, January, there were also full-scale anti-British riots in the WSBA at Akrotiri and Episkopi. These were contained by 10 GR's affiliated* British Regiment, the 1st Battalion, the Royal Scots, with 4 Platoon, 'B' Company, 10 GR, in support. Refugees in Athna Forest threatened to riot but were dissuaded. Mount Trudos Ski Centre was attacked and bombed by rioters and had to be defended by Gurkha soldiers there on a ski course. The Turks became more aggressive and objectionable, and the Greeks more and more unrealistic in their demands. Talks that were in progress broke down, anti-British feelings developed and there were rumours of Turkish plans for further advances. This period coincided with the formal farewell party to

*Regimental affiliations, approved by Her Majesty the Queen, are a prevalent feature in the British and Commonwealth armies, commemorating some joint achievement of arms or some historical connection. A variation on this theme is an alliance between regiments. In the Brigade of Gurkhas these are:

	Affiliated Regiment/Corps	Allied Regiment
2 GR	The Royal Green Jackets	Royal Brunei Malay Regiment
6 GR	14th/20th King's Hussars The Royal Green Jackets	
7 GR	The Cameronians (The Scottish Rifles) Queen's Own Highlanders (Seaforth & Camerons) The Queen's Own Rifles of Canada	Pacific Islands Regiment, Papua New Guinea
10 GR	The Royal Scots (The Royal Regiment)	
QGE	The Corps of Royal Engineers	
QGS	Royal Corps of Signals 32nd (Scottish) Signal Regiment (Volunteers) [Official Association with] 6 Signal Regiment Royal Australian Corps of Signals	
GTR	Royal Corps of Transport	

Cyprus which the battalion hosted. One hundred and thirty guests were scheduled to arrive for 1830 hours on 7 February, but one hour before an alert threatened. By 1800 hours all orders had been given in the event of a Turkish attack, but nothing happened and the party continued as normal. In the very early hours of the following morning a call to duty came, so the battalion officers held orders dressed in pyjamas – all were to be ready to move within two hours. The order was later cancelled – to everybody's relief.

By 27 February 1975 the battalion was once more back in England. Any sober judgement of the efficacy of its work in Cyprus has to conclude that, if it had not been for the complete military competence, impartial steadfastness, untiring efforts and obvious fearlessness shown by 10 GR, the Turkish Army would most certainly have occupied the major Greek Cypriot city and post of Larnaca and might well have overrun the ESBA, with untold consequences. As it was, 10 GR was the only battalion on the island that did not actually have to engage other armies in combat.

Not only that; the High Commissioner in Cyprus wrote to the Foreign and Commonwealth Office concerning the political sensitivities often encountered in committing Gurkhas to an operational role in a British dependency. Part of the letter reads:

'You will remember that certain reservations had to be overcome before the final decision was taken to send out a Gurkha battalion for an Internal Security role in the BSBAs. The Gurkhas have been so effective that I feel that I would like to record my views in case consideration is given in future to sending other Gurkhas out here to perform a similar task . . .

. . . Therefore, I am glad to be able to tell you that in my opinion, the choice of a Gurkha battalion . . . was not only justified – it was most successful. They were able to adapt lessons learned on the China border to the different needs of the BSBA.'*

The lessons referred to by the High Commissioner concern the prevention of escalation of tension by cool deliberate and controlled action, which contains rather than exacerbates.

As a result of the 1975 Defence Review 2 GR was to form the amalgamated battalion of 1/2 GR and 2/2 GR, and the new figure was to be achieved by 1 April 1979. The Hong Kong garrison was to be slimmed of its British personnel which meant that the three Gurkha corps units took on almost the entire engineer, communication and transport commitments. The Brigade of Gurkhas was seen to have a

*This letter is quoted in 10 GR's official history.

role for at least the following ten years, in support of the Hong Kong Government.

In Hong Kong refugees from Vietnam and illegal immigrants from the mainland flooded into the already overcrowded community. In all this, Gurkha battalions and corps units were deployed in many areas, helping to accommodate and administer the refugees and to deter and deflect illegal immigrants. Both were on-going commitments and involved much hard, humane yet firm treatment of bewildered people and much disruption of normal life. As the editor of the Brigade journal, *The Kukri*, put it:

The Gurkha soldier continues to display the remarkable versatility which has made his name a byword. The success of the Vietnamese relief operation, which coincided with the Queen's visit to Hong Kong, is a just tribute to the energy and understanding of our soldiers, to quote but one example. Likewise, the operations against illegal immigrants on the Hong Kong-China border have been a great, if played down, success story. The man himself is changing. He is more technically aware, better trained and better educated. He is also better paid than before and in spite of all the pressures put upon him, he remains the same delightful professional companion, which has always made service with Gurkhas such a pleasure . . .

. . . who could possibly have predicted that, in 1975, the whole mournful process of redundancy would have to be started up again?'

One of the highlights of 1977 was the Silver Jubilee of Her Majesty, Queen Elizabeth II, when Royal titles were given to The Gurkha Engineers, making them The Queen's Gurkha Engineers, and the Gurkha Signals, making them the Queen's Gurkha Signals. HRH Prince Charles, The Prince of Wales, was appointed as Colonel-in-Chief of 2 GR.

1978 was a very successful year for the Brigade of Gurkhas. The amalgamation of 1/2 GR and 2/2 GR was cancelled and it was announced that a Gurkha battalion would be in Brunei until 1983 (this was subsequently extended for a further five years until 1988) and that a tactical headquarters and two rifle companies, with small detachments of sappers and signalmen, were to be sent to Belize. The first unit to go was 6 GR.

It is interesting to note that, in 1982, after the Falklands campaign, Argentina backed the United Nations General Assembly's resolutions upholding Belize's right to independence and calling for appropriate action 'to guarantee its security and territorial integrity [against Guatemala] thereafter.'

This Gurkha commitment was still in operation in 1986.

In 1977, as in many other years, elements of the Brigade of Gurkhas were deployed in a 'community relations-cum-international aid' role. The Queen's Gurkha Engineers sent a sub-unit to the New Hebrides, to a remote island called Meawo, to build some bridges and thus help communications and the copra trade. A goup of QGE also went to the Solomon Islands to help clear up earthquake damage. The type of work the Gurkhas did is well shown in the citation for a British Empire Medal (BEM) for a junior NCO whose work, good in all respects, showed a degree of initiative, intelligence, reliability and courage beyond that of a man of his rank and experience while in Guadalcanal:

'Lance-Corporal Imanhang Limbu, a patrol leader, was given the task of reconnoitring some of the afflicted areas to report the position and state of landslides and advise on the safety of the villagers. He moved into his different areas by air, sea or river together with his rations, equipment and radio. He was left alone to set up his patrol by hiring bushmen as guides, carriers and interpreters. He patrolled on foot along the hot, steep landslides. He spent the nights in native villages at a time when tremors were still occurring and the rain was intense causing further landslides daily. His only link with his commander was the radio set which he used at the end of each day's patrol. His reporting, which involved cross-examining bushmen who at best could speak only pidgin English, and relied on keen observation and map reading, was complete, accurate and clearly presented. This was a remarkable achievement for a Nepalese in such a foreign environment.'

HONG KONG – ILLEGAL IMMIGRANTS

More than ten years after the troubles with the Red Guards in Hong Kong and when the revolutionary madness had burnt itself out in China, countless folk in that country were at their wits' end; it was to Hong Kong that they turned for sanity and freedom. Masses of miserable humanity had fled and continued to flee, not only from China but from another communist state, as refugees from Vietnam; the storm-tossed, pirate-ravaged and water-weary boat-people. And how many of those who had previously extolled the virtues of living in a workers' paradise sung its praises now?

Waves of misery were brought to Hong Kong in the International Year of the Child. Refugees were not a new problem in the Administration but the sheer weight of numbers threatened to overwhelm them. Apart from those from Vietnam, who came by frail boat, exhausted by sea, politics and the eternal irony of man's seeming indifference to fellow men, masses of illegal immigrants from mainland China arrived on foot having swum across the shallow bays. Many died in the attempt. Their bloated bodies drifted before the wind in the Sham Chun River, the dividing line between hate and hope. Hong Kong did respond to the influx, if only because it had no option. Camps were established to feed and care for the ever-arriving thousands. It seemed that the flow of refugees into the already crowded colony would extend the administrative sources of endeavour. But Hong Kong managed. It did so by absorbing these thousands, offering them temporary jobs and setting about the business of repatriation of the illegal immigrants when it could, with a balanced sense of reality.

The Brigade of Gurkhas was inevitably involved. The role of stopping this tide of Chinese humanity entailed many long hours of ambush, patrolling, lack of sleep and disruption of normal day-to-day activities, to say nothing of the more peaceful, non-military relations with the Vietnamese, often with no prior warning. The response called for a change in the Brigade's way of thinking. The pros and cons of the moral issues were not the subject of debate or dispute. The task in hand was what had to be dealt with. The task was well met. The strength of the Gurkha to adapt to new situations, devise better ways of meeting the job in hand, sustained the Brigade through a difficult chapter of its history. To say that anti-illegal immigrant operations left the Brigade better prepared for its primary role would be a lie. The long border tours inevitably meant less time to train, less to relax.

Battalions' instructions were 'To deter and arrest people attempting to enter Hong Kong illegally.' Each battalion on the border was allocated an area of responsibility and that was sub-divided into company areas and, in the normal way, those areas had to be carefully studied on the map and then reconnoitred. The company area was then further divided up where possible into platoon areas of responsibility. This was where the first problem occurred. Inevitably there were never three evenly sized, neat geographical areas. Sometimes a large area could not be allocated to more than one platoon. Often there were additional tasks to cope with, such as manning static observation posts and the border police posts. It was from these that valuable Intelligence was frequently acquired. Inevitably men were detached from one platoon to another and all too often platoon commanders found they were no longer commanding their own soldiers. The familiar platoon structure sometimes disappeared almost entirely.

When the company headquarters was forward at one of the original border locations such as Sha Tau Kok or Man Kam To, a ready-made company base with an operations room would be available and this would then become the home of the company for the duration of the border tour. In the other areas the company 'commuted' to work each evening from the lines and a company operations room would then be set up in the company office. Each night a company tactical head-quarters moved forward with the platoons and acted as the overall co-ordinator and sometimes as an extra patrol. Regardless of which way the company operated, it was essential that the company commander got out on the ground so that he became completely familiar with the whole area and fully understood the varying problems which affected his patrols. Normal daily life also had to continue, so a compromise was usually reached whereby the field work and the office work alternated between the company commander and his second-in-command.

As the majority of illegal immigrants came across the border at night the bulk of the effort to catch them was during the hours of darkness. However, it was also necessary to have observation posts established by day and at least a reaction force ready to be called forward in case illegal immigrants were seen. At night the standard technique was to deploy troops in three- or four-man groups. These were, in effect, small ambush parties that could operate on their own or in conjunction with others. From the outset of the anti-illegal immigrant campaign, the small covert ambush party proved to be the most successful use of manpower. The illegal immigrants had to move to attempt to reach their objective and, as always, the advantage lay with the man who could remain still and quiet.

Actual patrol locations were normally decided by the platoon com-manders but the company commander often liked to have the final say. In a number of cases certain locations proved their worth over many months. Illegal immigrants tended to favour certain routes, probably because many of them simply chose the easiest ones. Some good patrol locations were on the junction of several tracks popularly used by the fugitives. Overall the military aim was for patrols to be able to see across one another's front, that is to say, to have interlocking arcs of fire. To assist the soldiers at night, troops were issued with an invaluable device, like a low-powered telescope, called an 'individual weapon sight'.

When the Chinese entered an area the patrol that saw them first would inform any other patrols that might have to be involved. Once the direction and route of the illegal immigrants were confirmed, one man stayed with the radio and the other men of the patrol moved into cut-off positions. Men from other patrols might also have been required to help and often some fast talking on the radio was required, using established nicknames as an aid to speed. Ideally the ambush was sprung when the Chinese had moved to a point where they were sur-rounded. Frequently that was not possible and a chase would probably ensue. The normal reaction of an illegal immigrant was to run a short distance and then hide. Once the element of surprise was lost, torches often had to be used and each patrol carried very powerful torches.

It was essential that all the men in the patrol knew the area in their patrol location. they had to be fully familiar with every path, rock, bush, hut and grave, chicken farm and fish pond, patch of marsh and quicksand and plot of dry ground, and they had to know all the distances involved. Once alerted, the Chinese could surprise even the fastest runner by a sudden turn of speed, and their ability to disappear into the undergrowth was amazing.

There were a number of cases of violence. At night most resistance was through fear rather than aggression and normally a quiet, firm approach was better than a war cry and a brandished truncheon.

As well as providing ambush patrols, which captured the majority of illegal immigrants, use was also made of small reconnaissance 'Scout' helicopters, Alsatian dogs and boats. Indeed, a special boat troop of QGE was established for this very task. To communicate with such a varied lot of people, it became essential that the majority of soldiers were able to use the current voice procedure and tune their patrol radios. The junior NCO had suddenly been given more responsibility and, as a result, higher standards of junior command were achieved.

As an example of these anti-illegal immigrant operations, the act that led to the Queen's Gallantry Medal – the first ever awarded to a Gurkha – being won by Lance Corporal Aimansing Limbu, 7 GR, is given by quoting the citation:

'On the night of 28 May 1979, Lance Corporal Aimansing Limbu was in charge of a four-man anti-illegal immigrant beach ambush party on the Tolo Peninsula in the north-east sector of the New Territories. The night was very dark and the weather very windy which, together with a high tide, made the rocky shoreline where the ambush was situated particularly treacherous and dangerous due to the rough state of the sea. At approximately 0200 hours the patrol sighted a group of people a hundred or so yards off the shore, some on a raft, some in the water. Almost immediately another person was spotted leaving the water fifty yards away from the ambush position. Lance Corporal Aimansing told the patrol to watch the large group and moved off to capture the lone man. As he was attempting to arrest the lone man, he was jumped upon by two others, who must have landed earlier, and was knocked to the ground. The three people then leapt back into the sea shouting a warning to the others and started to swim towards the raft which began to head out to sea again. Lance Corporal Aimansing, quickly recovering his senses and without a thought to his own safety, slipped on a rubber ring left by the illegal immigrants and jumped into the sea after them. Two of the illegal immigrants who were still swimming then attempted to drown Lance Corporal Aimansing, but were discouraged by blows from his baton and were rendered capable only of clinging onto the raft. With considerable difficulty Lance-Corporal Aimansing then managed to get on board the raft despite kicks, blows and bites and subdued the six men on the raft. He then forced them to paddle the raft to the shore where all eight were apprehended.

Throughout this incident Lance Corporal Aimansing Limbu displayed not only a very high degree of personal courage in the face of very clear danger, both from drowning and the vicious assaults of eight desperate men, but also acted promptly and with complete disregard for his own safety. His actions went far beyond those which might reasonably be expected and were in the very highest traditions of active service.'

There were a number of other gallantry awards and commendations earned by Gurkha soldiers, all a variation on the above theme. Although minimum force was always observed by the Security Forces, who were mainly Gurkha units, this principle was not adhered to by the hapless Chinese who were trying to escape. Two Gurkha soldiers met their deaths and a number were injured.

However, as a result of the superb work done by the Gurkhas, the Hong Kong Government decided to pay for another Gurkha battalion, without which they feared that law and order in the colony could not be maintained. Thus it came about that 2/7 GR was again re-raised (in 1916, after the battalion had been captured at Kut-al-Amara and in 1942, after it had been taken in Tobruk, 2/7 GR was formed from scratch). In 1980, the Governor declared an end to what was known as the 'touch base' policy – the policy that allowed illegal immigrants the right to remain in the colony if they were not discovered within a certain time frame. This change in policy turned the tide of fleeing humanity into a trickle, with a drop in captures from a daily 400 to four within a week.

THE SOUTH ATLANTIC

In 1982, events in the South Atlantic captured the world's attention as Argentina invaded South Georgia and the Falkland Islands. It is not the concern here to evaluate the political pros and cons, argument and counter-argument and other such matters, which are far better left, if they have to be evaluated, to those whose particular business it is. The interest here is the inclusion in the Task Force, as part of 5 Brigade, of 1/7 GR, and the differing reactions to a battalion of Gurkhas in a Task Force made up entirely of British servicemen and in an environment, both politically and geographically, so entirely different from what had been seen before.

It is no secret that, in some sections of the British Government, notably the Foreign and Commonwealth Office, the use of Gurkhas – citizens of an independent nation that has never been the colony of another – as an implement of carrying out British foreign policy, has been an embarrassment from time to time. This was certainly true during the Cyprus involvement in 1974–5, when the Turkish Government asked the British, in no uncertain terms, about the use of Gurkhas and their status in the British Army. An extract of the Tripartite Agreement of 1947 was shown to them and, in future references to the Gurkhas, the Turks claimed that their name was misspelt and that they were, in fact, of Turkish origin. It is a strict rule that Gurkhas should never be used in the trouble in Northern Ireland, presumably because the political disadvantages would outweigh the military advantages. However, with the vagaries of defence planning and the fluctuating numbers of servicemen – that, paradoxically, has been the only constant since the end of the Second World War – there has always been a struggle for the defence planners to have enough troops for all eventualities, many which never arise, some which do unexpectedly, and a few which are known about in enough time to be properly planned, over and above the obvious 'fixed requirements' for home defence and the NATO alliance. So it was in the case of troops to be sent to the Falklands; on the one hand, as an integral part of the British Army, there was absolutely no reason why the Gurkhas should not be used; on the other, there were doubts in very high places that, were the Gurkhas to be used, the reactions of both the Argentines and certain peripheral states of the Third World might be too high a political price to pay (whatever it was thought to be) after the military requirements had been met. In the event, the military requirement superseded any political fears that had been entertained – to the discomforture of the Argentines and the enhancement of the Gurkhas.

The interest of 1/7 GR's deployment can be seen when their name was dragged into the world forum by Argentina, who lost no opportunity of attacking Nepal. For instance, during a Security Council debate on the Seychelles, an area of the globe not immediately of much concern to either country, the Argentine Representative devoted much of his statement to an attack on the United Kingdom for deploying that battalion as 'mercenaries' in the British 'aggression' against Argentina.

Apart from any dusty answer the Nepalese Representative gave, the British representative, in replying, made the following points:

'We reject totally the analogy between the mercenaries referred to in the Commission report and regiments of Gurkhas with long and distinguished records of service with the British Army, under agreements which had been reached freely and honourably between the Governments of Nepal and the United Kingdom.'

The British Representative then quoted the internationally agreed definition of mercenaries as laid down in the Geneva Convention of 1949. This definition excludes anyone who is 'a member of the Armed Forces of a party to the conflict'.

'We were astonished to hear such slurs in the Security Council from the Representative of a Government which had unleashed armed aggression in the South Atlantic on 2 April and was in flagrant violation of a mandatory resolution of the Council.'

In the Ad Hoc Committee of the United Nations General Assembly which, at the end of 1982, was currently considering a possible draft convention against the use of mercenaries, general agreement had been given to this new definition: 'A mercenary:
1. Is not a member of the regular forces of a country;
2. Is paid more than the regular forces of that country;
3. Cannot be a person bound by treaties between two countries.'

Examples of this third point are Nepal and Britain, Nepal and India, and Switzerland and the Vatican, for the papal guard. Thus it can be seen that by neither the old nor the new convention can Britain's Brigade of Gurkhas be called 'mercenaries' by any stretch of the imagination.

Reading between the lines of the Ad Hoc Committee's recommendation, it is clear that the target of their definition is the European mercenary who so disfigured the African scene in the 1960s, 1970s and the early 1980s. The Brigade of Gurkhas remains completely unsullied by insinuation and in fact is a great reflection on the wisdom of the late Maharaja Padma Shamsher Jang Bahadur Rana, the then prime minister of Nepal, who insisted in the negotiations on the recruitment of Nepalese citizens for service in the British and Indian armies, that they should be regarded as full members thereof and so should never have the stigma of the name mercenary attached to them, and nor should Nepal for having supplied them.

In the Security Council the Argentines and the Cubans were told to stop calling the Brigade of Gurkhas 'mercenaries' and that word was expunged from the records as it was obviously factually and morally incorrect. It did not escape anyone's notice that, when on the five occasions India had used Nepalese subjects against Pakistan and China, Argentina never raised any objections. Certainly, when Nepal and Argentina were debating the issue in the United Nations General Assembly, Nepal did not let this point slip, to Argentina's discomforture. India, a champion of the non-aligned movement and the Third World, also kept significantly quiet about the use of Gurkhas during the Falklands campaign.

Nevertheless, all that having been pointed out, the Falklands crisis, in different ways, was a test case both for the United Kingdom and for Nepal. For the former, had 1/7 GR been withdrawn from 5 Brigade when it was detailed for the South Atlantic, doubt would have been cast on the credibility of Gurkhas as fighting units of the British Army and great damage would have been done to morale, certainly at unit level, to say nothing of Britain's sincerity of purpose. Had the Nepalese Government given any sign, however informal, that there was concern about the use of British Army Gurkhas in this context, this would have signalled the end of the connection as it had been known by both governments. As it was, the Government of Nepal stuck firmly to its commitments; this, apart from any other reason, was because there was no genuine popular feeling against the recruitment of Gurkhas into the British Army. In any case, the Nepalese Government regarded the Falkland issue as one of 'self-determination' and not one of 'decolonization'.

The issue was raised, outside Nepal, because the Argentines went in mortal fear of the Gurkhas (the untruths they spread about 1/7 GR were so implausible as to be ridiculous – probably never before in recent history has any one unit played such an inconspicuous military role yet achieved such results by reputation alone); while, in Nepal, it was an opportunity for those who wanted, for whatever reasons, to embarrass Authority.

Despite good coverage of events in the Brigade of Gurkhas' own newspaper, copies of which find their way into the Hills, rumours in the east of Nepal, where 1/7 GR soldiers come from, were spread to the effect that every man except one had been killed and he was a prisoner of war. It does not take much imagination to see that rumour as a deliberate disinformation campaign and although proof as to source would be almost impossible to obtain, it is not difficult to guess which unfriendly power stood to profit most from launching that and fuelling student protests by payment out of party funds from its overblown embassy in Kathmandu.

1/7 GR, on a two-year spell of duty in the United Kingdom, had been deployed in 5 Infantry Brigade which had been formed as a 'fire brigade' for 'out of area' contingencies, with special emphasis to operations in the Third World. The idea was to have two parachute battalions, one in its parachute role at all times, and the third battalion as the air/land battalion in support, that is to be used to protect the paratroops' withdrawal and provide a series of secure bases from which the paratroops could operate in an infantry role. 1/7 GR had no role in mainland Europe.

There was nothing definite about the Gurkhas' operational future for some time after the Argentines had invaded the Falklands on 2 April 1982, although they had been part of 5 Infantry Brigade for some time before that incident. The crippling of HMS *Sheffield* on 4 May made all realize the gravity of the situation and gave an added impetus, were one needed, when the soldiers went to Sennybridge, in Wales, for extensive and concentrated field firing exercises. On the last morning, after a particularly foul night, news of the sinking of the *General Belgrano*, on 2 May, shocked the British officers. The Gurkhas gave no outward appearance of being moved by the news, giving the impression of non-chalance, but secretly very much hoping that they would be involved. The battalion then went back to Church Crookham where it received definite orders that it was to be committed in the Task Force. Between then and embarkation of RMS *Queen Elizabeth 2* on 12 May, there were a frantic few days for the many remaining preparations for a long sea voyage to a very cold climate. Arctic clothing was brought in from all over the country and the men were taught how to wear it. 'B' Company, which had been in tropical Belize for the past six months, managed to reach England just in time to be included in the kitting-out programme.

The Gurkhas were very impressed at their send off from South-ampton. All the soldiers' talk beforehand about 'the renown of the Gurkhas', 'we've reached a high standard of training' and 'the good name of the battalion', reflecting, yet again, the faith they had in them-selves and the intrinsic belief that they were better than anyone else, all clicked into sharper focus as everyone realized that they were 'news'. The importance of glory and medals was very much under the surface and, at the boarding ceremony, they were as proud as ever a battalion of Gurkhas has been.

1/7 GR had indeed trained very hard since its arrival in England in 1981 and the soldiers were both in a different frame of mind and fitter, militarily and physically, than the other two battalions of 5 Infantry Brigade which had been deployed on Household Duties and so had not been able to exercise their skills to the same extent. Once the voyage had started and a routine established, all were kept very busy with strenuous and essential training on such activities as helicopter drills with Sea Kings and, for selected men, familiarization with the new radio sets that, like the anti-tank 'Milan' wire-guided missiles (the battalion had only Wombats and Carl Gustav anti-tank weapons till then) and the .50 Browning machine-guns, had been issued in those last frenzied days on land. Much time was spent in doing life-saving drills blind-folded and the men were able, in the end, quite happily to wander about QE2 in the dark. Some British soldiers laughed at them for taking such precautions. The Gurkhas were very scornful at what they regarded as the lax attitude on the part of the British troops and their apparent disinclination for training on all possible occasions.

For the planners in battalion headquarters there were also endless conferences, but seldom with anything but frustration resulting as the many conflicting orders – doubtless reflecting a state of affairs in all circles, political and military, from the very top – caused confusion and irritation. Indeed, that facet and the appalling weather experienced below the 40th parallel were unchanging.

On 16 May the 80th anniversary of the battalion's raising was celebrated. It was described by one of those taking part as 'electric, with the atmosphere quite eerie – I felt that they could have taken on the lot that night – and so did they.' The pipes and drums played and the soldiers, clustered on the sports deck, jumped up and down with such fervour that the deck started cracking. The party was very popular and half the ship's crew seemed to be there.

Two days later they sailed past Freetown and crossed the Equator on 19 May, reaching Ascension Island the next day. Tension increased, certainly among the officers, as it became obvious that QE2 was a prime target of the Argentinians. Atlantic Conveyor and HMS Coventry had been hit on 25 May, and the news of 2 Para's battles at Goose Green and Darwin on 28 May, reinforced the sense of isolation, vulnerability and the magnitude of the whole perilous undertaking, particularly as it was realized that the helicopters on Atlantic Conveyor were the prime link in the logistic chain.

What really excited the Gurkhas, however, were the icebergs and the penguins, with many men wondering whether the birds would make good sport and better eating.

The four days after being transferred from QE2 to the MV Norland for the voyage from South Georgia to the Falklands were the unhappiest of all – gale force winds, very rough seas, a rolling, yawing boat, seasickness, with the Tannoy continually telling the men about action to be taken in the event of air raids, all made life exciting, if miserable and, whatever the dangers to be faced on shore, they would be a relief from the wretched, gut-heaving conditions on that storm-tossed ferryboat, with the attendant fears of being caught on a ship without the means to fight back. In the early hours of 1 June disembarkation started at San Carlos and, to everybody's intense relief, there was no devastating harassment from aerial bombardment, although bombing was experienced that day by other vessels and after the main body had disembarked.

Men were very heavily laden, weights of over 120 pounds being the norm.* The first tactical requirement was to establish themselves within the bridgehead that had already been formed. The Mortar Platoon, under Captain A. N. Price, were enjoying a mid-morning meal having, for the first time, dug their 81mm mortars in when a tractor and trailer bounded past them. Piled in the trailer were a dozen or so bodies, with the booted legs sticking out of the back. Price remembers the men gaping in mid-mouthful, as the truth sank in that this was not going to be like Salisbury Plain. Price also recalls his platoon 'digging in after their first shelling – arms like pneumatic drills! Being mortarmen, they had probably the heaviest loads to carry, especially the No. 1 with the barrel as well as arctic kit, rations, radio batteries, rifle and ammunition. In places, over difficult tussock grass, it was only possible to walk a few hundred yards before resting.' Later on, the soft peat proved to be a most difficult and hazardous platform for the base plates and resulted in their having to be moved every eight to ten rounds.

The reliability of the Gurkha in any situation that calls for stamina and calmness is a quality that commanders rely on. Despite the buffeting of shortages, last-minute changes, difficult terrain, very inclement weather and a large proportion of young soldiers, it was the staunchly phlegmatic and solid senior Gurkha ranks that kept everything as smooth as it was. Apart from the fact that a Gurkha battalion was working with two British battalions as a tactical brigade for the first time for many years – with the regional accents of the Scots and the Welsh exacerbating the Gurkhas' English-language weaknesses, which would have made combined smooth functioning difficult back at Sennybridge under peacetime conditions – the whole affair was made vastly more opaque by the complicated nature of the operation, the damage caused by Argentine air attacks and the consequent administrative nightmare for the staff planners. It was off-putting, for instance, when eventually a helicopter did turn up to find out that, instead of long

---

*1/7 GR carried more because they had more weapons and more ammunition than anyone else in the theatre. They had 2×GPMGs per section, 4 MMG 51mm Brownings (for example) and the battalion had learnt, on their last exercise in Wales, that they could not trust helicopters or the weather, to help them move heavy gear forward, so they had to carry it all themselves. Only in the attack were they stripped down to 'fighting order'. (Letter from CO to me, 30 August 1985.)

overdue and urgently needed radio batteries, grenades, pyrotechnics and rations, it contained a television camera crew. Such incidents and the fact that the battalion never closed with the enemy generated an atmosphere of unreality which, along with the hardships of hunger, dirt and bitter cold throughout the whole brief campaign, gave a dimension of insubstantiality to an already most unusual and taxing situation. None the less, the ability of the Gurkha to sustain high morale under adverse conditions, to improvise where possible and to rise to the occasion all helped to soften the impact of sometimes needless, other times inevitable, frustrations.

By 3 June the Gurkhas were deployed at Darwin and Goose Green and, as befitting troops who were used to operating in small groups, many men were used to clear small pockets of Argentines, starting at Lafonia, the 'near island' peninsula south of the isthmus. Launched on raids to winkle out any pockets of resistance, often by helicopter, the Gurkhas – especially the Reconnaissance Platoon under 2nd Lieutenant Q. E. Oates, a soft-spoken, young Australian – effectively prevented any resurgence of Argentinian harassment by stay-behind parties or artillery observation posts in the area of Mount Usbourne and the Wickham Heights, which dominate the road from Darwin to Port Stanley. It was during this phase of the conflict that a kukri was flourished in front of three Argentines at last light as they made their unsuspecting way towards where Oates and his men were. The kukri was later auctioned for £1,500.

Prior to the actual landings on the Falklands, the Argentine propaganda machine had indulged in much macabre comment and detailed description of the beastliness, barbarity and brutishness of the Gurkhas: how they 'topped' people with their kukris, how they ate their prisoners and how they went into batle high on drugs. This propaganda was firmly believed and the blacker it was, the more fearful did the Gurkhas become to the young Argentine conscripts. It certainly made the three men Oates's group brandished kukris all horribly servile. It played an adverse part in preparing these conscripts for battle and there was, in fact, no need for the British to engage in psychological warfare to any extent as the Argentine authorities did the job for them, albeit unwittingly and unwisely.

Meanwhile Goose Green and Darwin had to be defended: the considerable chaos of much abandoned equipment, light vehicles and ammunition was aggravated by the many dead Argentines who had to be collected for disposal by prisoners of war. The Gurkhas' task was not made any the easier by a shortage of rations at this juncture. Soldiers were fed by sheep and geese being shot and cooked with natural peat as fuel. Even when rations were delivered, it was sometimes the case that no solid fuel was supplied and the size and contents of the ration packs meant that they could not easily be broken down.

Individual officers carry their own personal recollections of how the Gurkhas reacted. The CO, Lieutenant Colonel D. P. de C. Morgan, told Lance Corporal Dilbahadur Limbu, who was sentry when an artillery duel started, to shout out 'incoming' and 'outgoing' as and how. He just could not get it right; 'ingoing' mixed with 'outcoming' until, as shells landed very near by, a pathetic 'ayoo' was heard which, if nothing else, broke the tension.

The second-in-command, Major W. J. Dawson, was at Goose Green with a group of Gurkhas when they came across the lone grave of a Harrier pilot. The Gurkhas immediately held a small religious ceremony, a 'puja', for the dead pilot, then made the same religious gesture over the graves of several Argentinians at the other end of the area, very possibly victims of the Harrier. Dawson was also involved in a drama at sea the day after the RFAs *Sir Galahad* and *Sir Tristram* had been sunk with such devastating casualties to the Welsh Guards. He and 180 Gurkhas had to board *Monsunan*, a small tramp steamer used to ferry sheep and, totally unprotected, go and try to salvage a landing craft that had been hit. Casualties had been evacuated by helicopter, except for one dead man whom the Gurkhas found, but radio kits and vehicles still on board were urgently needed. It was reached about a dozen miles off shore and efforts to tow it back were thwarted when a rope fouled *Monsunan*'s propeller. The two boats, unable to move under their own power, were stuck together like a pair of grotesque Siamese twins. Despite using a 'one time wet suit' more than once and trying to cut the rope with kukris so that *Monsunan* could get back to the shore by dawn so as not to be a sitting duck for aerial attack, all efforts were in vain. The world service radio in England had already announced that the vessel was carrying troops and dawn was, by then, not far off. It was an unenviously fraught situation so Dawson decided to break radio silence and call the Royal Navy over. With experienced divers the offending rope was cleared in time for *Monsunan* to regain the shore unscathed, abandoning the precious cargo but preventing further carnage. The Gurkhas ended up where they had started from, not where they were meant to arrive, but safe. Dawson recalls that the men all took the extraordinary episode totally in their stride, as well as the subsequent ride in a Chinook helicopter the next day at zero feet without gyro compasses and with over 80 men inside the machine.

The Gurkhas' ability to go to sleep anywhere was well demonstrated, and the casual gesture of awareness when it was pointed out to a QGO that his jacket had been torn by a piece of shrapnel both showing that, as ever, the Gurkhas' blood does not rise until the enemy has been closed with. At times like this the macabre side of Gurkha humour can be witnessed and was exemplified when a Mortar Fire Controller, standing by an Argentinian corpse, prodded it, saying 'Eh, stand to!'

All the while the brunt of the fighting was being borne by the other brigade, with the Marines and the Paras, who fought bravely and suffered casualties. On the night of 9 June, about six miles from Stanley, the Gurkhas came under intensive artillery fire and four men were wounded.

On 13 June, 1/7 GR moved to an area just below the Two Sisters feature for the attack on Mount William, which is a continuation of the Mount Tumbledown feature and, as such, part of the vital ground overlooking Stanley, the final objective. The Scots Guards were in front of the Gurkhas, who could not move into their final position until the Scots Guards were clear. However, the Scots Guards were held up and the start time for 1/7 GR was delayed five hours, from 0400 hours, when they would have been able to move in darkness, until 0900 hours, when they could be observed.

So that the operational timetable should not be slowed down the CO took a bold decision to move to the objective in the dark by another route, along the edge of Tumbledown while the Guards were still fighting for possession of the heights. This decision was bold because a minefield was known to lie across the axis of the Gurkhas' advance. As luck would have it, the obstacle was slightly farther north than had been thought and only one company actually entered the minefield. This caused no casualties but eight men were wounded by artillery fire before it was light.

As their attack was going in, the Argentines realized that it was the dreaded Gurkhas who were about to fall on them, so they ran away and surrendered to the Scots Guards rather than face a fate they imagined must be worse. There was then no point in the battalion going on any further and they were ordered to discontinue their advance once they were upon their objective. At 1100 hours, 14 June, the enemy surrendered. News was passed to Dawson, who was manning the radio set at the time and who let everybody in the area know in no uncertain fashion. The television crew heard the commotion and came over to find out what had happened. They wanted to get the news to the outside world . . . and when Dawson's happy face and cheerful voice boomed the news to the world, those watching their sets were not to know that the announcement was, in fact, the third rehearsal for the camera crew, who wanted it 'just right'. As the officers and soldiers said afterwards, the announcement was one of the most frustrating things that had ever happened to them – all the training, the preparations, the slog of it all, to say nothing of the considerable mental stress that comes to everyone before a battle were suddenly no more – it was a most extraordinary mixture of relief and frustration.

It will be a brave, and very foolish, man to suggest that the final surrender came about when it did because 1/7 GR were poised in front of the capital, Stanley, but their presence must have played a significant part in the Argentine decision to stop fighting.*

In the Falklands war the Gurkhas saved lives, prevented casualties and won their battles on their reputation alone; there can be few soldiers of any other country or army who can make that claim. However, the Gurkhas fully realize that a high standard brings its own penalties of expectation; as long as they are soldiers of the Queen they know what is expected from them, and they are determined to continue to give to Her Majesty their best for as long as they are allowed to. That the people of Britain feel similarly was amply demonstrated by the reception accorded the battalion at Southampton on their return. Normally saturnine dockers told anyone who might be interested how they had fought with the Gurkhas in Burma, even, on occasion, producing worn photographs to prove their claim. On the coach drive to Fleet motorists honked their horns and flashed their lights as they drove past the convoy (only observed by those few who had not dropped off to sleep), and at the climax of the day the Gurkhas were overwhelmed even more at the reception given to them by the good citizens of Fleet. The battalion marched through the town, the men poker-faced, the regimental priest bringing up the rear and the crowd ecstatic, the helicopter fly-past and the words of welcome from the Chief of the Defence Staff (his first appearance in uniform as a Field Marshal) and the Colonel of the Regiment, all made the Gurkhas really feel part of Britain as the incredible show of warmth, gratitude and spontaneous friendship accorded them so obviously came from the heart.

The Mortar Platoon Commander, three years later when adjutant of 2/7 GR, nicely summed up feelings when he wrote, '. . . the lasting thing I personally came away with was the knowledge that the lads in the Brigade today are every bit the men their fathers were. Times and situations change, weapons and uniforms develop, but given the right circumstances, the Gurkha of today will prove himself and face challenges as he has always done. It was my privilege to be there to see it.'

*The lack of involvement with the enemy is emphasized, especially when compared with the other units in the campaign, by the paucity of awards made to 1/7 GR. Apart from the CO being made OBE, only the Medical Officer and the Mechanical Transport Officer, a QGO, were recognized, both receiving a Mention-in-Despatch.

8
THE FUTURE

After the agreement on the future, post-1997, status of Hong Kong had been signed between the governments of the United Kingdom and the People's Republic of China, many people, not least the Nepalese at many levels of society, started wondering what the future of the Brigade of Gurkhas would be, although the majority of Gurkhas serving at the time of the announcement would be away home on pension by 1997.

In Hong Kong itself, however, the decision to disband 2/7 GR by 1987 was taken in 1985. This was separate from any long-term plans for the Brigade as a whole. The reasons for this decision were seen to be three-fold: the overall security situation has so improved that normal force levels could cope; 2/7 GR's barracks, at Lyemun, were right in the projected path of a badly needed new highway so had to be demolished; while it was obviously not worthwhile spending a lot of money on new barracks with such a shortened life span.

The lessons learnt from the decrease in the size of the Brigade in the late 1960s – evident signs of which are still visible with those who left the army then with no pension still forming the bulk of the chronic welfare cases – have not been forgotten. For 2/7 GR, the plans are to reabsorb its men in their original units whence they were drafted on the battalion being re-raised, a fair distribution to other units of those soldiers posted directly to 2/7 GR after their recruit training, and the minimum voluntary redundancies; all with recruitment being adjusted to balance the overall strength.

This the Secretary of State for Defence announced, in 1985; that being so, two questions spring to mind: how many Gurkhas will be needed? and where will they serve? with a third question about any political ramifications between the governments of Nepal and the United Kingdom?

Apart from both the British and Nepalese governments being satisfied with the arrangement on a purely political level, what, for Britain, will be the military commitments? What of the Falklands, Belize, Gibraltar, Cyprus and Brunei, to name but five of today's places where there are British forces outside the United Kingdom? Who can tell? And if anyone could tell, would it be revealed so far ahead and before it was necessary? What new commitments might crop up? Again, who can tell? Whatever the problem is and wherever it might be, as far as the Brigade of Gurkhas is concerned, its one and only task must be to continue to be ready, in every possible respect, to meet whatever challenge of arms is presented to it. Wherever service may be and however many or few Gurkhas will be serving, a continuation of realistic training, an enhancement of proficiency in English and a maintenance of all the very high standards that are expected, collectively and individually, are indispensable prerequisites.

There are some who would wish that the Brigade fold up and quietly disappear. There are others with the opposite view. There are those who feel that both the image and the reality of present-day Britain and Nepal being joined by soldiers is not right and that the money Britain spends on Nepal through the Brigade (third in the table of earners of hard currency) is too much or should be added to the already considerable total obligated to aid. These are legitimate thoughts.

Others regard the comparatively few Nepalese citizens who make up the Brigade of Gurkhas as acting as an 'equation of balance' for Nepal, hemmed in as it is by countries which, however much friendship they profess for Nepal, are guided chiefly by scoring points for or against each other than for any altruistic wish for Nepal itself. The same cannot be said of Britain. In the game of power politics it could be argued that the British Army Gurkhas have an element of political clout for stability in Nepal that equals, if not outweighs, the purely military benefit accruing to Britain. In the context of the Cold War between the two communist giants in Asia and their associates this is important.

Apart from wondering about the problems of tomorrow, how many of today's leaders, with their ideas of today, will be around to give definitive answers when they are due? A day in politics can be a long time.

None of these points is of any concern to the soldier with the kukri on his belt and British money in his pocket; his concern must be to continue with the required mixture of maintenance of the old discipline, acquisition of new skills and an act of faith that Gurkhas will always prove better than even the most optimistically minded felt they were capable of performing. Remember, more people regard the Gurkhas as being among the best soldiers in the world, if not the best, than regard them in any other light. Remember, also, that many political decisions are based more on expediency than on rationality.

APPENDIX 1
ORDER OF BATTLE
OF THE BRIGADE OF GURKHAS

On 1 January 1948, four Gurkha regiments became an integral part of
the British Army, forming the Brigade of Gurkhas, although they were
known as the 'Gurkha Regiment' for the first two years. These regiments
were:

2nd King Edward VII's Own Gurkha Rifles (The Sirmoor Rifles)	2 GR
6th Gurkha Rifles	6 GR
7th Gurkha Rifles	7 GR
10th Gurkha Rifles	10 GR

each with a 1st and a 2nd Battalion, abbreviated by putting the battalion
number first and the regimental number second (e.g., 1/2 GR, 2/6 GR,
1/7 GR and 2/10 GR).

   After 1948, additional units were raised to join the eight battalions,
namely:

Gurkha Independent Parachute Company	GURKHA PARA
5 Gurkha Guard Dog Company, that formed from, when disbanded	
Gurkha Military Police	GMP
The Gurkha Engineers	GE
Gurkha Signals	
Gurkha Army Service Corps	GASC
Major Staff Band.	

   As at the end of this history, the Brigade of Gurkhas was organized as
follows:

1st Battalion, 2nd King Edward VII's Own Gurkha Rifles (The Sirmoor Rifles)	1/2 GR
2nd Battalion, 2nd King Edward VII's Own Gurkha Rifles (The Sirmoor Rifles)	2/2 GR
(Within the Regiment 'Gurkha Rifles' is not used, but the older form of 'Goorkhas' is.)	
6th Queen Elizabeth's Own Gurkha Rifles	6 GR
1st Battalion, 7th Duke of Edinburgh's Own Gurkha Rifles	1/7 GR
2nd Battalion, 7th Duke of Edinburgh's Own Gurkha Rifles	2/7 GR

10th Princess Mary's Own Gurkha Rifles	10 GR
The Queen's Gurkha Engineers	QGE
Queen's Gurkha Signals	QG SIGNALS
Gurkha Transport Regiment	GTR

APPENDIX 2
HONOURS AND AWARDS TO GURKHAS
OF THE BRIGADE OF GURKHAS

Gurkhas have been admitted into two British Orders: The Royal Victorian Order, as Member, 5th Class (MVO); and The Most Excellent Order of the British Empire, in the 4th Class, as Ordinary Officers (OBE), and 5th Class, as Ordinary Members (MBE). Allied to, but not part of, this Order is an award made to soldiers: The British Empire Medal (BEM).

When the Gurkhas joined the British Army, there were some Gurkha Officers who were of an Order of the old Indian Army that became extinct on 1 January 1948: The Order of British India (OBI). Those who were awarded the First Class of the Order used the title of 'Sardar Bahadur', while the Second Class of the Order attracted the title of 'Bahadur'.

There then come the Gallantry Awards. Some of the old Indian Army awards had been won by members of the British Army Gurkhas; the list of precedence of both British and Indian Armies runs:

Victoria Cross	The supreme award which, together with the	VC
George Cross	are senior to all grades of the Orders of Chivalry	GC
Distinguished Service Order	For commissioned officers only	DSO
Indian Order of Merit	Ceased on 15 August 1947	IOM
Military Cross	Normally for commissioned officers only	MC
Distinguished Conduct Medal	For soldiers only, equivalent to the DSO	DCM
Indian Distinguished Service Medal	Ceased on 15 August 1947	IDSM
Military Medal	For soldiers only, equivalent to the MC	MM
Queen's Gallantry Medal		QGM

The four 'main' bravery awards are made on the basis of how much one single individual does to influence the outcome of the battle being fought. The greater the influence, the higher the award.

Victoria Cross: undisputed and personal influence that was critical to success.
Distinguished Service Order and *Distinguished Conduct Medal*: very significant influence, but not uniquely individual.
Military Cross and *Military Medal*: significant influence.
Mention in Dispatches: some influence.

APPENDIX 3
RANKS IN THE BRIGADE OF GURKHAS

The Rank and File and the Warrant Officers in the Brigade of Gurkhas are designated in the same way as their British counterparts. It is only the officer bracket that is different, as there is no counterpart to the Queen's Gurkha Officer in the British services now there is no longer a Commissioned Petty Officer in the Royal Navy. The three ranks concerned are:

Lieutenant (Queen's Gurkha Officer); Lt (QGO) or, unofficially, G/Lt
Captain (Queen's Gurkha Officer); Capt (QGO) or, unofficially, G/Capt
Major (Queen's Gurkha Officer); Maj (QGO) or, unofficially, G/Maj or GM.

These officers wear two stars, three stars and a crown respectively, on a piece of ribbon in the Brigade colours of green, black and red, stitched vertically underneath.

In addition, there are normally two Captains (Queen's Gurkha Officer) in attendance on Her Majesty the Queen during the summer months as Queen's Gurkha Orderly Officers.

Further to the officers already listed are the following:

Honorary Lieutenant (Queen's Gurkha Officer)	Hon Lt (QGO)
Lieutenant (Gurkha Commissioned Officer)	Lt (GCO)
Honorary Lieutenant (Gurkha Commissioned Officer)	Hon Lt (GCO)
Captain (Gurkha Commissioned Officer)	Capt (GCO)
Honorary Captain (Gurkha Commissioned Officer)	Hon Capt (GCO)
Major (Gurkha Commissioned Officer)	Maj (GCO)

All the above, except the first named, are on a par in status with British Army ranks.

Gurkha Commissioned Officers who have received a Quartermaster's commission are appropriately designated, e.g. Lt (GCO) (QM).

For Nepalese citizens who go through the British Army commissioning system in the United Kingdom, the categories of Regular and Short

Service apply to them in the same way as to their British counterparts.

Theoretically there is no limit to how high a 'Sandhurst commissioned' Gurkha can rise. To date, the officer who has risen the highest is Lieutenant Colonel Lalbahadur Pun, OBE, MC, of 2 GR; he is also the only such officer to have been to the Staff College at Camberley, England.

APPENDIX 4
GURKHA FESTIVALS AND CELEBRATIONS

The major religion in Nepal is Hinduism, with very nearly four out of every five people of that faith; Buddhism has many of the remaining people as its adherents. There are pockets of Muslims to be found. Christianity is scarcely tolerated. The two major religions hold as a tenet of faith that a person's luck is governed by what the gods have written on the forehead; illegible, unalterable and permanent. Inescapably, one must blindly follow what Fate has decreed, with the wheel of life reflecting past conduct and demanding adherence to rituals without which the gods' displeasure will be incurred. One definition of such religions could well be 'conduct directed towards salvation'.

In a Gurkha unit, the outward trappings of religion do not play a significant part of everyday life. There is a Brahman, known as 'pandit', in each major unit as a 'religious teacher' and it is he who is responsible for maintaining the inescapable minimum observations required by Hinduism. There are, however, certain festivals that play a significant part of every Gurkha's life, the three principal of which are *Dashera, Diwali* and *Holi*.

In brief, *Dashera* celebrates the victory of right over wrong and involves the sacrifice of goats and buffaloes. The battalion and other units serving in England were the first to discontinue this practice and now all units observe such sacrifices by proxy, with the actual rites being performed by the British Gurkhas in Nepal. During this ceremony, battalion weapons are blessed. There is also much revelry as well as family prayers. *Dashera* lasts for ten days.

Diwali is celebrated on the first full moon after *Dashera.* A myriad of candles and other lights are placed outside dwellings to guide the goddess Laxmi back after one of her victories. Gambling is officially allowed during the period of this festival, five days in all.

Holi commemorates the rebirth of the year and is an ancient fertility celebration. Coming after the winter, it is the season of marriages. Red dye is thrown everywhere, but this habit is not observed by the Brigade of Gurkhas.

In a Gurkha unit, the family lines need the help of the 'pandit' with birth, weaning, name-giving, and the first haircut all needing his presence. Death is also laden with rites: the death of a near relative in Nepal causes great concern to a serving soldier and, if he is the only person who can perform the necessary obsequies, he is allowed to return on compassionate leave. Like other aspects of a soldier's welfare, such treatment is a great factor in maintaining morale.

SELECT BIBLIOGRAPHY

FURTHER READING ON THE BRITISH ARMY GURKHAS:

Adshead, Robin, *Gurkha: The Legendary Soldier*, Singapore and London, 1970.

Chant, Christopher, *Gurkha* The Illustrated History of an Elite Fighting Force, Poole and New York, 1985.

Farwell, Byron, *The Gurkhas*, London and New York, 1984.

James, Harold, and Denis Sheil-Small, *A Pride of Gurkhas* The 2nd King Edward VII's Own Goorkhas, 1948–1971, London 1974.

McAlister, Major General R. W. C., *Bugle and Kukri* The Story of the 10th Princess Mary's Own Gurkha Rifles, vol. II, 1948–1975, Isle of Wight, 1978.

Messenger, Charles, *The Steadfast Gurkha* Historical Record of the 6th Queen Elizabeth's Own Gurkha Rifles, vol. III, 1948–1982, London, 1986.

Perowne, Major General L. E. C. M., *Gurkha Sapper* The Story of the Gurkha Engineers, 1948–1970, Hong Kong, 1973.

Smith, E. D., *Britain's Brigade of Gurkhas*, London, 1982.

—— *East of Kathmandu* The Story of the 7th Duke of Edinburgh's Own Gurkha Rifles, Vol. II, 1948–1973, London, 1976.

—— *Johnny Gurkha* 'Friends in the Hills', London, 1985.

Tucci, Sandro, (with Introduction by J. P. Cross), *Gurkhas* London, 1985.

BOOKS THAT INCLUDE REFERENCES TO GURKHAS:

Blaxland, Gregory, *The Regiments Depart*, London, 1971.

James, Harold, and Denis Sheil-Small, *The Undeclared War*, London, 1971.

Pocock, Tom, *Fighting General* The Public and Private Campaigns of General Sir Walter Walker, London, 1973.

Smith, E. D., *Malaya and Borneo*, Shepperton, 1985.

BOOKS WITH ESPECIAL SLANTS:

Limbu, Lieutenant (QGO) Rambahadur, V. C., *My Life Story*, Isle of Wight, 1978; (published by The Gurkha Welfare Trust, MOD (Army), Room 8, Archway North, Spring Gardens, London SW1A 2BE).

Marks, J. M., *Ayo Gurkha*, Oxford, 1971.

A very comprehensive bibliography compiled by Lieutenant General Sir John Chapple is with the Curator of the Gurkha Museum, Queen Elizabeth's Barracks, Church Crookham, Aldershot, Hampshire GU13 0BE, England.

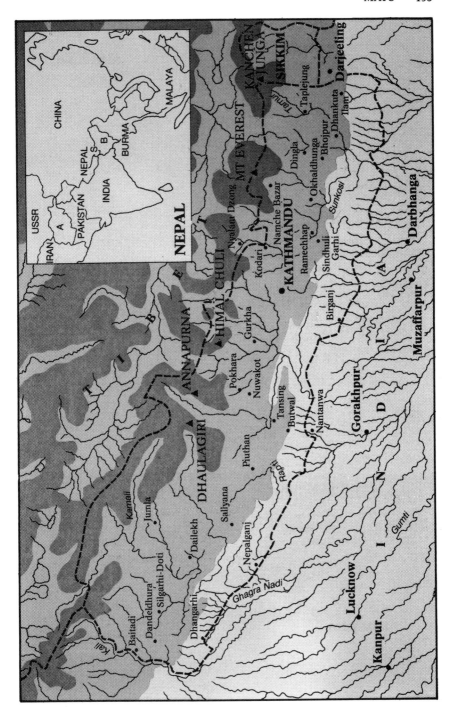

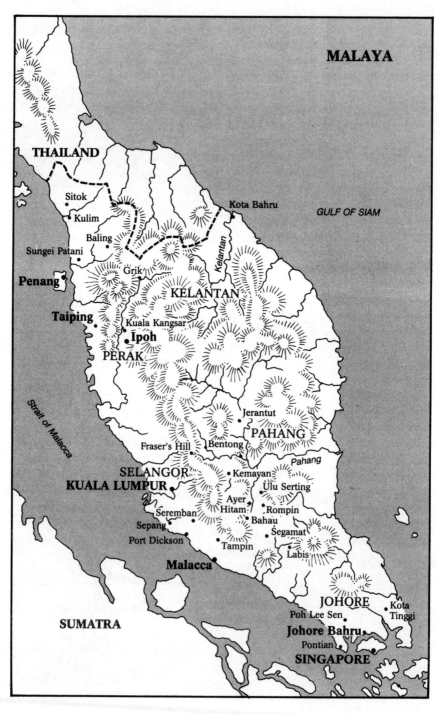

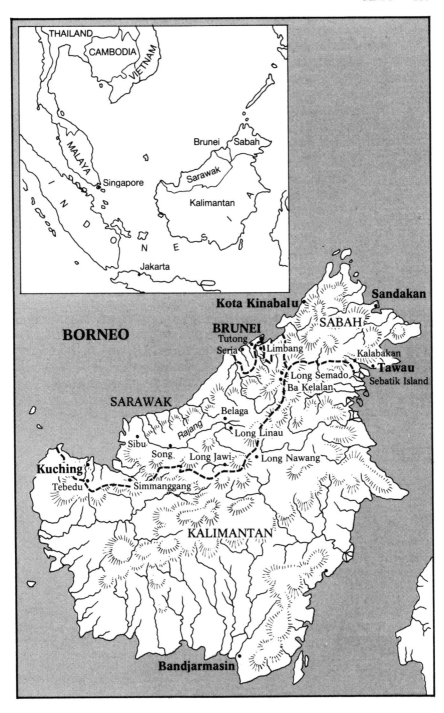

THAILAND

CAMBODIA

VIETNAM

MALAYA

Singapore

INDONESIA

Jakarta

Brunei

Sabah

Sarawak

Kalimantan

BORNEO

Kota Kinabalu

Sandakan

BRUNEI

SABAH

Tutong

Seria

Limbang

Kalabakan

Long Semado

Tawau

Ba Kelalan

Sebatik Island

SARAWAK

Belaga

Rajang

Long Linau

Sibu

Song

Long Jawi

Long Nawang

Kuching

Tebedu

Simmanggang

KALIMANTAN

Bandjarmasin

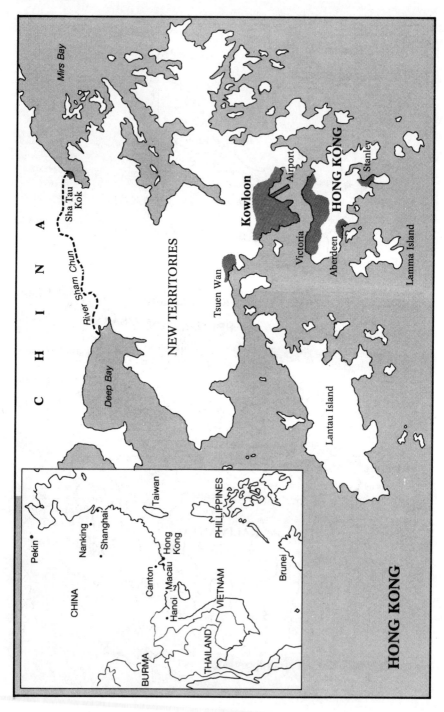

HONG KONG

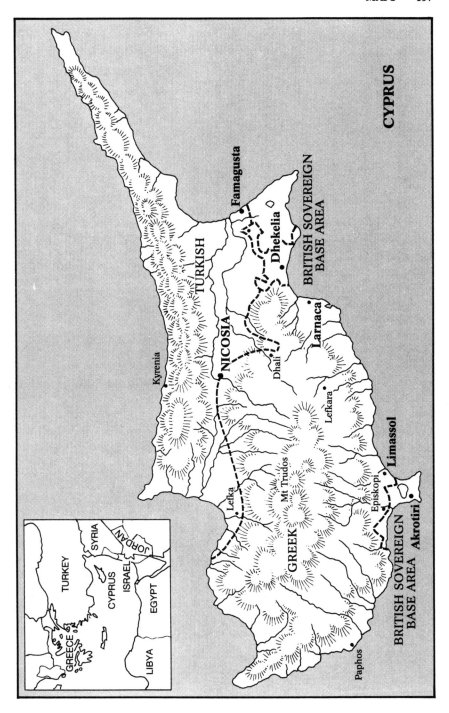

CYPRUS

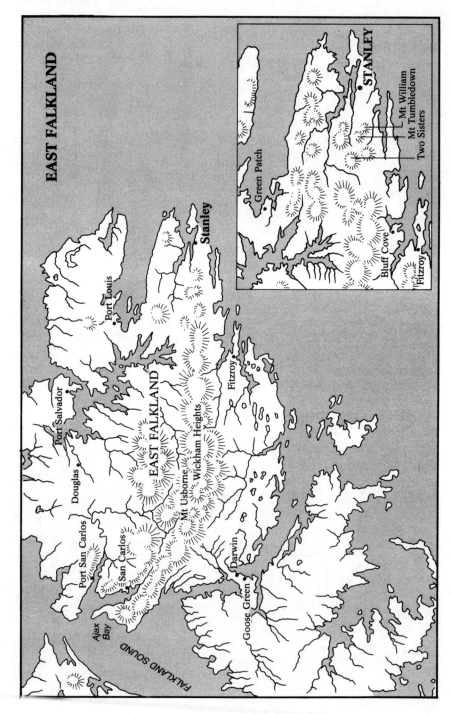

EAST FALKLAND

STANLEY

Mt William
Mt Tumbledown
Two Sisters

Green Patch

Bluff Cove

Fitzroy

Port Louis

Stanley

Port Salvador

EAST FALKLAND

Douglas

Fitzroy

Mt Usborne
Wickham Heights

Port San Carlos

San Carlos

Darwin

Ajax
Bay

Goose Green

FALKLAND SOUND

INDEX

Only those place names that are critical to the narrative are listed here; those not listed will be found on the appropriate maps.